Fair Trial Rights
of the Accused

FAIR TRIAL RIGHTS
OF THE ACCUSED

A Documentary History

Edited by RONALD BANASZAK, SR.

Primary Documents in American History and Contemporary Issues

GREENWOOD PRESS
Westport, Connecticut • London

Library of Congress Cataloging-in-Publication Data

Fair trial rights of the accused : a documentary history / edited by
Ronald Banaszak, Sr.
     p. cm. — (Primary documents in American history and contemporary issues,
ISSN 1069–5605)
   Includes bibliographical references and index.
   ISBN 0–313–30525–0 (alk. paper)
   1. Fair trial—United States—History—Sources. 2. Due process of law—United
States—History—Sources. I. Banaszak, Ronald A. II. Series.
KF9223.4.F35 2002
345.73′056—dc21   2001023304

British Library Cataloguing in Publication Data is available.

Library of Congress Catalog Card Number: 2001023304
ISBN: 0–313–30525–0
ISSN: 1069–5605

First published in 2002

Greenwood Press, 88 Post Road West, Westport, CT 06881
An imprint of Greenwood Publishing Group, Inc.
www.greenwood.com

Printed in the United States of America

The paper used in this book complies with the
Permanent Paper Standard issued by the National
Information Standards Organization (Z39.48–1984).

10 9 8 7 6 5 4 3 2 1

Contents

Series Foreword

This series is designed to meet the research needs of high school and college students by making available in one volume the key primary documents on a given historical event or contemporary issue. Documents include speeches and letters, congressional testimony, Supreme Court and lower court decisions, government reports, biographical accounts, position papers, statutes, and news stories.

The purpose of the series is twofold: (1) to provide substantive and background material on an event or issue through the texts of pivotal primary documents that shaped policy or law, raised controversy, or influenced the course of events, and (2) to trace the controversial aspects of the event or issue through documents that represent a variety of viewpoints. Documents for each volume have been selected by a recognized specialist in that subject with the advice of a board of other subject specialists, school librarians, and teachers.

To place the subject in historical perspective, the volume editor has prepared an introductory overview and a chronology of events. Documents are organized either chronologically or topically. The documents are full text or, if unusually long, have been excerpted by the volume editor. To facilitate understanding, each document is accompanied by an explanatory introduction. A selected bibliography of related sources appears at the end of this volume.

It is the hope of Greenwood Press that this series will enable students and other readers to use primary documents more easily in their research, to exercise critical thinking skills by examining the key documents in American history and public policy, and to critique the variety of viewpoints represented by this selection of documents.

Introduction

Everyone has experienced the thrill of a courtroom scene in a movie or television show. It is clear that rules and procedures must be followed. Many of these are familiar to the youngest Americans—public trial by jury, right to counsel, due process of law, and so forth. The source of these rights in the United States is the Bill of Rights in the Constitution and the guarantees of rights in state constitutions. In the U.S. Constitution the Fifth and Sixth Amendments contain a list of citizens' rights related to trials intended to provide justice for the accused and for the country. Included are the following rights:

Fifth Amendment
- Grand jury indictment is required for a capital or other infamous crime, except for military cases during time of war or public danger
- No double jeopardy
- No one can be compelled to witness against himself
- No one can be deprived of life, liberty, or property without due process of law
- No private property can be taken for public use without just compensation

Sixth Amendment
- Accused has right to speedy trial
- Accused has right to public trial
- Accused has right to impartial jury from area wherein the crime was committed
- Accused has right to be informed of the nature and cause of the accusation
- Accused has right to confront witnesses against him
- Accused has right to compulsory process for obtaining witnesses in his favor
- Accused has right to assistance of counsel for his defense

This is an impressive list of rights. These trial rights did not originate with the writers of the amendments. They have a long past. Historically, the story of trial rights is really the story of the relationship of citizens and their rulers. It is the story of the balance between the authority of government and the rights of people. For if a ruler can imprison citizens without constraint, then the citizens have no other rights. In modern times, there is also a conscious balancing of the rights of the accused and the rights of victims.

At one time in human history, the will of the ruler was the law. Citizens had no rights or protection against a capricious ruler. Hammurabi, an ancient Babylonian ruler, is credited with creating the first written laws to "hold back the strong from oppressing the weak" (Warren 1955, 224). A nearer ancestor of the legal system of the United States is English law. Englishmen fought hard and long to gain each of their rights. Each right prevented government treatment considered unfair by the people. The colonists brought with them this tradition of rights dating back centuries.

ENGLISH ROOTS

Three major documents helped guarantee rights in England. The first of these was the Magna Carta. It resulted from a confrontation between the barons and King John in 1215. John was a cruel and arbitrary ruler described so well in the stories about Robin Hood. The heavy taxes that Robin Hood fought against were in real life levied by John to finance a series of wars to attempt to win back his land holdings in France. In 1214 he was defeated by France and immediately began laying plans for another war and, of course, for new taxes to finance it. Instead the barons revolted. They had had enough and even discussed offering the crown to the son of Philip of France, which would certainly end warfare with France. Those loyal to the king and those in revolt met in a meadow named Runnymede. All were armed for battle. Actually, King John had little alternative but to give in to the barons' demands. He quickly lost popular support once the rebellion started and his forces were outnumbered at Runnymede. Even the city of London and the clergy sided with the barons.

John signed the Magna Carta (see Document 1), or great charter, at Runnymede. It was a list of restrictions on the actions of the king. Many were minor or obscure, meaningful only to those affected, but had little in common with our Bill of Rights. The significance of the Magna Carta is its establishment of limits on the actions the king can take. For the first time, the barons had forced the king to agree that his actions were limited by law. Because the Magna Carta is also a written document, the king found it difficult to later deny his concessions. Immediately after signing it, the king attempted to have it overturned, with no success. In fact, he was compelled to reissue the charter in 1217 and again in 1225 to certify his continuing obligation to abide by its terms. The document stands today as a testament to the efforts of English citizens to secure their rights. Note, however, that the rights in the Magna Carta applied only to freemen, not to commoners or serfs. One of the great trends over time has been the continual extension of rights to additional classes of individuals.

After the Magna Carta, of course, the king still ruled England and had most of the power. During the following centuries a struggle ensued between kings trying to preserve their power and Englishmen trying to check the king's power. In these confrontations, sometimes the king maintained power and authority; on other occasions the people gained additional protections in the form of new guarantees of rights. Still, Parliament provided the most important protection from arbitrary treatment by a king. In John's day and for centuries to follow, Parliament could meet only when the king convened it. Once Parliament met, it used its power to approve taxes. The kings needed income to provide for their lifestyle, provision the military, and support wars. In exchange for their agreement to pay taxes without resistance, Englishmen gained the power to decide which taxes should be imposed on them. Naturally, the kings did not easily give up their independent power to tax. The 1600s was a pivotal century both for the rights of Englishmen and for American colonists. As the English colonies were being founded, dramatic events were taking place in England.

In the early 1600s, King Charles I and Parliament faced off. Confronted with a need for income to support war efforts and with the opposition of Parliament to approving those taxes, Charles insisted he had the ability to raise money without Parliament's consent. King Charles forced citizens to loan him money. He saved military expenses by billeting soldiers in citizens' homes, requiring his subjects to feed and provide sleeping arrangements for the soldiers. The fate for anyone who refused was jail; any judges who did not enforce the king's orders were removed. Martial law was imposed, and those who opposed the king were jailed indefinitely without charges. They were given no common law trial or permitted to use bail.

King Charles used his prerogative courts to imprison opponents. These were courts through which the discretionary powers of the king were exercised. Originally formed in the 1400s, they became progressively more powerful as the kings used them to carry out their sovereign powers and bypass the common, or ordinary, courts, which are the more direct ancestors of today's trial courts. The most hated was the Court of Star Chamber, which dealt with offenses against public order. This was the mechanism that Charles frequently used to imprison his opponents.

Its procedures were less rigid than those followed in common law courts. Juries were not used either for indictment or for verdict. Protections for the accused practiced in common law courts were absent. Cases could begin with a complaint from the king or others. Witnesses gave depositions. The accused could be placed under oath and asked detailed questions without knowing what witnesses had said or even what the criminal charge was. The Star Chamber was famous for arbitrary punishments that included fines, imprisonment, whipping, branding, mutilation, and the pillory. In 1627, the judges refused bail for the accused in the Five Knights case, since they were not accused of any specific offenses!

Even these efforts were unable to provide sufficient funds for King Charles. In 1628, his need forced him to convene Parliament to secure its assistance in raising taxes. Unbelievably, Charles and his ministers had embroiled England in war simultaneously with France and Spain. Under the leadership of Sir Edward Coke, Parliament used the situation to secure the king's agreement to new guarantees of rights. Fully twenty-seven of Parliament's members had been imprisoned earlier by Charles for opposition to him. The Petition of Rights (see Document 2) that he accepted limited him and future kings by guaranteeing Englishmen's rights. It specifically barred imprisonment by order of the king, tax collection without parliamentary consent, martial law, and the billeting of troops in private citizens' homes. Charles may have felt that he did not have to live by the new rights outlined in the Petition, but Parliament did.

During the following two years, peace treaties were made removing England from continental wars. The 1630s were largely peaceful, but the elite in England resented the continual taxation of Charles. Trouble began again in the 1640s. Faced with a Scottish war, Charles summoned Parliament in 1640 to approve new taxes, but Parliament instead began listing grievances against Charles. He quickly dismissed Parliament. Losses in battle with the Scots led Charles to sign a humiliating treaty that required him to pay for the upkeep of the Scottish army. He had no choice but to reconvene Parliament for a second time in 1640. This Parliament immediately used its leverage to limit the king's authority. It brought down the king's advisers, ended the king's use of counselors to rule, and eliminated the Star Chamber. It also mandated that Parliament could not be suspended without its own consent and that Parliament would be required to meet every three years. Shortly, England descended into civil war between Charles and Parliament. Charles lost and was executed in 1649. There followed various governmental forms that ended with Charles's son being invited to become monarch. With his death in 1685, his Catholic brother James II ascended the throne.

Protestant England was worried about James's Catholicism. When an heir was born—thus opening the prospect for a series of Catholic monarchs—seven prominent Protestants invited William of Orange to investigate the birth; in effect, they invited a foreign prince to invade their land. William promptly complied, arriving with his army in 1688. Catholic King James II fled England, allowing William of Orange and his wife, Mary, to ascend to the throne. As part of the terms of assuming the throne, William and Mary agreed to a Bill of Rights (see Document 3) passed by Parliament. This document guaranteed a great variety of rights. The nobles wanted to prevent William and Mary and their successors from ever threatening these rights again. Relating to trials, the Bill of Rights eliminated excessive bail, excessive fines, and cruel and unusual punishments. It also prevented forfeiture of property or fines without conviction of a crime and required jurors to be impartially selected.

These three documents provide a broad outline of the struggle for rights, but many other events contributed. The right of an accused person to have the aid of learned counsel was recognized by the twelfth century. By 1342, the twelve-man jury was a regular legal fixture in common law courts. A law in 1444 compelled sheriffs to release prisoners on bail unless their crime was extremely serious. Another law in 1275 warned officers against extortion from prisoners.

COLONIAL ROOTS

These events in England were happening at the time of the founding of the North American colonies. Although in many ways the English colonists came to North America to start over, they carried with them fresh memories of the battle for rights. In North America, the first permanent English settlement was Jamestown, started in 1607, followed in 1620 by the Pilgrims' settlement in Plymouth. Others were settled in rapid succession.

The English settling in the New World wanted all the rights guaranteed to them in England. They wanted the authorities prohibited from depriving citizens of life, liberty, or property without due process of law. In 1641, the same year in which Parliament eliminated the hated Star Chamber, Massachusetts colony enacted the first written guarantee of specific liberties in the colonies. Known as the Massachusetts Body of Liberties (see Document 4), it was a remarkable document that influenced all that followed. Fully twenty-five of the twenty-eight rights included in the Bill of Rights were present in it. Although impressive, the rights were guaranteed only for Christians, not even all Christians. Protestants known as Quakers and Anabaptists were specifically excluded.

Guarantees of rights were sometimes used to attract settlers to sparsely settled regions. When Quakers gained control of the western half of New Jersey, they issued the Concessions and Agreements of West New Jersey (see Document 5) to attract settlers. Due process of law was guaranteed, as was trial by jury. Two witnesses were required for the establishment of guilt in criminal cases, and citizens were allowed to represent themselves in court. An original feature was the right to challenge and dismiss potential jurors.

Between 1682 and 1701, Pennsylvania and New York, two of the most influential colonies, established legal statements of citizens' rights. These are important because they help establish a specific list of rights to be guaranteed from the many rights that might be guaranteed. Pennsylvania created two documents. The Frame of Government (see Document 6) was written by William Penn, a Quaker, who had personal experience with religious discrimination. Pennsylvania was intended to be an open colony accepting anyone and protecting everyone's rights. The second part of this document contains a statement of rights. Religious freedom was guaranteed and also the rights of public trial by jury, right to bail, and right for the accused to appear in court to plead his or her case. Court fees and fines had to be moderate and stated in a published public schedule. A common feature of English prisons of the day was to charge prisoners for their food and lodging. Penn outlawed such a practice. Court records were required to be kept in English to make them available to all. In 1701, Penn created a new Charter of Privileges (see Document 8), which created a one-house legislature elected by the citizens to involve them more in the government of the colony. Although the list of included rights was small, it did contain several rights that laid the foundation for the Sixth Amendment and the due process clause. It allowed the accused the right to call witnesses and have counsel. These rights were not guaranteed by any other colony, but they would be included in the Sixth Amendment. The Charter of Privileges also guaranteed that every person would be entitled to "ordinary Course of Justice," meaning due process.

New York's contribution was the Charter of Libertyes and Priviledges (see Document 7), created in 1683. New York was a royal colony that belonged to the duke of York, who later became King Charles II. At first New York was not allowed any self-rule, but in 1683 the duke of York allowed the election of a General Assembly in exchange for the promise that it would tax the colony and thus make the colony self-supporting. The General Assembly's first action was to draft the Charter of Libertyes and Privileges giving a variety of rights. Criminal rights included trial by jury, right to bail, and indictment by grand jury. The duke of York promptly vetoed the law, but later when he fled from England the colonies issued a new, almost identical law. The new law did have one major change: It did not permit religious freedom for Roman Catholics.

In the ensuing decades, the colonies grew in population, sophistication, and economic vigor. Not much innovation in the expansion of rights was expressed during these tranquil periods, though they tended to be implemented in practice more vigorously, but most felt their rights were largely secure, as a result of general agreement and written expression. In some cases, they were far ahead of the rights in England. For example, the right to a lawyer for all criminal defendants did not exist in England until implemented by Parliament in 1836 (Beaney 1955).

REVOLUTIONARY AMERICA

By the time of the American Revolution, every colony had established a list of rights, either in a constitution or in law. There were many similarities between these statements, and some differences, but their purpose was to protect life, liberty, and property. In the dispute with England that led to the revolution, grievances about taxation without representation are famous. But colonists also complained of imprisonment without proper trial, general warrants of search and seizure, denial of habeas corpus, lack of bail, and even billeting of troops. They objected to being subjected to treatment that would not be allowed in England.

When the first Continental Congress met in 1774, one of its first actions was to draft a declaration of rights. In another form, those rights were stated in the Address to the Inhabitants of Quebec (see Document 9). The colonists hoped, in vain, that those in Quebec would join them in their protests against British treatment. They listed the specific trial rights of a jury trial and the right to habeas corpus, that is, the right to a legal proceeding, to not being held indefinitely in jail.

Six months later, the battle of Lexington and Concord marked the first battle of the Revolutionary War. As the situation worsened with England, more colonists, but certainly not all, began to think and act independently. The debate about revolution turned on issues of freedom and rights of citizens. With the rejection of British rule, the forms of government in the colonies needed rebuilding. In May 1776, Virginia recommended to the Continental Congress that independence should be declared from England. That same month the Continental Congress called for the colonies to each form new state governments. Virginia approved a new state constitution in June. The first part of this document contained a Declaration of Rights (see Document 10) that expanded the personal rights of citizens more than any other previously adopted official statement. It included numerous trial rights, including the right against self-incrimination. Other states freely adopted Virginia's statement into their own constitutions. A few days later, New Jersey approved its new constitution (see Document 11), which contained a list of rights in the body of the document. It guaranteed a trial by jury and stated that that right "shall remain confirmed as part of the law of this

Colony, without repeal, forever." In July, the Declaration of Independence was approved. There was no turning back.

One of the last states to have a constitution was Massachusetts. Its citizens rejected the first proposed constitution because it lacked a bill of rights. In 1779, a new constitution was proposed with a detailed Declaration of Rights (see Document 12) modeled after the Virginia Bill of Rights, and the constitution was approved the following year (Bodenhamer 1992). It was the only state constitution submitted to its citizens for approval.

These state constitutions provide a summary of the rights Americans expected from their government on the eve of writing the Constitution of the United States. When the war ended in 1783 with the colonists victorious, the state constitutions and their guarantees of rights gained full legitimacy.

The Articles of Confederation, the first national constitution, was ratified in March 1781. It had no provisions guaranteeing fundamental rights, assuming those protections were provided through state constitutions. In the Northwest Ordinance (see Document 13), which set up procedures for dealing with the unsettled regions north and west of the existing states, Congress did include a list of rights. These rights were to "forever remain unalterable, unless by common consent." Included were the now familiar rights of trial by jury, writ of habeas corpus, due process of law, bail, and freedom from cruel or unusual punishment.

The Articles of Confederation quickly lost support, however, and calls for revision increased in intensity. In May 1787, delegates met in Philadelphia and emerged five months later with a new constitution. Remarkably, it did not contain a bill of rights either. Only a few rights of citizens were mentioned, and the only trial right was contained in a single section (see Document 14). It required a jury trial in the location where the crime was committed.

The new federal Constitution had to be submitted to states for ratification, and it was hotly debated. Those who supported the Constitution became known as Federalists and its opponents as Anti-Federalists. The Federalists published a series of insightful essays arguing for the Constitution. In Federalist No. 83 (see Document 15), concerns about the absence of mention of jury trials in civil courts, which handle cases other than criminal, are addressed. Anti-Federalists had claimed that no mention of jury trials in civil courts meant they were eliminated. If jury trials could be eliminated for civil cases, why not for criminal cases as well? Alexander Hamilton, the author of Federalist No. 83, dismissed these fears. Hamilton argued that jury trials in civil cases were not eliminated; they were just not mentioned. Doing so allows the new government freedom to establish civil courts and the procedures of those courts.

As with the Massachusetts Constitution, the Constitution was widely denounced for lacking a statement of rights. During the ensuing debate, commitments were made that the new government would append a list of rights. The Constitution was ratified and the first ten amendments listing the rights of citizens promptly approved. The Fifth and Sixth Amendments (see Document 16) contain the trial rights listed at the beginning of this introduction. These rights included most of the trial rights contained in earlier statements and in state constitutions, with the addition of double jeopardy. The language of these rights sounded familiar, for it was based on previous statements. Although aware of legal theory, the authors of these rights constructed them primarily from experience.

CONSTITUTIONAL RIGHTS

In the federal system established by the Constitution, power is shared between the national government and the state governments. Rights of individuals are guaranteed by the Constitution and by state constitutions. The rights listed in each are not identical, however. The state and federal courts are charged with interpreting the law and constitutions to explain their meaning in specific cases. The debate over rights now becomes a legal matter and is expressed primarily through court decisions.

Initially, it was assumed that the rights in the Constitution restrained only the federal government and that each state was guided by its own list of rights contained in its constitution or laws. Some began to reason that since federal rights apply to the entire country, they should be applied in state courts as well as in federal courts. In *Barron v. Mayor & City Council of Baltimore* (see Document 17), the Supreme Court decided otherwise. Chief Justice John Marshall reasoned that the Constitution established the national government and that its provisions applied only to that government. Had the writers of the Constitution intended otherwise, they would have so stated. The Court used language to express its reasoning in this case to imply that this decision applied to the entire Bill of Rights. This issue was generally considered settled—the Bill of Rights restricts the actions of only the federal government.

In the ensuing decades, the Supreme Court had little to say about trial rights. With a belief that the best federal government is one that rules least, Congress let the states deal with most criminal matters. Since few criminal statutes were enacted by Congress and since the Bill of Rights applied only to federal cases, there were almost no decisions involving trial rights (Bodenhamer 1992).

During the 1820s and again in the 1850s, many states revised their constitution. Most of the federal protections for criminal defendants were incorporated in these new constitutions. But what states included differed, and, to a surprising degree, the meaning of the rights varied from state to state as their state courts interpreted them (Bodenhamer 1992).

In the tumult of the Civil War and the following decades of adjustment, the Supreme Court began to deal with trial rights more frequently. The Civil War began in 1861. The unprecedented action of some states withdrawing from the Union to form another country created fear and confusion everywhere. It was unclear which states would remain loyal to the Union. There were individuals in the Northern states, particularly those that bordered the Confederate states, who argued for withdrawal. The federal government decided it must act decisively to secure as many states as possible in the Union. Lincoln ordered that the writ of habeas corpus could be suspended. The right of habeas corpus, preventing a person from being held in jail indefinitely without charges, dates back to the Magna Carta and is guaranteed in the Constitution except in cases of "rebellion or invasion." The actions of the Confederate States of America certainly constituted a rebellion, and so Lincoln proceeded to suspend the writ of habeas corpus in those parts of the country that were wavering about joining or supporting the Confederacy. By suspending the writ, Lincoln could have groups of people gathered up and put in jail, thus preventing them from aiding the Confederacy. The Constitution, however, was unclear regarding who had the power to suspend. Supreme Court Chief Justice Taney and some members of Congress claimed only Congress could. Other members of Congress were content to allow that power to rest with the president (Hyman and Wiecek 1982). When Taney ordered Lincoln to release an individual held when the writ was suspended, Lincoln refused. The crisis was resolved when Congress passed legislation in 1863 regulating how the writ of habeas corpus could be suspended (see Document 18). The law asserted the right of Congress to suspend the writ but delegated that power to the president. It also required indictment by a grand jury to continue holding anyone beyond a specific time limit.

The Supreme Court also reaffirmed trial rights in another Civil War case, *Ex Parte Milligan* (see Document 19). Milligan, a civilian, had been tried in military court, found guilty of disloyal activities, and sentenced to death. In a military court judges decide on guilt; thus Milligan was denied a jury trial. Milligan lived and was tried in Indiana, not a state in rebellion, though martial law had been declared there. The civilian courts were functioning in Indiana. The Supreme Court ruled that the case "involves the very framework of the government and the fundamental principles of American liberty." Since civilian courts were functioning, Milligan should have been tried in them. No other courts can be substituted for functioning civilian courts, even in time of distress. The Court thus preserved the power of civilian, common law courts and all the trial rights attached to them. Even in the difficult times of the Civil War, it called the use of military courts "a gross usurpation of power."

With the war ending in 1865, the victorious North had to determine how to deal with the defeated Confederacy. A group of congressmen known as "Radical Republicans" desired to punish the South and treat it as a conquered foreign country. They declared martial law, stationed troops, and replaced civil authority with military authority. Congress passed the Civil Rights Act of 1866 to guarantee rights to former slaves, but President Andrew Johnson, believing that the 1866 act violated the rights of states by requiring them to apply a federal standard in their state courts, vetoed the law. Congress promptly passed the law over his veto. Congress also proposed constitutional amendments. The Thirteenth Amendment ended slavery everywhere in the country forever. Concerned that the Civil Rights Act would be declared unconstitutional, Congress proposed the Fourteenth Amendment (see Document 20), which used virtually the same language. It was easily approved, partially because former Confederate states had to ratify the amendment as a condition of rejoining the Union.

The Fourteenth Amendment redefined the relationship between the national and state governments. Its goal was to protect the former slaves, now freedmen, from discrimination based on their former status. It stated that "all persons born or naturalized in the United States . . . are citizens of the United States and of the State wherein they reside." Thus citizens have dual citizenship, national and state. It also prevented states from doing anything that would "abridge the privileges or immunities of citizens of the United States." Further, it stated that states cannot "deprive any person of life, liberty, or property, without due process of law; nor deny to any person within its jurisdiction the equal protection of the laws." It, therefore, also provided for federal involvement in preserving citizens' rights, an area that had belonged exclusively to states. It was generally believed that the amendment had no effect on the states' historical control of criminal process (Beth 1971).

In the aftermath of the Civil War and the determined efforts of the ex-Confederate states to deprive freedmen of their rights, the federal government enacted new criminal legislation. The explosion of economic development after the war also contributed to increased federal criminal legislation, primarily to control economic activity.

An example is the Slaughterhouse cases (1873). In New Orleans a monopoly was granted by the city in the slaughtering trade. Other butchers sued claiming that the action deprived them of liberty and property without due process of law guaranteed under the Fourteenth Amendment. In a far-reaching ruling, the Supreme Court reasoned that federal and state citizenship were different. The Fourteenth Amendment applied only to federal rights, and most rights belonging to Americans came from state citizenship. There was no infringement of due process, since the city had acted in accordance with its own laws. This was known as procedural due process. Due process results from following appropriate procedures. Some justices dissented, arguing that substantive due process was required. Substantive due process refers to the outcome of the case being consistent with understanding of the meaning of rights. In time, substantive due process won out.

Only a few cases tested the idea that federalism and dual citizenship meant that the Fourteenth Amendment did not apply the entire federal Bill of Rights as a restraint on the actions of states. One case that did was *Hurtado v. California* (see Document 21). In this case, the Court ruled that the Fifth Amendment guarantee of a grand jury indictment in criminal proceedings did not apply in state trials, only in federal trials. "The Fourteenth Amendment does not profess to secure to all persons in the United States the benefit of the same laws and the same remedies. Great diversities may exist . . . in two States separated only by an imaginary line. On one side there might be a right of trial by jury, and on the other side no such right. Each state prescribes its own modes of judicial proceeding," the Court explained.

The lone dissenter, on this and other cases involving the application of the Bill of Rights to the states, was Justice Harlan, who believed that the intent of the Fourteenth Amendment was to require the states to abide by all the rights in the Bill of Rights. His dissents remain important because his reasoning became the majority opinion in the twentieth century.

The Supreme Court decisions of this era did not break new ground, but they did reaffirm the contemporary understanding of the authority of states and the federal government (dual federalism) and of defendants' rights.

The Court was presented with an increasing number of federal criminal rights cases as Congress passed new legislation to deal with the development of national businesses and other organizations. In *Ex Parte Wilson* (see Document 22), the Court ruled that a grand jury indictment was needed in federal court for any infamous crime, meaning a crime punishable by up to fifteen years' imprisonment. In another case, the Supreme Court had previously found that the indictment was invalid for three men, two of whom had been found guilty of murder. The third was found innocent. The state retried all three. On appeal, the Supreme Court ruled in *Ball v. United States* (see Document 23) that the retrial of the third man violated his double jeopardy rights. In *Bram v. United States* (see Document 25), the Court found that the confession given by the defendant was not freely given and could not be introduced as evidence in his federal trial.

When *Chicago, B. & Q. R. Co. v. City of Chicago* (see Document 24) came to the Court in 1897, the justices agreed with the defendants that the Fourteenth Amendment guarantee of due process meant that government could not take away private property without just compensation, which is also a guarantee of the Fifth Amendment. Chicago wanted to expand a street and cross the railroad's tracks, and a jury determined that just compensation to the railroad was $1.00. The railroad appealed the case. Although the Court agreed with the valuation offered by Chicago, it also established that the Fourteenth Amendment due process provision requires just compensation. Although the Court never mentioned the Fifth Amendment in its decision, it was generally believed that the Court had applied the just compensation provision of the Fifth Amendment to the states through the Fourteenth Amendment. This was the slow start of a rethinking of the meaning of the Fourteenth Amendment's due process clause.

In *Twining v. State of New Jersey* (see Document 26), the Court took another step. Twining was convicted of misrepresentation and was convicted largely because the judge drew a negative inference from Twining's refusal to testify. Whereas in New Jersey, the judge was permitted to do so, in other states and in federal courts such a conclusion would not be allowed. On hearing his case, the Supreme Court ruled once again that the Fifth Amendment's language concerning self-incrimination and due process is not applicable to state courts. However, the Court did volunteer the belief that personal rights like those in the Bill of Rights might be applied to the states through the Fourteenth Amendment "because they are of such a nature that they are included in the conception of due process of law."

A trend in state courts was an emphasis on efficiency that led to new procedures such as plea bargaining. This is a pre-trial agreement between the prosecutor and the defendant to exchange a guilty plea for a lighter sentence. Another innovation was the bench trial, in which a judge decided the defendant's guilt and punishment instead of a jury. In other states, the role of the jury was limited to a determination of facts only. These innovations tended to challenge the traditional rights of the accused (Bodenhamer 1992).

Another challenge was based on the treatment of immigrants and African Americans. Both found that their rights were not protected in the same way as those of Anglo-Saxons. In the Red Scare of 1919 after World War I, Americans feared that the Bolsheviks who had taken control in Russia were causing labor and social strife in the United States. In a xenophobic response, citizens engaged in left-wing activities were harassed and arrested, many were deported, and documents of radical organizations were burned. When African Americans committed crimes against others of their own race, the crimes were often treated lightly, frequently ignored. But should an African American commit a crime against whites, punishment was swift and fierce. This dual standard in state courts was noticed and documented, along with other shortcomings, often shocking shortcomings, in a series of criminal justice studies in the 1920s (Bodenhamer 1992). In 1919, race riots involving African Americans and whites occurred in twenty cities, most in the North. In the aftermath, reports revealed discriminatory law enforcement before and during the riots. In 1931, the report of the National Commission on Law Observance and Enforcement appointed by President Hoover presented evidence of widespread police brutality (National Commission 1931).

These abuses of the rights of individuals enraged many Americans. In the 1920s, numerous organizations were formed to protect individuals from these abuses. Prominent among these was the American Civil Liberties Union (ACLU). Founded during World War I, it quickly grew into a national organization focused on defending the rights of individuals. It planned to use the Fourteenth Amendment's due process clause to extend the Bill of Rights of the states. This reasoning became known as incorporation (Bodenhamer 1992). Numerous other organizations adopted the same strategy, including the National Association for the Advancement of Colored People (NAACP) and the International Labor Defense.

The Supreme Court redefined the rights of the accused in a series of cases beginning in the 1930s through the 1950s. By the end of these three decades, the Bill of Rights provision for no coerced confessions, public trial, impartial jury, and counsel were required in state courts. During this time, the Court in deciding a variety of cases identified which rights from the Bill of Rights were required of states and which were not. One of the difficulties for the Court was the absence of a clear theoretical basis for their decisions. The Court articulated the reasoning that in a federal system the states have the primary responsibility in their own courts to provide for fair trials. Only those rights fundamental to a fair trial are required by the Fourteenth Amendment's due process clause. Since the Court had no clear list or rationale for others to determine which rights are fundamental to a fair trial, those rights had to be determined case by case. This left state courts unsure which federal rights the Court would decide they had to honor.

A minority on the Court argued that all of the Bill of Rights should be applied to the states. Justice Black articulated this position. He asked, how is it possible for some parts of the Bill of Rights to be more fundamental to a fair trial than other parts? This position was known as total incorporation. Total incorporation had the benefit of providing a clear standard for state courts, but the majority of the Court did not embrace total incorporation for decades. Instead, the Court's decisions wavered regarding the incorporation of the Bill of Rights, with some decisions seeming to limit the rights applied to the states and some decisions expanding the list of rights applied to the states through the due process clause of the Fourteenth Amendment.

The Fourteenth Amendment had been enacted to prevent discriminatory treatment of African Americans, but segregation and discrimination existed throughout the country. It is appropriate that the case that first caused the Court to apply the Fourteenth Amendment to trial rights involved African Americans. A small group of African American young men aged 13 to 19 were hiding in a freight train traveling across Alabama in 1931. The Great Depression had started, and many young men traveled the rails hoping to find something better. These youths were found in the cars in Scottsboro, Alabama, with two teenage white girls who, when found, claimed they had been raped repeatedly. The Scottsboro Boys, as they were called in newspaper stories, were charged, tried, and sentenced to death in four separate trials that together took four days. More than three thousand people came to watch, and the National Guard had to be called out to control the crowd. The National Guard even felt compelled to mount machine guns on the courthouse.

Groups as diverse as the Communist Party of the United States and the NAACP lent support to the Scottsboro Boys to help in their appeals (Bodenhamer 1992). In *Powell v. Alabama* (see Document 27), decided in 1935, the Supreme Court was asked to rule that the protections for defendants in the Bill of Rights should be applied in state courts through the due process clause of the Fourteenth Amendment. The Court agreed, focusing on the lack of adequate counsel. It ruled that having counsel in a capital case was essential to due process, and the Fourteenth Amendment prevented the states from denying due process. The Court had already ruled in other cases that the rights of speech and press were applied to the states by the amendment. The Court reasoned that they were fundamental to the liberty that states could not deprive of its citizens. This was the first case in which the Court applied Bill of Rights criminal procedures to the states. It would not be the last.

In another Scottsboro Boys case, *Norris v. Alabama* (see Document 28), decided the next year, the systematic exclusion of African Americans from juries was found to be a violation of the defendant's right to due process guaranteed by the Fourteenth Amendment. In that same year, the Court ruled in *Brown v. Mississippi* (see Document 29) that the treatment of the defendants was a "wrong so fundamental that it made the whole proceeding a mere pretense of a trial." Brown and two co-defendants had been convicted of murder. The only evidence was their confessions, which had been given only after the three were tortured. Brown had been hanged several times and beaten. He still had rope burns on his neck at his trial.

But not all the rights of the accused were applied to the states, just those considered fundamental to due process, the Court explained in

Palko v. Connecticut (see Document 30). Palko was tried, convicted of second-degree murder, retried because of errors in the first trial, and found guilty of second-degree murder in the second trial. He appealed, claiming he was subject to double jeopardy. The Court disagreed because double jeopardy was not fundamental to due process. Only those rights are protected if their denial imposed "hardships so shocking that our polity will not endure it." States were still free to follow a great variety of criminal procedures so long as the result was a fair trial.

Thus in *Betts v. Brady* (see Document 31), the Court found that the trial court's refusal to appoint an attorney was not a denial of due process. Admiral Dewey Adamson (see Document 32) refused to testify at his murder trial, and his refusal to testify was used to suggest to the jury that he was guilty. The Court ruled that Adamson's treatment was not a violation of the Fourteenth Amendment. This was a close, 5 to 4 decision. The four justices who dissented did so with the argument that the entire Bill of Rights should be incorporated by and required of the states. The Court majority maintained the fundamental fairness reasoning. The Court did find in *Cole v. Arkansas* (see Document 33) that a defendant must be informed of the crime for which he is tried; and in *In Re Oliver* (see Document 34), the secret proceeding and the defendant's inability to offer any defense were found unconstitutional. Yet in *Bute v. People of State of Illinois* (see Document 35), the circumstances were different and the absence of counsel was not found to be unconstitutional. In this case, four justices did dissent, arguing that the state procedure should comply with the federal procedure that would have required the defendant to have counsel. The Court found that the defendant in *Griffin v. Illinois* (see Document 36) was denied due process and equal protection. In Illinois to have an appellate review, various documents must be prepared. Those documents can be expensive, and Griffin, being indigent, could not afford them. Under Illinois law only those indigents sentenced to death were entitled to free documents. Thus those who could afford the documents could have an appeal and those who could not were denied the appeal. The Supreme Court found the Illinois procedure to be unfair and unconstitutional.

DUE PROCESS REVOLUTION

Earl Warren was appointed chief justice by President Eisenhower in 1953 to repay a political debt. Only a few chief justices merit having their name applied to the Court (as in "Warren Court") during their tenure. Warren was the only chief justice in the twentieth century worthy of the honor. He served until his retirement in 1969. Warren was a politician, not a judge, but his view of court activism to champion the individual, especially those normally ignored, would dramatically change the course of the Court. Warren believed, in reasoning that sounded much like that of America's founding fathers, that people have natural rights that need to be protected against arbitrary government. These rights are guaranteed in the Bill of Rights, but their meaning needs to be revisited over time as circumstances change. He predicted, "Thus it is that when the generation of 1980 receives from us the Bill of Rights, the document will not have exactly the same meaning it had when we received it from our fathers" (Warren 1955, 226). No one predicted how sweeping the changes would be.

After World War II, American society was returning to peacetime. Prosperity had returned, and there was no repetition of the Great Depression after this world war. The Great Depression and World War II had contributed to a great strengthening of the federal government's role in the everyday life of Americans. This was consistent with a new nationalization of many institutions. Businesses sold the same goods in all parts of the country; a McDonald's hamburger was the same everywhere. Nationally circulated magazines and network television began to bind all parts of the country together into more of a national whole. Warren's activist views were supported by these and similar developments.

The Warren Court's first blockbuster decision was *Brown v. Board of Education* in 1954. The decision eliminated segregation in public schools and led to additional laws and decisions that eliminated the legal foundations for a segregated society. The Warren Court made decisions on the electoral process, public support of religion, obscenity, free speech, public representation, and other issues that were just as revolutionary and controversial. Between 1961 and 1969, the Warren Court made rulings that incorporated almost the complete Bill of Rights in the meaning of the due process clause of the Fourteenth Amendment. The same restraints on government action then existed in both federal and state courts.

In 1963, the Court decided in *Gideon v. Wainwright* (see Document 37) that the Fourteenth Amendment requires every defendant in capital and noncapital cases in state and federal courts to have an attorney. If the defendant is indigent, as was Gideon, the trial court must appoint counsel. Thus, *Betts v. Brady* (see Document 31) was overturned and the counsel requirement of *Powell v. Alabama* (see Document 27) was extended to noncapital cases. That same year, in *Douglas v. California* (see Document 38), the Court found that indigent defendants were entitled to counsel for their first appeal also.

The right to counsel for a fair trial was returned to again and again. Could a suspect be questioned by police without a lawyer? That was common practice, but in *Escobedo v. Illinois* (see Document 42) the Court found that the accused was entitled to a lawyer during questioning, since incriminating statements could be made and used later in the defendant's trial. Having counsel at the trial would do little good if the defendant had already been incriminated by his own statements. Any statements made by the defendant without the presence of counsel could not be entered into evidence at the trial. Of course, the defendant could waive the right to counsel.

This decision left confusion with police. What constituted a waiver? Can no questions be asked before counsel is present? The Court clarified its ruling in *Miranda v. Arizona* (see Document 46). The now famous phrase "You have the right to remain silent. Anything you say can and will be used against you in court. You have the right to an attorney, and if you cannot afford one, one will be appointed" was dictated by the Court to be given to every individual as soon as police start questioning. As soon as the defendant asks for counsel, all questioning should stop until counsel is present. This decision angered many who thought it would be nearly impossible to secure confessions in the future. Police were particularly upset, not only because the task of questioning individuals was made more complex but also because police questioning techniques were severely criticized by the Court. By now many called for Earl Warren's impeachment. Billboards declared, "Save America. Impeach Earl Warren." Others welcomed the expanded protections for the accused.

The right to counsel has many manifestations. Massiah's incriminating comments to an associate were broadcast over a hidden radio transmitter to nearby federal agents who later testified in court about the comments. The Court ruled in *Massiah v. United States* (see Document 39) that eavesdropping constituted testimony taken without the advice of counsel.

Another thorny issue for the Court was self-incrimination. In *Malloy v. Hogan* (see Document 40), in a 5 to 4 decision, the Court ruled for the first time that the Fifth Amendment protection from self-incrimination applied in state as well as federal courts. Following quickly was the case of *Murphy v. Waterfront Commission* (see Document 41). In this case, the accused was granted immunity from prosecution in the state court and compelled to give testimony. He refused, since he could also be charged in federal court for the same crime. The Court overruled its previous decisions that immunity did not pass jurisdictions and decided that a grant of immunity applied in both federal and state courts. Griffin had claimed his Fifth Amendment right against self-incrimination in a California court and refused to answer questions. The judge commented to the jury that his refusal could be interpreted as evidence of guilt. The Court ruled in *Griffin v. California* (see Document 44) against such comments because they were a violation of Fifth Amendment rights.

Confrontation of witnesses is a Sixth Amendment right that the Court applied to the states in *Pointer v. Texas* (see Document 43). Pointer was questioned at a preliminary hearing. He had no counsel and did not cross-examine the complaining witness. By the time of his trial, the witness had moved to California and refused to return. Prosecutors entered into evidence the transcript of the preliminary hearing, but the Court found that violated Pointer's right to confront and question witnesses. Similarly, in *Bruton v. United States* (see Document 51), a confession of a co-defendant that implicated Bruton was entered into evidence, but the co-defendant did not testify under his Fifth Amendment right. The Court found that this violated Bruton's right to confront and question witnesses against him. This was true even though the trial judge ordered the jury to consider only the confession as evidence against Evans.

The Warren Court also had the opportunity to rule about fairness in trials. In 1966, it considered the case of *Sheppard v. Maxwell* (see Document 45), which involved the role of the media in covering trials. Sheppard was a respected doctor whose pregnant wife was killed while he slept in another room. He was immediately suspected though he claimed he had awoken to struggle with a man he could not describe. This dramatic case was seized on by the local press and then by the national press and television. The stories before his trial consistently featured Sheppard in an unfavorable light, often clearly implying that he was guilty. The actual trial was a media circus with reporters filling most of the seats in the courthouse and wandering through the halls of the courthouse interviewing everyone. Their noise and confusion often interfered with the trial court's proceeding. This outrageous behavior prevented Sheppard from having a fair trial, the Supreme Court ruled. The judge had a responsibility for controlling the media coverage, and the Court included specific advice about how to do so. The Court also carefully expressed appreciation for the role the press plays in a free society, recognizing its protection under the First Amendment.

In *Parker v. Gladden* (see Document 47), the Court considered the consequence of a bailiff's making comments to jurors about the guilt of the accused. This was found to be unconstitutional behavior under the Sixth Amendment right to an impartial jury. And in *Duncan v. Louisiana* (see Document 52), decided in 1968, the Warren Court found that a jury trial is needed even in state misdemeanor trials. It required the same rule in state courts as is used in federal courts, namely, that any crime punishable by more than six months in jail requires a jury trial.

The Sixth Amendment guarantees a speedy trial, but how speedy is that? In *Klopfer v. North Carolina* (see Document 48), the Court found that Klopfer had been denied a speedy trial. He was tried once, but the jury could not reach a verdict. The prosecutor indicated he would retry, but after eighteen months the prosecutor filed a motion that would allow the trial to be delayed indefinitely using an unusual feature of North Carolina law. The Court decided that this violated Klopfer's right to a speedy trial and applied the speedy trial right to all state courts.

The Warren Court revolutionized the treatment of minors in juvenile courts with its decision in *In Re Gault* (see Document 49). Juvenile courts were established to treat youth in especially appropriate ways. Sometimes, however, youths were denied fair trial rights according to the Court. Gault was 15 years old when he was charged with making obscene phone calls. Police seized him from his home, questioned him, and held him without his parents' knowledge. He was charged with delinquency and sentenced to the State Industrial School for six years, until he was 21. He was denied an attorney and a jury trial. An adult convicted of the same crime would have been fined $5 to $50 and imprisoned for no more than two months. The Court ordered that youths as well as adults must receive fair treatment and dictated specific due process rights that must be incorporated into juvenile procedures.

By the mid-1960s, the Warren Court had included almost all the Bill of Rights in the meaning of due process required of states by the Fourteenth Amendment. In 1967, the right to obtain witnesses was extended to state proceedings, and in 1969, to protection from double jeopardy. Texas state laws prevented a participant's testimony during the trial of a co-participant. The Court found that in *Washington v. Texas* (see Document 50), the testimony of a co-participant would have been helpful and so struck down the Texas law. The ruling also noted that the right to obtain witnesses in the accused's favor is included in the due process clause of the Fourteenth Amendment. Double jeopardy, namely, being placed in jeopardy twice for the same crime, does not apply to cases in which the defendant is retried as the result of a mistrial or because on appeal a retrial has been ordered. *Benton v. Maryland* (see Document 53) clarified that a defendant found innocent of a charge cannot be retried on the same charge when a retrial is ordered. Benton had been tried and found guilty of burglary and innocent of larceny. Because of an invalid constitutional provision of the Maryland Constitution, the grand jury and petit jury in his case were improperly impaneled. He was retried on both charges and convicted of both. He maintained, and the Warren Court agreed, that since he had been found innocent of larceny in his first trial and since that trial had been fair, retrying him on the larceny charge was double jeopardy. Double jeopardy was added to the list of rights contained in the due process clause.

AFTER THE WARREN COURT

Earl Warren resigned in 1969. Many feared that the Court under new leadership would reverse many of the Warren Court's decisions. There was plenty of cause for concern. Nixon had been elected president with law-and-order campaign promises. He vowed to appoint conservative justices to the Supreme Court and blamed judicial permissiveness as a cause of crime (Bodenhamer 1992). Congress passed the Omnibus Crime Control and Safe Streets Act of 1968, designed to reverse recent Court decisions. The law allowed voluntary confession to be used as evidence even if an attorney was not present. Police could hold suspects for six hours or longer without arraignment and use in trial any confession that was given (Murphy 1972).

These concerns were ill-founded. In the decades after the Warren Court, its decisions relating to defendants' rights were not overturned. The new chief justice, Warren Burger, was more conservative and did not advocate judicial activism, believing reform was more properly a function of legislatures. His successor, William Rehnquist, was similarly conservative. Although the Court did not undo the due process revolution, it was less willing to expand the rights of defendants. This can be seen in the cases over the three decades since Warren retired.

For example, in 1970, the Court ruled in *Williams v. Florida* (see Document 54) that a twelve-member jury is not required. This reversed a series of decisions dating back to 1898. Two years later the Court ruled in *Johnson v. Louisiana* (see Document 55) that unanimity of a jury verdict was not required to convict in state courts. Louisiana law permitted conviction if nine out of twelve jurors agreed. And in *Lewis v. United States* (see Document 63), the Court found that Lewis was not entitled to a jury trial because the penalty for his crime was six months in jail. This was despite his conviction carrying a total sentence of twelve months, since he was charged with two counts of the offense.

In *Gideon,* the Court had ruled that in every trial involving imprisonment of six months or more, the accused was entitled to be represented by counsel. In *Argersinger v. Hamlin* (see Document 57), the Court expanded *Gideon,* calling for counsel when the accused could be sentenced to a prison term of any length.

In 1970, Congress enacted a new more limited immunity law. The law set procedures for offering immunity from prosecution so defendants could testify even if that testimony was self-incriminating. The old immunity rule provided that the individual offered immunity could not be prosecuted for the crime. The new rule allowed prosecution, but the government had to show that the evidence used was not based on the testimony or derived from it. In *Kastigar v. United States* (see Document 56), the Court found the new law did not violate self-incrimination rights.

In *Barker v. Wingo* (see Document 58), the Court ruled regarding the right to a speedy trial. Barker's trial began five years after his arrest as a result of an unusual series of events. His co-defendant was tried separately, and his first five trials were not completed. The sixth trial ended in his conviction. Barker's trial was further delayed by illness. When he was tried, he was found guilty. He appealed, saying he was denied a speedy trial. The Court reasoned that no fixed timetable could be imposed to define a speedy trial, since cases varied so much. A key consideration in evaluating a delay is its prejudicial effect on the defendant's case. Barker's delay did adversely affect his defense, so the delays in his case were acceptable. Congress responded to this case by passing the Speedy Trial Act of 1974 (see Document 59), which provided guidelines for acceptable delays. The Court has not had an opportunity to rule on the constitutionality of this law.

In another case, the Court found delays unacceptable. Doggett was indicted for drug trafficking, but he was not tried until eight years later because he left the country and, though he openly returned unaware of his indictment, the government was unable to find him for years. The Court ruled in *Doggett v. United States* (see Document 62) that this delay was attributable to government error and did violate the Sixth Amendment.

The Fifth Amendment guarantee of counsel for the accused is not meaningful if the counsel is inadequate. The Court addressed this issue in *Strickland v. Washington* (see Document 61). Strickland appealed his case on a variety of reasons, including inadequate counsel. Upon careful review, the Court found that his counsel had acted appropriately, but laid down guidelines regarding how to judge the competence of an attorney.

One of the most controversial decisions of the Warren Court was in the *Miranda* case. Twice there have come before the Court cases that would have allowed it to reduce or overturn *Miranda*. The first case, *Edwards v. Arizona* (see Document 60), was heard by the Burger Court and involved the waiver of Miranda rights. Edwards had been arrested and was being questioned when he asked for an attorney. Questioning immediately stopped, but the next morning different police began questioning him again. At first he refused to talk, but then he did, and in the course of that questioning he confessed. The appeal of his case argued that he had been denied his Miranda rights. The police argued that when he consented to questioning on the second day, he waived his Miranda rights. The Court found that a waiver must be more explicit and involve knowingly giving up rights. Once Edwards asked for an attorney, no questioning should have been conducted until an attorney was present.

The second case came in 2000 when William Rehnquist was chief justice. As a lawyer, Rehnquist had strongly objected to *Miranda*, and many wondered what he would do when *Dickerson v. United States* (see Document 64) provided him the opportunity to overturn *Miranda*. In the Omnibus Crime Control and Safe Streets Act of 1968, Congress had attempted to overturn *Miranda* by providing that confessions given voluntarily without the presence of counsel could be used at trial. Tried for bank robbery and related federal crimes, Dickerson claimed that his statement used against him was inadmissible because he had not received his Miranda warnings. Chief Justice Rehnquist wrote the opinion strongly supporting *Miranda*. He reasoned that the portion of the Omnibus Crime Control and Safe Streets Act of 1968 that did not require presence of counsel was unconstitutional, since it was contrary to a constitutional finding of the Supreme Court. Rehnquist was joined in this decision by six other justices, showing that the Court still strongly supported *Miranda*.

CONCLUSION

Trial rights of Americans have a long and adventuresome history. From the signing of the Magna Carta, through the Middle Ages, the wrangling of Parliament and English kings, and the founding and development of English colonies to the list of rights contained in our Bill of Rights, the trip was treacherous with the outcome never certain. Trial rights began as a way to protect the people from the will of an arbitrary government. First the concept that people had any rights at all needed to be established. Then over centuries a list of fundamental rights emerged. The American colonies helped refine their own list of basic rights. Once these were codified in the Bill of Rights, they were applied in federal cases. Then to provide consistency in justice, they were expanded to state cases as well. Finally, trial rights were used to protect the accused from arbitrary government action. Today we enjoy our trial rights because of the courage and wisdom of countless predecessors who over the centuries fought for justice.

Significant Events in the History of Fair Trial Rights

1215	Magna Carta signed by King John granting rights to nobles including the first guarantee of right to trial and of due process in British history
1607	First permanent English colony in North America was established in Jamestown
1628	King Charles agreed to the Petition of Rights which guaranteed Englishmen's rights including barring imprisonment by order of the king, martial law, and billeting of troops in citizens' homes
1640–1688	England suffered political turmoil which included a civil war, execution of a king, establishment of a republic, reestablishment of monarchy, and installation of a new line of succession of kings
1641	Massachusetts Body of Liberties was first written guarantee of colonial rights and provided for protection against double jeopardy and guarantee of just compensation for property taken by the government
1677	First colonial guarantee of public trial in Concessions and Agreements of West New Jersey
1682	Pennsylvania Frame of Government provided for a public trial by jury, right to bail, right for accused to appear in court to plead case, and limited fines stated publicly
1683	First colonial guarantee of grand jury indictment in New York Charter of Liberties
1688	England's turmoil ended with the installation of William of Orange and his wife Mary as king and queen in exchange for their agreement to abide by the Bill of Rights which eliminated excessive bail, excessive fines, cruel and unusual punishment, and fines without conviction of a crime and guaranteed impartial selection of jurors
1701	Pennsylvania Charter of Liberties provided the accused with the right to call witnesses and to have counsel

1701   Most of the rights of the accused later included in the Fifth and Sixth Amendments were guaranteed in some colonial statement, though no colony had all the trial rights included in those amendments

1701– Rights already guaranteed were more consistently implemented as the
1770   colonies grew in size and independence

1750– Conflicts between the rights of the colonists and the power of the Eng-
1776   lish king to rule the colonies them led to a revolution

1774   Colonists attempt to gain support of the Canadian colonies by arguing in Address to the Inhabitants of Quebec that their rights, including trial rights, could be abridged by the English king

1776   Colonists declare their independence from England

1776   First colonial guarantees of due process, speedy trial, right to know cause and nature of accusation, and protection against self-incrimination in the Virginia Declaration of Rights, a new state constitution. These and other listed rights are repeated in constitutions approved by other states

1781   Colonists win the Revolutionary War

1781   Articles of Confederation contains no guarantee of rights

1787   New Constitution written which guarantees few rights

1787– U.S. Supreme Court has limited opportunity to rule on trial rights cases
1850s   since few federal criminal laws were passed

1791   Bill of Rights approved. Fifth and Sixth Amendments contain trial rights. These amendments were viewed as applying only to the federal government

1820s– Many states revised their constitutions modeling state trial rights after
1850s   those contained in the U.S. Bill of Rights

1833   In *Baron v. Baltimore* the Supreme Court ruled that the Bill of Rights applies only to the federal government. Individual states govern the rights of citizens in their courts

1861– U.S. Civil War
1865

1861– President Abraham Lincoln suspended the right of habeas corpus lead-
1863   ing to a debate regarding his power to do so. U.S. Congress passed legislation giving him the power, but regulating its use

1866   In *Ex Parte Milligan* the Supreme Court ruled that military courts could not be used when civilian courts were functioning

1868   Amendment Fourteen was ratified guaranteeing due process of law and equal protection by states

1884   In *Hurtado v. California* ruled that Fourteenth Amendment does not require states to follow the trial rights of the Bill of Rights

1897   In *Chicago, B. & Q. R. Co. v. City of Chicago* ruled states are bound by the Fourteenth Amendment due process guarantee and cannot take property without just compensation

1908   In *Twining v. State of New Jersey*, ruled that states are not bound by federal trial rights, but provided that they could be depending on the circumstances

1910s–   Various First Amendment rights are required of states through the due
1920s   process clause of the Fourteenth Amendment

1932–   In three cases, Supreme Court found that treatment by states so fun-
1936   damentally violated trial rights that the due process clause of the Four-teenth Amendment was violated

1937–   In series of cases, Supreme Court selectively requires states to follow
1963   specific provisions of the Fifth and Sixth Amendments by deciding that some are fundamental to due process

1948   The public trial clause of the Sixth Amendment was applied to the states in *In Re Oliver*

1948   In *Cole v. Arkansas* the notice clause of the Sixth Amendment was ap-plied to the states

1960s   In numerous cases, the Supreme Court consistently ruled that the due process clause of the Fourteenth Amendment required states to apply the trial rights of the Fifth and Sixth Amendments in their courts

1963   The right to counsel clause of the Sixth Amendment was required of states in cases involving possible imprisonment of six months or more in *Gideon v. Wainwright*

1964   Self-incrimination clause of the Fifth Amendment was applied to the states in *Malloy v. Hogan*

1964   In *Escobedo v. Illinois*, accused found entitled to lawyer during question-ing

1965   The confrontation clause of the Sixth Amendment was required of states in *Pointer v. Texas*

1966   In *Sheppard v. Maxwell*, ruled that prejudicial news coverage made a fair trial impossible

1966   In *Miranda v. Arizona*, police were required to warn suspects that their statements would be used against them and they were entitled to a lawyer

1966   The Sixth Amendment requirement of an impartial jury was required of states in *Parker v. Gladden*

1967   In *Washington v. Texas* the compulsory process clause of the Sixth Amendment was applied to the states

1967   In *Klopfer v. North Carolina* the Sixth Amendment clause for a speedy trial was applied to the states

1967   Juveniles entitled to due process rights, *In Re Gault*

1968   Jury trial clause of the Sixth Amendment was required of states in cases involving possibility of six months or more of jail sentence in *Duncan v. Louisiana*

Part I

Trial Rights in America's Founding Era

DOCUMENT 1: Magna Carta (1215)

Runnymede is an ordinary appearing meadow next to the Thames River in England near Windsor, where King John of England lived. It is remembered today for a remarkable meeting that occurred there. King John reluctantly came to Runnymede to deal with a group of rebellious barons and on June 15, 1215, signed the Magna Carta, the Great Charter. The king had little choice. The revolt of the barons had spread quickly from its start the previous fall. The king lost support quickly as others joined the barons in their revolt, including the city of London and even the clergy. King John had brought this on himself. His rule was marked by cruel and arbitrary behavior described so well in the stories about the legendary Robin Hood.

The Magna Carta is generally recognized as the first in the series of English documents that guarantees the rights of citizens. It is important for what it said and because it was a written agreement. The Magna Carta is most significant because it stated the principle that the king is subject to the law, as are all others. King John was fond of saying, "The law is in my mouth." After the Magna Carta, he and other kings could no longer say that without being challenged. The Magna Carta is a rambling document that lists solutions to many of the complaints against King John. The clauses included in the selection below are the ones most pertinent for establishing trial rights of citizens.

Under feudal law, these rules applied only to freemen; commoners were called villeins and had to wait for their rights. Slowly as villenage died out, these rights were extended to more people. The Magna Carta laid a foundation for the concept of due process. Although the Magna

Carta is the start of the history of our Bill of Rights, it shares only a few rights in common with it. Only four of the twenty-eight rights in the Bill of Rights are in the Magna Carta. There are an additional fifty-nine provisions in the Magna Carta that are not in the Bill of Rights. The language below has been modernized, and the original document had no numbering.

* * *

THE MAGNA CARTA

1. To all free men of our kingdom we have also granted, for us and our heirs forever, all the liberties written out below, to have and to keep for them and their heirs, of us and our heirs:

17. Ordinary lawsuits shall not follow the royal court around, but shall be held in a fixed place.

20. For a trivial offence, a free man shall be fined only in proportion to the degree of his offence, and for a serious offence correspondingly, but not so heavily as to deprive him of his livelihood. In the same way, a merchant shall be spared his merchandise, and a husbandman the implements of his husbandry, if they fall upon the mercy of a royal court. None of these fines shall be imposed except by the assessment on oath of reputable men of the neighbourhood.

24. No sheriff, constable, coroners, or other royal officials are to hold lawsuits that should be held by the royal justices.

28. No constable, or other royal official shall take corn or other moveable goods from any man without immediate payment, unless the seller voluntarily offers postponement of this.

29. No sheriff, royal official, or other person shall take horses or carts for transport from any free man, without his consent.

38. In future no official shall place a man on trial upon his own unsupported statement, without producing credible witnesses to the truth of it.

39. No free man shall be seized or imprisoned, or stripped of his rights or possessions, or outlawed or exiled, or deprived of his standing in any other way, nor will we proceed with force against him, or send others to do so, except by the lawful judgement of his equals or by the law of the land.

40. To no one will we sell, to no one deny or delay right or justice.

63. It is accordingly our wish and command that the English Church shall be free, and that men in our kingdom shall have and keep all these liberties, rights, and concessions, well and peaceably in their fullness and entirety for them and their heirs, of us and our heirs, in all things and all places for ever.

Both we and the barons have sworn that all this shall be observed in good faith and without deceit. Witness the abovementioned people and many others.

Given by our hand in the meadow that is called Runnymede, between Windsor and Staines, on the fifteenth day of June in the seventeenth year of our reign.

Source: Translations and Reprints from the Original Sources of European History (n.d.), "English Constitutional Documents," ed. by Edward P. Cheyney, I, No. 6, 6–17. Philadelphia: n.p. Based on Stubbs's reprint of the Latin text. Reprinted in Perry, Richard L., and John C. Cooper, eds., *Sources of Our Liberties.* Chicago: American Bar Foundation, 1959, 11–22.

DOCUMENT 2: Petition of Right (1628)

Another great document of English liberty, the Petition of Right grew out of a dispute between King Charles I and Parliament. The dispute, once again, was over the power of the king. By now Parliament had grown in importance, was composed of a House of Commons and a House of Lords, and imposed taxes. The Parliament of 1626 did not vote adequate funding for the king's military adventures.

King Charles insisted that he could continue to charge some taxes without Parliament's consent. He further raised funds through a forced loan. Those who refused to pay were imprisoned, and judges who refused to enforce the loan were dismissed. He billeted soldiers in people's homes, meaning that the people had to provide food and sleeping arrangements for the soldiers without compensation. Martial law, law enforced by the military, was imposed. Men were imprisoned on the order of the king without trial or bail. Even with these measures his finances were exhausted, and Charles convened the Parliament of 1628. This Parliament used Charles's need for money as a tool to establish limits on his power. Twenty-seven of its members had been imprisoned by the king for refusing the loan.

The king's chief adversary in Parliament was Sir Edward Coke. Coke led Parliament in drafting a Petition of Right that condemned arbitrary government. The Petition of Right made imprisonment by order of the king illegal and prohibited tax collection without parliamentary consent. The petition also prohibited the use of martial law and the billeting of troops in homes. The arguments and leadership of Coke in this dispute became a model for American colonial leaders in their dispute with England over taxation and billeting of troops in the next century. King Charles accepted the Petition of Right, but he insisted that it merely confirmed old liberties without creating any new ones.

* * *

Petition of Right, 1628

The petition exhibited to his majesty by the lords spiritual and temporal, and commons in this present parliament assembled, concerning divers rights and liberties of the subjects with the king's majesty's royal answer thereunto in full parliament.

To the king's most excellent majesty: Humbly show unto our sovereign lord the king the lords spiritual and temporal, and commons in parliament assembled, that, whereas it is declared and enacted by a statute made in the time of the reign of King Edward the First, commonly called *Statutum de Tallagio non Concedendo*, that no tallage or aid should be laid or levied by the king or his heirs in this realm without the goodwill and assent of the archbishops, bishops, earls, barons, knights, burgesses, and other freemen of the commonalty of this realm; and, by authority of parliament holden in the five-and-twentieth year of the reign of King Edward III, it is declared and enacted that from thenceforth no person should be compelled to make any loans to the king against his will, because such loans were against reason and the franchise of the land; and by other laws of this realm it is provided that none should be charged by any charge or imposition, called a benevolence, or by such like charge; by which the statutes before mentioned, and other the good laws and statutes of this realm, your subjects have inherited this freedom, that they should not be compelled to contribute to any tax, tallage, aid, or other like charge not set by common consent in parliament: yet, nevertheless, of late divers commissions directed to sundry commissioners in several counties with instructions have issued, by means whereof your people have been in divers places assembled and required to lend certain sums of money unto your majesty; and many of them, upon their refusal so to do, have had an oath administered unto them, not warrantable by the laws of statutes of this realm, and have been constrained to become bound to make appearance and give attendance before your privy council and in other places; and others of them have been therefor imprisoned, confined, and sundry other ways molested and disquieted; and divers other charges have been laid and levied upon your people in several counties by lord lieutenants, deputy lieutenants, commissioners for muster, justices of peace, and others, by command or direction from your majesty or your privy council, against the laws and free customs of the realm.

And where also, by the statute called the Great Charter of the Liberties of England, it is declared and enacted that no freeman may be taken or imprisoned, or be disseised of his freehold or liberties or his free customs, or be outlawed or exiled or in any manner destroyed, but by the lawful judgment of his peers or by the law of the land; and in the eight-and-twentieth year of the reign of Kind Edward III it was declared and enacted by authority of parliament that no man, of what estate or condition that he be, should be put out of his land or tenements, nor taken, nor imprisoned, no disherited, nor put to death, without being brought to answer by due process of law: nevertheless, against the tenor of the said statutes and other the good laws and statutes of your realm to that end provided, divers of your subjects have of late been imprisoned without any cause showed; and when for their deliverance they were brought before your justices by your majesty's writs of *habeas corpus*, there to undergo and receive as the court should order, and their keepers commanded to certify the causes of their detainer, no cause was certified, but that they were detained by your majesty's special command, signified by the lords of your privy council; and yet were returned back to several prisons, without being charged with anything to which they might make answer according to the law.

And whereas of late great companies of soldiers and mariners have been dispersed into divers counties of the realm, and the inhabitants against their will have been compelled to receive them into their houses, and there to suffer them to sojourn, against the laws and customs of this realm, and to the great grievance and vexation of the people: and whereas also, by authority of parliament in the five-and-twentieth year of the reign of Kind Edward III, it is declared and enacted that no man should be forejudged of life or limb against the form of the Great Charter and the law of the land; and, by the said Great Charter and the other laws and statutes of this your realm, no man ought to be adjudged to death but by the laws established in this your realm, either by the customs of the same realm or by acts of parliament; and whereas no offender of what kind soever is exempted from the proceedings to be used, and punishments to be inflicted by the laws and statutes of this your realm: nevertheless of late divers commissions under your majesty's great seal have issued forth, by which certain persons have been assigned and appointed commissioners, with power and authority to proceed within the land according to the justice of martial law against such soldiers or mariners, or other dissolute persons joining with them, as should commit any murder, robbery, felony, mutiny, or other outrage or misdemeanour whatsoever and by such summary course and order as is agreeable to martial law and as is used in armies in time of war, to proceed to the trial and condemnation of such offenders, and them to cause to be executed and put to death according to the law martial; by pretext whereof some of your majesty's subjects have been by some of the said commissioners put to death, when and where, if by the laws and statutes of the land they had deserved death, by the same laws and statutes also they might, and by no other ought to have been, adjudged and executed; and also sundry grievous offenders, by colour thereof claiming an exemption, have escaped the punishments due to them by the laws and statutes of this your realm, by reason that divers of your officers and ministers of justice have unjustly refused or forborne to proceed against such offenders according to the same laws and statutes, upon pretence that the said offenders were punishable only by martial law and by authority of such commissions as aforesaid; which commissions and all other of like nature are wholly and directly contrary to the said laws and statutes of this your realm.

They do therefore humbly pray your most excellent majesty that no man hereafter be compelled to make or yield any gift, loan, benevolence, tax, or such like charge without common consent by act of parliament; and that none be called to make answer, or take such oath, or to give attendance, or be confined, or otherwise molested or disquieted concerning the same, or for refusal thereof; and that no freeman, in any such manner as is before mentioned, be imprisoned or detained; and that your majesty would be pleased to remove the said soldiers and mariners; and that your people may not be so burdened in time to come; and that the foresaid commissions for proceeding by martial law may be revoked and annulled; and that hereafter no commissions of like nature may issue forth to any person or persons whatsoever, to be executed as aforesaid, lest by colour of them any of your majesty's subjects be destroyed or put to death, contrary to the laws and franchise of the land (all of which they most humbly pray of your most excellent majesty as their rights and liberties according to the laws and statutes of this realm); and that your majesty would also vouchsafe and declare that the awards, doings, and proceedings to the prejudice of your people in any of the premises shall not be drawn hereafter into consequence or example; and that your majesty would be also graciously pleased, for the further comfort and safety of your people, to declare your royal will and pleasure that in the things aforesaid all your officers and ministers shall serve you according to the laws and statutes of this realm, as they tender the honour of your majesty and the prosperity of this kingdom.

Source: 3 Car. I, C. I. Danby Pickering, ed. *Statues at Large*. Vol. 7. Cambridge: n.p. 1726–1807, 317–20. Reprinted in Perry, Richard L., and John C. Cooper, eds., *Sources of Our Liberties*. Chicago: American Bar Foundation, 1959, 73–75.

DOCUMENT 3: Bill of Rights (1689)

The U.S. Bill of Rights is a clear descendant of the English Bill of Rights of 1689. The English Bill of Rights, entitled "An Act Declaring the Rights and Liberties of the Subject and Settling the Succession of the Crown," was one outcome of the conflict known as the Glorious

Revolution of 1688. King James II, a staunch Catholic, attempted to end discrimination against Catholics, a religious minority. He replaced Protestants with Catholics in many leadership positions in the military, as civil servants, and as local governors. When Parliament resisted, he dismissed it. He issued a Declaration of Indulgence declaring full equality of religious practice to all Christians. He ordered that it be read from the pulpits of all churches for two weeks. An archbishop and six bishops of the Anglican Church (Church of England) asked him to rescind his order to have it read, since they believed it was illegal. James arrested them for sedition. They were tried and acquitted, and on the day of their acquittal, a messenger was dispatched by the English nobility to invite William of Orange to come to England with his army to depose James.

The invitation to William had some justification. He was the grandson of a previous English king, Charles I, and his wife Mary was the daughter of James. Even though Mary was Protestant, she was the logical successor to the throne until James had a son, a Catholic heir. Faced with the threat of William and his loss of support, James fled England. As he left, he tried to disrupt civil government. He threw the Great Seal of England into the Thames River and did not abdicate his kingship. With James gone and the Great Seal lost, there was no legal government of England.

To solve this dilemma, William convened an assembly that drew up and approved a Declaration of Rights, which William and Mary agreed to abide by. The now vacant throne was offered to and accepted by William and Mary as co-rulers provided they agreed to abide by the Declaration of Rights. The assembly was declared to be an official Parliament, and it quickly enacted the Declaration of Rights as the Bill of Rights.

Among the rights guaranteed by the English Bill of Rights were the following related to trials: elimination of excessive bail, excessive fines, and cruel and unusual punishments; duly impaneling jurors; and no forfeitures of property or fines before conviction. These rights are included in the fifth paragraph of the document.

* * *

Bill of Rights, 1689

An act declaring the right and liberties of the subject and settling the succession of the crown. Whereas the lords spiritual and temporal and commons assembled at Westminster, lawfully, fully, and freely representing all the estates of the people of this realm, did upon the 13th day of February, in the year of our Lord 1688, present unto their majesties, then called and known by the names and style of William and Mary, prince and princess of Orange, being present in their proper persons, a certain declaration in writing made by the said lords and commons in the words following, *viz.*:

Whereas the late King James II, by the assistance of divers evil counselors, judges, and ministers employed by him, did endeavour to subvert and extirpate the Protestant religion and the laws and liberties of this kingdom by assuming and exercising a power of dispensing with and suspending of laws and the execution of laws without consent of parliament, by committing and prosecuting divers worthy prelates for humbly petitioning to be excused from concurring to the said assumed power, by issuing and causing to be executed a commission under the great seal for erecting a court called the court of commissioners for ecclesiastical causes, by levying money for and to the use of the crown by pretence of prerogative for other time and in other manner than the same was granted by parliament, by raising and keeping a standing army within this kingdom in time of peace without consent of parliament and quartering soldiers contrary to law, by causing several good subjects being Protestants to be disarmed at the same time when papists were both armed and employed contrary to law, by violating the freedom of election of members to serve in parliament, by prosecutions in the court of king's bench for matters and causes cognizable only in parliament, and by divers other arbitrary and illegal courses;

And whereas of late years partial, corrupt, and unqualified persons have been returned and served on juries in trials, and particularly divers jurors in trials for high treason, which were not freeholders, and excessive bail hath been required of persons committed in criminal cases to elude the benefit of the laws made for the liberty of the subjects, and excessive fines have been imposed, and illegal and cruel punishments inflicted, and several grants and promises made of fines or forfeitures before any conviction or judgment against the persons upon whom the same were to be levied, all which are utterly and directly contrary to the known laws and statutes and freedom of this realm;

And whereas the said late King James II having abdicated the government, and the throne being thereby vacant, his highness the prince of Orange (whom it hath pleased Almighty God to make the glorious instrument of delivering this kingdom from popery and arbitrary power) did, by the advice of the lords spiritual and temporal and divers principal persons of the commons, cause letters to be written to the lords spiritual and temporal being Protestants, and other letters to the several counties, cities, universities, boroughs, and Cinque Ports for the choosing of such persons to represent them as were of right to be sent to parliament to meet and sit at Westminster. . . . in order to [provide] such an establishment as that their religion, laws, and liberties might not again be in danger of being subverted, upon which letters elections having been accordingly made:

And thereupon the said lords spiritual and temporal and commons, pursuant to their respective letters and elections being now assembled in a full and free representative of this nation, taking into their most serious consideration the best means for attaining the ends aforesaid, do in the first place (as their ancestors in like case have usually done) for the vindicating and asserting their ancient rights and liberties, declare that the pretended power of suspending of laws or the execution of laws by regal authority without consent of parliament is illegal; . . . that jurors ought to be duly impanelled and returned, and jurors which pass upon men in trials for high treason ought to be freeholders; that all grants and promises of fines and forfeitures of particular persons before conviction are illegal and void; and that, for redress of all grievances and for the amending, strengthening, and preserving of the laws, parliaments ought to be held frequently. . . .

Having therefore an entire confidence that his said highness the prince of Orange will perfect the deliverance so far advanced by him and will still preserve them from the violation of their rights which they have here asserted and from all other attempts upon their religion, rights, and liberties, the said lords spiritual and temporal and commons assembled at Westminster do resolve that William and Mary, prince and princess of Orange, be and be declared king and queen of England, France, and Ireland, and the dominions thereunto belonging, to hold the crown and royal dignity of the said kingdoms and dominions to them, the said prince and princess, during their lives and the life of the survivor of them; and that the sole and full exercise of the regal power be only in and executed by the said prince of Orange in the names of the said prince and princess during their joint lives, and after their deceases the said crown and royal dignity of the said kingdoms and dominions to be to the heirs of the body of the said princess, and for default of such issue to the princess Anne of Denmark and the heirs of her body, and for default of such issue to the heirs of the body of the said prince of Orange. . . .

Upon which their said majesties did accept the crown and royal dignity of the kingdoms of England, France, and Ireland and the dominions thereunto belonging, according to the resolution and desire of the said lords and commons contained in the said declaration; . . .

Now, in pursuance of the premises, the said lords spiritual and temporal and commons in parliament assembled, for the ratifying, confirming, and establishing the said declaration and the articles, clauses, matters, and things therein contained by the force of a law made in due form by authority of parliament, do pray that it may be declared and enacted that all and singular the rights and liberties asserted and claimed in the said declaration are the true, ancient, and indubitable rights and liberties of the people of this kingdom and so shall be esteemed, allowed, adjudged, deemed, and taken to be; and that all and every the particulars aforesaid shall be firmly and strictly holden and observed as they are expressed in the said declaration, and all officers and ministers whatsoever shall serve their majesties and their successors according to the same in all times to come. . . .

And for preventing all questions and divisions in this realm by reason of any pretended titles to the crown, and for preserving a certainty in the succession thereof, in and upon which the unity, peace, tranquillity, and safety of this nation doth under God wholly consist and depend, the said lords spiritual and temporal and commons do beseech their majesties that it may be enacted, established, and declared that the crown and regal government of the said kingdoms and dominions, with all and singular the premises thereunto belonging and appertaining, shall be and continue to their said majesties and the survivor of them during their lives and the life of the survivor of them; . . . and after their deceases the said crown and premises shall be and remain to the heirs of the body of her majesty, and, for default of such issue, to her royal highness the princess Anne of Denmark and the heirs of her body and, for default of such issue, to the heirs of the body of his said majesty. And thereunto the lords spiritual and temporal and commons do, in the name of all the people aforesaid, mostly humbly and faithfully submit themselves, their heirs, and posterities forever; and do faithfully promise that they will stand to maintain and defend their said majesties, and also the limitation and succession of the crown herein specified and contained, to the utmost of their powers with their lives and estates against all persons whatsoever that shall attempt anything to the contrary.

And whereas it hath been found by experience that it is inconsistent with the safety and welfare of this Protestant kingdom to be governed by a popish prince or by any king or queen marrying a papist, the said lords spiritual and temporal and commons do further pray that it may be enacted that all and every person and persons that is, are, or shall be reconciled to, or shall hold communion with, the see or Church of Rome, or shall profess the popish religion, or shall marry a papist shall be excluded and be forever incapable to inherit, possess, or enjoy the crown and government of this realm and Ireland and the dominions thereunto belonging or any part of the same, or to have, use or exercise any regal power, authority, or jurisdiction within the same. . . .

All which their majesties are contented and pleased shall be declared, enacted, and established by authority of this present parliament; and shall stand, remain, and be the law of this realm forever. And the same are by their said majesties, by and with the advice and consent of the lords spiritual and temporal and commons in parliament assembled and by the authority of the same, declared, enacted, and established accordingly. And be it further declared and enacted by the authority aforesaid that, from and after this present session of parliament, no dispensation ... of or to any statute, or any part thereof, shall be allowed; but that the same shall be held void and of no effect—except a dispensation be allowed of in such statute, and except in such cases as shall be specially provided for by one or more bill or bills to be passed during this present session of parliament. Provided that no charter or grant or pardon granted before the three-and-twentieth day of October, in the year of our Lord 1689, shall be anyways impeached or invalidated by this act; but that the same shall be and remain of the same force and effect in law and no other than as if this act had never been made.

Source: I Will. and Mary, sess. 2, c.2. Danby Pickering, ed. *Statues at Large*. Vol. 9. Cambridge: n.p., 1726–1897, 67–73. Reprinted in Perry, Richard L., and John C. Cooper, eds. *Sources of Our Liberties*. Chicago: American Bar Foundation, 1959, 11–22.

DOCUMENT 4: Massachusetts Body of Liberties (1641)

With the colonial charter had come the right of the colonists to rule from the colonies, not from England. The colonists wanted laws that would guarantee "such liberties Immenities and priveledges as humanitie, Civilitie, and Christianitie call for as due to every man in his place and proportion." Following a large influx of immigrants in 1630, the colonists pushed for a more representative government. Though resisted at first, one was established and then came the cry for a statement of liberties.

Governor John Winthrop of the Massachusetts Bay colony explained the need for the Body of Liberties in his journal. They were intending, Winthrop recorded, to "frame a body of grounds of laws, in resemblance to a Magna Carta." They succeeded in this attempt admirably. This was a most remarkable document for its time. Fully twenty-five of the twenty-eight rights included in the Bill of Rights are present in the Massachusetts Body of Liberties. This is the first colonial document guaranteeing specific liberties.

Most importantly, the Body of Liberties was the first colonial effort to express the idea that fundamental rights of the people should be contained in a written instrument enacted by their representatives. Nothing like it existed in England.

This statement of rights influenced subsequent statements in other colonies and the Bill of Rights itself. Nevertheless, it was not perfect.

The statement of rights, while phrased in enlightened ways, had different meaning for the colonists than for us. For example, these rights applied only to Christians, not to "hereticks" such as Anabaptists and Quakers. Still this list of rights is quite enlightened for its time.

* * *

Massachusetts Body of Liberties, 1641

The free fruition of such liberties Immunities and priveledges as humanitie, Civilitie, and Christianitie call for as due to every man in his place and proportion without impeachment and Infringement hath ever beene and ever will be the tranquillitie and Stabilitie of Churches and Commonwealths. And the deniall or deprivall thereof, the disturbance if not the ruine of both.

We hould it therefore our dutie and safetie whilst we are about the further establishing of this Government to collect and expresse all such freedomes as for present we foresee may concerne us, and our posteritie after us. And to ratify them with our sollemne consent.

We doe therefor this day religiously and unanimously decree and confirme these following Rites, liberties and priveledges concerneing our Churches, and Civill State to be respectively impartiallie and inviolably enjoyed and observed throughout our Jurisdiction for ever.

1. No mans life shall be taken away, no mans honour or good name shall be stayned, no mans person shall be arested, restrayned, banished, dismembered, nor any wayes punished, no man shall be deprived of his wife or children, no mans goods or estaite shall be taken away from him, nor any way indammaged under coulor of law or Countenance of Authoritie, unlesse it be by vertue or equitie of some expresse law of the Country waranting the same, established by a generall Court and sufficiently published, or in case of the defect of a law in any parteculer case by the word of god. And in Capitall cases, or in cases concerning dismembring or banishment, according to that word to be judged by the Generall Court.

2. Every person within this Jurisdiction, whether Inhabitant or forreiner shall enjoy the same justice and law, that is generall for the plantation, which we constitute and execute one towards another without partialitie or delay.

3. No man shall be urged to take any oath or subscribe any articles, covenants or remonstrance, of a publique and Civill nature, but such as the Generall Court hath considered, allowed, and required. . . .

5. No man shall be compelled to any publique worke or service unlesse the presse be grounded upon some act of the gnerall Court, and have reasonable allowance therefore.

6. No man shall be pressed in person to any office, worke, warres or

other publique service, that is necessarily and suffitiently exempted by any naturall or personall inpediment, as by want of yeares, greatnes of age, defect of minde, fayling of sences, or impotencie of Lymbes. . . .

8. No mans Cattle or goods of what kinde soever shall be pressed or taken for any publique use or service, unlesse it be by warrant grounded upon some act of the generall Court, nor without such reasonable prices and hire as the ordinarie rates of the Countrie do afford. And if his Cattle or goods shall perish or suffer damage in such service, the owner shall be suffitiently recompenced. . . .

12. Every man whether Inhabitant or fforreiner, free or not free shall have libertie to come to any publique Court, Councel, or Towne meeting, and either by speech or writeing to move any lawfull, seasonable, and materiall question, or to present any necessary motion, complaint, petition, Bill or information, whereof that meeting hath proper cognizance, so it be done in convenient time, due order, and respective manner. . . .

Rites Rules and Liberties concerning Juditiall proceedings

18. No mans person shall be restrained or imprisoned by any Authority whatsoever, before the law hath sentenced him thereto. If he can put in sufficient securitie, bayle or mainprise, for his appearance, and good behaviour in the meane time, unleasse it be in Crimes Capital, and Contempts in open Court, and in such cases where some expresse act of Court doth allow it. . . .

25. No Summons pleading Judgement, or any kinde of proceeding in Court or course of Justice shall be abated, arested or reversed upon any kinde of cercumstantiall errors or mistakes. If the person and cause be rightly understood and intended by the Court.

26. Every man that findeth himselfe unfit to plead his owne cause in any Court shall have Libertie to imploy any man against whom the Court doth not except, to helpe him, Provided he give him noe fee or reward for his paines. This shall not exempt the partie him selfe from Answering such Questions in person as the Court shall thinke meete to demand of him.

27. If any plantife shall give into any Court a declaration of his cause in writeing. The defendant shall also have libertie and time to give in his answer in writeing. And so in all further proceedings betwene partie and partie. So, it doth not further hinder the dispach of Justice then the Court shall be willing unto. . . .

41. Everie man that is to Answere for any Criminall cause, whether he be in prison or under bayle, his cause shall be heard and determined at the next Court that hath proper Cognizance thereof, And may be done without prejudice of Justice.

42. No man shall be twise sentenced by Civill Justice for one and the same Crime, offence, or Trespasse. . . .

45. No man shall be forced by Torture to confesse any Crime against

himselfe nor any other unlesse it be in some Capitall case where he is first fullie convicted by cleare and suffitient evidence to be guilty. After which if the cause be of that nature, That it is very apparent there be other conspiratours, or confederates with him, Then he may be tortured, yet not with such Tortures as be Barbarous and inhumane. . . .

55. In all suites or Actions in any Court, the plaintife shall have libertie to make all the titles and claims to that he sues for he can. And the Defendant shall have libertie to plead all the pleas he can in answere to them, and the Court shall judge according to the entire evidence of all. . . .

57. Whensoever any person shall come to any very suddaine untimely and unnaturall death, Some assistant, or the Constables of that Towne shall forthwith sumon a Jury of twelve free men to inquire of the cause and manner of their death, and shall present a true verdict thereof to some neere Assistant, or the next Court to be helde for that Towne upon their oath. . . .

64. Everie Action betweene partie and partie, and proceedings against delinquents in Criminall causes shall be briefly and destinctly entereed on the Rolles of every Court by the Recorder thereof. That such actions be not afterwards brought againe to the vexation of any man. . . .

98. Lastly because our dutie and desire is to do nothing suddainlie which fundamentally concerne us, we decree that these rites and liberties, shall be Audably read and deliberately weighed at every Generall Court that shall be held, within three yeares next insueing. And such of them as shall not be altered or repealed they shall stand so ratified, That no man shall infringe them without due punishment.

And if any Generall Court within these next thre yeares shall faile or forget to reade and consider them as abovesaid. The Governor and Deputy Governor for the time being, and every Assistant present at such Courts shall forfeite 20sh. a man, and everie Deputie 10sh. a man for each neglect, which shall be paid out of their proper estate, and not by the Country or the Townes which choose them, and whensoever there shall arise any question in any Court amonge the Assistants and Associates thereof about the explanation of these Rites and liberties, The Generall Court onely shall have power to interprett them.

Source: Whitmore, W. H. *The Colonial Laws of Massachusetts, 1672*. Boston: Rockwell & Churchill, City Printers, 1890.

DOCUMENT 5: Concessions and Agreements of West New Jersey (1677)

To attract colonists, the proprietors of the New Jersey colony provided for freedom of religion and self-government through an elected legislature in 1664. In 1674, one of the original proprietors sold his interest in the colony to a group of Quakers, including William Penn, who later founded Pennsylvania. The Quakers gained control of the unoccupied western half. To make settlement attractive, they issued the Concessions and Agreements of West New Jersey in 1677. This document was remarkable because it contained clauses that made it the fundamental law of the region and prohibited any law from being enacted by the legislature in contradiction to it. This is very close to the concepts of a binding written constitution and of unconstitutional legislation.

This document required due process, trial by jury, and two witnesses for the establishment of guilt in criminal cases. In addition, it allowed citizens to represent themselves in the court without retaining legal advice. The right to challenge and dismiss potential jurors was a unique feature. Up to thirty-five individuals could be dismissed without cause, and with cause any number could be dismissed. The proprietors also required that the document be displayed to the public in court throughout West Jersey and read out loud four times each year.

It is not clear who wrote the concessions, but the author might well have been William Penn, who later wrote two additional documents guaranteeing individual rights for his Pennsylvania colony.

* * *

Concessions and Agreements of West New Jersey, 1677
The Charter of Fundamental Laws, of West New Jersey, Agreed
Upon

Chapter XIII

That these following concessions are the Common Law, or Fundamental Rights, of the Province of West New Jersey.

That the common law or fundamental rights and privileges of West New Jersey, are individually agreed upon by the Proprietors and freeholders thereof, to be the foundation of the government, which is not to be altered by the Legislative authority, or free Assembly hereafter mentioned and constituted, but that the said Legislative authority is constituted according to these fundamentals, to make such laws as agree with, and maintain the said fundamentals, and to make no laws that in the least contradict, differ or vary from the said fundamentals, under what pretence or alligation soever.

Chapter XV

That these Concessions, law or great charter of fundamentals, be recorded in a fair table, in the Assembly House, and that they be read at the beginning and dissolving of every general free Assembly: And it is further agreed and ordained, that the said Concessions, common law, or great charter of fundamentals, be writ in fair tables, in every common hall of justice within this Province, and that they be read in solemn manner four times every year, in the presence of the people, by the chief magistrates of those places.

Chapter XVII

That no Proprietor, freeholder or inhabitant of the said Province of West New Jersey, shall be deprived or condemned of life, limb, liberty, estate, property or any ways hurt in his or their privileges, freedoms or franchises, upon any account whatsoever, without a due tryal, and judgment passed by twelve good and lawful men of his neighbourhood first hand: And that in all causes to be tryed, and in all tryals, the person or persons, arraigned may except against any of the said neighbourhood, without any reason rendered, (not exceeding thirty five) and in case of any valid reason alleged, against every person nominated for that service.

Chapter XVIII

And that no Proprietor, freeholder, freedenison, or inhabitant in the said Province, shall be attached, arrested, or imprisoned, for or by reason of any debt, duty, or thing whatsoever (cases felonious, criminal and treasonable excepted) before he or she have personal summon or summons, left at his or her last dwelling place, if in the said Province, by some legal authorized office, constituted and appointed for that purpose, to appear in some court of judicature for the said Province, with a full and plain account of the cause or thing in demand, as also the name or names of the person or persons at whose suit, and the court where he is to appear, and that he hath at least fourteen days time to appear and answer the said suit, if he or she live or inhabit within forty miles English of the said court, and if at a further distance, to have for every twenty miles, two days time more, for his and their appearance, and so proportionably for a larger distance of place.

That upon the recording of the summons, and non-appearance of such person and persons, a writ or attachment shall or may be issued out to arrest, or attach the person or persons of such defaulters, to cause his or their appearance in such court, returnable at a day certain, to answer the penalty or penalties, in such suit or suits; and if he or they shall be condemned by legal tryal and judgment, the penalty or penalties shall be paid and satisfied out of his or their real or personal estate so condemned, or cause the person or persons so condemned, to lie in execution till satisfaction of the debt and damages be made. Provided always, if such person or persons so condemned, shall pay and deliver such estate, goods, and chattels which he or any other person hath for his or their use, and shall solemnly declare and aver, that he or they have not any further estate, goods or chattels wheresoever, to satisfy the person or persons, (at whose suit, he or they are condemned) their respective judgments, and shall also bring and produce three other persons as compurgators, who are well known and of honest reputation, and approved of by the commissioners of that division, where they dwell or inhabit, which shall in such open court, likewise solemnly declare and aver, that they believe in their consciences, such person and persons so condemned, have not werewith further to pay the said condemnation or condemnations, he or they shall be thence forthwith discharged from their said imprisonment, any law or custom to the contrary thereof, heretofore in the said Province notwithstanding. And upon such summons and default of appearance, recorded as aforesaid, and such person and persons not appearing within forty days after, it shall and may be lawful for such court of judicature to proceed to tryal, of twelve lawful men to judgment, against such defaulters, and issue forth execution against his or their estate, real and personal, to satisfy such penalty or penalties, to such debt and damages so recorded, as far as it shall or may extend.

Chapter XIX

That there shall be in every court, three justices or commissioners, who shall sit with the twelve men of the neighbourhood, with them to hear all causes, and to assist the said twelve men of the neighbourhood in case of law; and that they the said justices shall pronounce such judgment as they shall receive from, and be directed by the said twelve men, in whom only the judgment resides, and not otherwise.

And in case of their neglect and refusal, that then one of the twelve, by consent of the rest, pronounce their own judgment as the justices should have done.

And if any judgment shall be past, in any case civil or criminal, by any other person or persons, or any other way, then according to this agreement and appointment, it shall be held null and void, and such person or persons so presuming to give judgment, shall be severely fin'd, and upon complaint made to the General Assembly, by them be declared incapable of any office or trust within this Province.

Chapter XX

That in all matters and causes, civil and criminal, proof is to be made by the solemn and plain averment, of at least two honest and reputable persons; and in case that any person or persons shall bear false witness, and bring in his or their evidence, contrary to the truth of the matter as shall be made plainly to appear, that then every such person or persons, shall in civil causes, suffer the penalty which would be due to the person or persons he or they bear witness against. And in case any witness or witnesses, on the behalf of any person or persons, indicted in a criminal cause, shall be found to have born false witness for fear, gain, malice or favour, and thereby hinder the due execution of the law, and deprive the suffering person or persons of their due satisfaction, that then and in all other cases of false evidence, such person or persons, shall be first severly fined, and next that he or they shall forever by disabled from being admitted in evidence, or into any publick office, employment, or service within this Province.

Chapter XXI

That all and every person and persons whatsoever, who shall prosecute or prefer any indictment or information against others for any person injuries, or matter criminal, or shall prosecute for any other criminal cause, (treason, murther, and felony, only excepted) shall and may be master of his own process, and have full power to forgive and remit the person or persons offending against him or herself only, as well before as after judgment, and condemnation, and pardon and remit the sentence, fine and punishment of the person or persons offending, be it personal or other whatsoever.

Chapter XXII

That the tryals of all causes, civil and criminal, shall be heard and decided by the virdict or judgment of twelve honest men of the neighbourhood, only to be summoned and presented by the sheriff of that division, or propriety where the fact or trespass is committed; and that no person or persons shall be compelled to fee any attorney or counciller to please his cause, but that all persons have free liberty to plead his own cause, if he please: And that no person nor persons imprisoned upon any account whatsoever within this Province, shall be obliged to pay any fees to the officer or officers of the said prison, either when committed or discharged.

Chapter XXIII

That in all publick courts of justice for tryals of causes, civil or criminal, any person or persons, inhabitants of the said Province may freely come into, and attend the said courts, and hear and be present, at all or any such tryals as shall be there had or passed, that justice may not be done in a corner nor in any covert manner, being intended and resolved, by the help of the Lord, and by these our Concessions and Fundamentals, that all and every person and persons inhabiting the said Province, shall, as far as in us lies, be free from oppression and slavery.

Source: Leaming, A., and J. Spicer. *The Grants, Concessions, and Original Constitutions of the Province of New Jersey.* 2nd ed., 393–98. Philadelphia: W. Bradford, 1812.

DOCUMENT 6: Pennsylvania Frame of Government (1682)

William Penn, the proprietor of the Pennsylvania colony, was a Quaker and had personal experience with the ways English courts could be used to persecute individuals with unpopular beliefs. He was tried in 1670 for preaching a prohibited sermon to a Quaker meeting in England.

In 1681 he was granted the charter to start Pennsylvania. The Frame of Government he wrote in 1682 had provisions to limit his power and that of later governors so "no power of doing mischief, that the will of one man may not hinder the good of a whole country." The first part of the Frame of Government set up the machinery of government. In the preface Penn declares, "Any government is free to the people under it (whatever be the frame) where the laws rule and the people are a party to those laws."

The second part is the more pertinent. "Laws Agreed upon in England, &c." was truly a Bill of Rights. It provided for religious freedom, of course, but also provided important guarantees for judicial procedure. It guarantees a jury trial, a public trial, right of bail, and the right to the accused to appear in court and personally plead their case or to plead through their friends. It also limits financial burdens of the English justice system: Court fees must be moderate and fixed in a public schedule, fines must be moderate and cannot affect a defendant's means of livelihood, and prisons are to be free with no fees for food or lodging. Court proceedings and records are to be plainly kept in English.

This Frame of Government lasted only a few years, being replaced in 1701 by the Charter of Privileges (see Document 8), written by Penn.

* * *

Pennsylvania Frame of Government, 1682

Laws Agreed Upon in England, &c.

I. That the charter of liberties, declared, granted and confirmed the five and twentieth day of the second month, called April, 1682, before divers witnesses, by William Penn, Governor and chief Proprietor of Pensilvania, to all the freemen and planters of the said province, is hereby declared and approved, and shall be for ever held for fundamental in the government thereof, according to the limitations mentioned in the said charter. . . .

V. That all courts shall be open, and justice shall neither be sold, denied nor delayed.

VI. That, in all courts all persons of all persuasions may freely appear in their own way, and according to their own manner, and there personally plead their own cause themselves; or, if unable, by their friends; and the first process shall be the exhibition of the complaint in court, fourteen days before the trial; and that the party, complained against, may be fitted for the same, he or she shall be summoned, no less than ten days before, and a copy of the complaint delivered him or her, at his or her dwelling house. But before the complaint of any person be received, he shall solemnly declare in court, that he believes, in his conscience, his cause is just.

VII. That all pleadings, processes and records in courts, shall be short, and in English, and in an ordinary and plain character, that they may be understood, and justice speedily administered.

VIII. That all trials shall be by twelve men, and as near as may be, peers or equals, and of the neighborhood, and men without just exception; in cases of life, there shall be first twenty-four returned by the sheriffs, for a grand inquest, of whom twelve, at least, shall find the complaint to be true; and then the twelve men, or peers, to be likewise returned by the sheriff, shall have the final judgment. But reasonable challenges shall be always admitted against the said twelve men, or any of them.

IX. That all fees in all cases shall be moderate, and settled by the provincial Council, and General Assembly, and be hung up in a table in every respective court; and whosoever shall be convicted of taking more, shall pay twofold, and be dismissed his employment; one moiety of which shall go to the party wronged.

X. That all prisons shall be work-houses, for felons, vagrants, and loose and idle persons; whereof one shall be in every county.

XI. That all prisoners shall be bailable by sufficient sureties, unless for capital offences, where the proof is evident, or the presumption great.

XII. That all persons wrongfully imprisoned, or prosecuted at law, shall have double damages against the informer, or prosecutor.

XIII. That all prisons shall be free, as to fees, food and lodging.

XIV. That all lands and goods shall be liable to pay debts, except where there is legal issue, and then all the goods, and one-third of the land only.

XV. That all wills, in writing, attested by two witnesses, shall be of the same force as to lands, as other conveyances, being legally proved within forty days, either within or without the said province.

XVI. That seven years quiet possession shall give an unquestionable right, except in cases of infants, lunatics, married women, or persons beyond the seas.

XVII. That all briberies and extortion whatsoever shall be severely punished.

XVIII. That all fines shall be moderate, and saving men's contenements, merchandize, or wainage. . . .

XXI. That all defacers or corrupters of charters, gifts, grants, bonds, bills, wills, contracts, and conveyances, or that shall deface or falsify any enrolment, registry or record, within this province, shall make double satisfaction for the same; half whereof shall go to the party wronged, and they shall be dismissed of all places of trust, and be publicly disgraced as false men. . . .

XXIV. That all lands and goods of felons shall be liable, to make satisfaction to the party wronged twice the value; and for want of lands or goods, the felons shall be bondmen to work in the common prison, or work-house, or otherwise, till the party injured be satisfied.

XXV. That the estates of capital offenders, as traitors and murderers shall go, one-third to the next of kin to the sufferer, and the remainder to the next of kin to the criminal

XXVI. That all witnesses, coming, or called, to testify their knowledge in or to any matter or thing, in any court, or before any lawful authority, within the said province, shall there give or deliver in their evidence, or testimony, by solemnly promising to speak the truth, the whole truth, and nothing but the truth, to the matter, or thing in questions. And in case any person so called to evidence, shall be convicted of wilful falsehood, such person shall suffer and undergo such damage or penalty, as the person, or persons, against whom he or she bore false witness, did, or should, undergo; and shall also make satisfaction to the party wronged, and be publicly exposed as a false witness, never to be credited in any court, or before any Magistrate, in the said province. . . .

XXXIV. That all Treasurers, Judges, Masters of the Rolls, Sheriffs, Justices of the Peace, and other officers and persons whatsoever, relating to courts, or trials of causes, or any other service in the government; and all Members elected to serve in provincial Council and General Assembly, and all that have right to elect such Members, shall be such as possess faith in Jesus Christ, and that are not convicted of ill fame, or unsober and dishonest conversation, and that are of one and twenty years of age, at least; and that all such so qualified, shall be capable of the said several employments and privileges as aforesaid. . . .

XXXVII. That as a careless and corrupt administration of justice draws the wrath of God upon magistrates, so the wildness and looseness of the people provoke the indignation of God against a country; therefore, that all such offences against God, as swearing, cursing, lying, prophane talking, drunkenness, drinking of healths, obscene words, incest sodomy, rapes, whoredom, fornication, and other uncleanness (not to be repeated) all treasons, misprisions, murders, duels, felony, seditions, maims, forcible entries, and other violences, to the persons and estates of the inhabitants within this province; all prizes, stage-plays, cards, dice, May-games, gamesters, masques, revels, bull-baitings, cock-fighting, bear-baitings, and the like, which escite the people to rudeness, cruelty, looseness, and irreligion, shall be respectively discouraged, and severly punished, according to the appointment of the Governor and freemen in provincial Council and General Assembly; as also all proceedings contrary to these laws, that are not here made expressly penal.

XXXVIII. That a copy of these laws shall be hung up in the provincial Council, and in public courts of justice; and that they shall be read yearly at the opening of every provincial Council and General Assembley, and court of justice; and their assent shall be testified, by their standing up after the reading thereof.

XXXIX. That there shall be, at no time, any alteration of any of these laws, without the consent of the Governor, his heirs, or assigns, and six parts of seven of the freemen, met in provincial Council and General Assembly.

XL. That all other matters and things not herein provided for, which shall, and may, concern the public justice, peace or safety of the said province; and the raising and imposing taxes, customs, duties, or other charges whatsoever, shall be, and are, hereby referred to the order, prudence and determination of the Governor and freemen, in provincial Council and General Assembly, to be held, from time to time, in the said province.

Signed and sealed by the Governor and freemen aforesaid, the fifth day of the third month, called May, one thousand six hundred and eighty-two.

Source: Thorpe, Francis N., ed. *The Federal and State Constitutions, Colonial Charters, and Other Organic Laws*. Vol. 5, 3052–63. Washington, D.C.: Government Printing Office, 1909.

DOCUMENT 7: New York Charter of Libertyes and Priviledges (1683)

New York was a royal colony that belonged to the duke of York, the future King James II. Relationships were strained between the future king and his colony. He thought popular government was not to be allowed, declaring to a friend in 1676 that it "would be of dangerous consequence, nothing being more knowne than the aptness of such bodyes to assume to themselves many priviledges wch prove destructive to . . . the peace of ye governmt" (Schwartz 1971). Of course the colonists wanted self-rule, just like the other colonies.

Despite his fears, he consented to the election of a General Assembly in 1683. He granted permission in exchange for a promise that the General Assembly would tax the colony to provide the funds needed to govern it. The first law passed, however, was the Charter of Libertyes and Priviledges. The Charter provided for the nature, election rules, and regular meeting of the General Assembly. It also provided a number of rights, including criminal rights and rights to protect property of arbitrary action by the government. Among the criminal rights guaranteed was a jury trial, bail in all cases except treason or felony (capital case), and grand jury.

Predictably, the duke of York, now king, was not pleased. He vetoed the law in 1684 and issued a new commission directing the governor and council to repeal the Charter of Libertyes and Privileges. The New York colonists ignored the king and continued to try to enforce the charter. After the king was expelled from England, the colony regained its self-rule and immediately issued a new law in 1691 that restated in almost the same language the rights of the charter.

* * *

New York Charter of Libertyes and Priviledges, 1683

The Charter of Libertyes and priviledges granted by his Royall Highnesse to the Inhabitants of New Yorke and Its Dependencyes

For The better Establishing the Government of this province of New Yorke and that Justice and Right may be Equally done to all persons within the same.

Bee It Enacted by the Governour Councell and Representatives now in Generall Assembly mett and assembled and by the authority of the same.

That The supreme Legislative Authority under his Majesty and Royall Highnesse James Duke of Yorke Albany &c Lord proprietor of the said province shall forever be and resaide in a Governour, Councell, and the people mett in General Assembly.

That The Exercise of the Cheife Magistracy and Administracon of the Government over the said province shall bee in the said Governour assisted by a Councell with those advice and Consent or with at least four of them he is to rule and Governe the same according to the Lawes thereof. . . .

That Noe freeman shall be taken and imprisoned or be disseized of his ffreehold or Libertye or ffree Customes or be outlawed or Exiled or any other wayes destroyed nor shall be passed upon adjudged or condemned But by the Lawfull Judgment of his peers and by the law of this province. Justice nor Right shall be neither sold denyed or deferred to any man within this province.

That Noe aid, Tax, Tallage, Assessment, Custome, Loane, Benevolence or Imposicon whatsoever shall be layed assessed imposed or levyed on any of his Majestyes Subjects within this province or their Estates upon any manner of Colour or pretence but by the act and Consent of the Governour Councell and Representatives of the people in Generall Assembly mett and Assembled.

That Noe man of what Estate or Condicion soever shall be putt out of his Lands or Tenements, nor taken, nor imprisoned, nor disherited, nor banished nor any wayes distroyed without being brought to Answere by due Course of Law.

That A ffreeman Shall not be amerced for a small fault, but after the manner of his fault and for a great fault after the Greatnesse thereof Saveing to him his freehold, And a husbandman saveing to him his Wainage and a merchant likewise saveing to him his merchandize And none of the said Amerciaments shall be assessed but by the oath of twelve honest and Lawfull men of the Vicinage provided the faults and misdemeanours be not in Contempt of Courts of Judicature.

All Tryalls shall be by the verdict of twelve men, and as neer as may be peers or Equalls And of the neighbourhood and in the County Shire or Division where the fact Shall arise or grow Whether the Same be by Indictment Infermacon Declaracon or otherwise against the person Offender or Defendant.

That In all Cases Capitall or Criminall there shall be a grand Inquest who shall first present the offence and then twelve men of the neighbourhood to try the Offender who after his plea to the Indictment shall be allowed his reasonable Challenges.

That In all Cases whatsoever Bayle by sufficient Suretyes Shall be allowed and taken unlesse for treason or felony plainly and specially Expressed and menconed in the Warrant of Commitment provided

Always that nothing herein contained shall Extend to discharge out of prison upon bayle any person taken in Execucon for debts or otherwise legally sentenced by his Judgment of any of the Courts of Record within the province. . . .

Source: Colonial Laws of New York. Vol. 1, 111–16. Albany, N.Y.: J. B. Lyon, 1894.

DOCUMENT 8: Pennsylvania Charter of Privileges (1701)

The Pennsylvania Charter of Privileges replaced the Pennsylvania Frame of Government. It is the second of the documents granting citizens rights written by William Penn, who returned from England to his colony and dealt with the discontent of colonists wanting more self-rule than the Frame of Government provided. The charter established a one-house legislature and excluded the council, appointed by the proprietor, from being involved in passing legislation.

Freedom of religion was made the first and primary freedom in the Pennsylvania Charter of Privileges. The charter does not specifically guarantee as many rights relating to trials as did the Frame of Government, but it does make a unique contribution. The most progressive clause in the document granted the accused the same right to call witnesses and have counsel as the prosecution. No other colony granted these rights until after the revolution. The charter thus laid the foundation for the Sixth Amendment. Another provision guaranteed that no person need answer any complaint or other matter relating to property except in "ordinary Course of Justice," meaning proper legal process. This clause is a precursor of the due process clause in the Constitution. Also, the property of any person committing suicide could not be taken by the state, a common practice in colonial times.

The Charter of Privileges remained in force until replaced by the Pennsylvania Constitution of 1776.

* * *

Pennsylvania Charter of Privileges, 1701

William Penn, Proprietary and Governor of the Province of Pensilvania and Territories thereunto belonging, To all to whom these Presents shall come, sendeth Greeting. Whereas King Charles the Second, by His Letters Patents, under the Great Seal of England, bearing Date the Fourth Day of March, in the year One thousand Six Hundred and Eight-one, was graciously pleased to give and grant unto me, and my Heirs and

Assigns for ever, this Province of Pensilvania, with divers great Powers and Jurisdictions for the well Government thereof.

And whereas the King's dearest Brother, James Duke of York and Albany, &c. by his Deeds of Feoffment, under his hand and Seal duly perfected, bearing Date the Twenty-Fourth Day of August, One thousand Six Hundred Eighty and Two, did grant unto me, my Heirs and Assigns, all that Tract of Land, now called the Territories of Pensilvania, together with Powers and Jurisdictions for the good Government thereof.

And Whereas for the Encouragement of all the Freemen and Planters, that might be concerned in the said Province and Territories, and for the good Government thereof, I the said William Penn, in the Year One Thousand Six Hundred Eighty and Three, for me, my Heirs and Assigns, did grant and confirm unto all the Freemen, Planters and Adventurers therein, Attests as now established by the Law made at New-Castle, in the Year One thousand and Seven Hundred, entitled, An Act directing the Attests of several Officers and Ministers, as now amended and confirmed this presented Assembly. . . .

V

That all Criminals shall have the same Privileges of Witnesses and Council as their Prosecutors.

VI

That no Person or Persons shall or may, at any Time hereafter, be obliged to answer any Complaint, Matter or Thing whatsoever, relating to Property, before the Governor and Council, or in any other Place, but in ordinary Course of Justice, unless Appeals thereunto shall be hereafter by Law appointed. . . .

VIII

If any person, through Temptation or Melancholy, shall destroy himself; his Estate, real and personal, shall notwithstanding descend to his Wife and Children, or Relations, as if he had died a natural Death; and if any Person shall be destroyed or killed by Casualty or Accident, there shall be no Forfeiture to the Governor by reason thereof.

And no Act, Law or Ordinance whatsoever, shall at any Time hereafter, be made or done, to alter, change or diminish the form or Effect of this Charter, or of any Part of Clause therein, contrary to the true Intent and Meaning thereof, without the Consent of the Governor for the Time being, and Six Parts of Seven of the Assembly met.

But because the Happiness of Mankind depends so much upon the Enjoying of Liberty of their Consciences as aforesaid, I do hereby solemnly declare, promise and grant, for me, my Heirs and Assigns, That the First Article of this Charter relating to Liberty of Conscience, and every Part and Clause therein, according to the true Intent and Meaning thereof, shall be kept and remain, without any Alteration, inviolably for ever.

And lastly, I the said William Penn, Proprietary and Governor of the Province of Pensilvania, and Territories thereunto belonging, for myself, my Heirs and Assigns, have solemnly declared, granted and confirmed, and do hereby solemnly declare, grant and confirm. That neither I, my Heirs or Assigns, shall procure or do any Thing or Things whereby the Liberties in this Charter contained and expressed, nor any part thereof, shall be infringed or broken: And if any thing shall be procured or done, by any Person or Persons, contrary to these Presents, it shall be held of no Force or Effect.

In witness whereof, I the said William Penn, at Philadelphia in Pensilvania, have unto this present Charter of Liberties, set my Hand and broad Seal, this Twenty-Eighth Day of October, in the Year of Our Lord One Thousand Seven Hundred and One, being the Thirteenth Year of the Reign of King William the Third, over England, Scotland, France and Ireland, &c. and the Twenty-First Year of my Government. . . .

I do hereby promise, grant and declare, That the Inhabitants of both Province and Territories, shall separately enjoy all other Liberties, Privileges and Benefits, granted jointly to them in this Charter, any Law, Usage or Custom of this Government heretofore made and practised, or any Law made and passed by this General Assembly, to the Contrary hereof, notwithstanding.

William Penn

This Charter of Privileges being distinctly read in Assembly; and the whole and every Part thereof, being approved of and agreed to, by us, we do thankfully receive the same from our Proprietary and Governor, at Philadelphia, this Twenty-Eight Day of October, One Thousand Seven Hundred and One, Signed on Behalf, and by Order of the Assembly.

Per Joseph Growdon, Speaker
Edward Shippen, Griffith Owen,
Phineas Pemberton, Caleb Pusey,
Samuel Carpenter, Thomas Story,
Proprietary and Governor's Council

Source: Thorpe, Francis N. *The Federal and State Constitutions, Colonial Charters, and Other Organic Laws.* Vol. 5, 3076–82. Washington, D.C.: Government Printing Office, 1909.

DOCUMENT 9: Address to the Inhabitants of Quebec (1774)

The Address to the Inhabitants of Quebec, passed by the First Continental Congress in 1774, failed to achieve its purpose. The First Continental Congress hoped that its appeal to the freeholders of Quebec would cause them to join in the effort to resist English threats to their freedom. Not understanding that Quebec had its own culture and did not need a lecture about basic rights, the address told them that they were entitled to the rights of Englishmen, described these rights, explained how in various ways England was denying them their rights (much of this description is largely omitted here), and invited them to join the resistance. The freeholders of Quebec declined to participate.

The Address to the Inhabitants of Quebec lists four rights: self-government, jury trial, habeas corpus, and freedom of the press. The fifth right deals with land ownership without the need to give service. This was an issue in Quebec and not in the colonies; its presence in this document was designed to appeal to the freeholders of Quebec and was not a right the colonists were concerned about.

This document is notable for several reasons. First, the description of trial rights in the eleventh paragraph is very detailed, much clearer than other statements of trial rights. Further, two of the other rights— right to habeas corpus and freedom of the press—are absent from other colonial documents. Habeas corpus prevents a person from being held in jail with no charge. The inclusion of freedom of the press is memorable because it is the first time it is mentioned in a document of an official assembly.

* * *

Address to the Inhabitants of Quebec, 1774

We, the Delegates of the Colonies of New-Hampshire, Massachusetts-Bay, Rhode-Island and Providence Plantations, Connecticut, New-York, New-Jersey, Pennsylvania, the Counties of Newcastle Kent and Sussex on Delaware, Maryland, Virginia, North-Carolina and South-Carolina, deputed by the inhabitants of the said Colonies, to represent them in a General Congress at Philadelphia, in the province of Pennsylvania, to consult together concerning the best methods to obtain redress of our afflicting grievances, having accordingly assembled, and taken into our most serious consideration the state of public affairs on this continent, have thought proper to address your province, as a member therein deeply interested.

When the fortune of war, after a gallant and glorious resistance, had incorporated you with the body of English subjects, we rejoiced in the truly valuable addition, both on your own and your account; expecting, as courage and generosity are naturally united, our brave enemies would become our hearty friends, and that the Divine Being would bless to you the dispensations of his over-ruling providence, by securing to you and your latest posterity the inestimable advantages of a free English constitution of government, which it is the privilege of all English subjects to enjoy. . . .

In this form, the first grand right, is that of the people having a share in their own government by their representatives chosen by themselves, and, in consequence, of being ruled by laws, which they themselves approve, not by edicts of men over whom they have no controul. . . .

The next great right is that of trial by jury. This provides, that neither life, liberty nor property, can be taken from the possessor, until twelve of his unexceptionable countrymen and peers of his vicinage, who from that neighbourhood may reasonably be supposed to be acquainted with his character, and the characters of the witnesses, upon a fair trial, and full enquiry, face to face, in open Court, before as many of the people as chuse to attend, shall pass their sentence upon oath against him; a sentence that cannot injure him, without injuring their own reputation, and probably their interest also; as the question may turn on points, that, in some degree, concern the general welfare; and if it does not, their verdict may form a precedent, that, on a similar trial of their own, may militate against themselves.

Another right relates merely to the liberty of the person. If a subject is seized and imprisoned, tho' by order of Government, he may, by virtue of this right, immediately obtain a writ, termed a Habeas Corpus, from a Judge, whose sworn duty it is to grant it, and thereupon procure any illegal restraint to be quickly enquired into and redressed.

A fourth right, is that of holding lands by the tenure of easy rents, and not by rigorous and oppressive services. . . .

These are the invaluable rights, that form a considerable part of our mild system of government; . . .

These are the rights, without which a people cannot be free and happy, and under the protecting and encouraging influence of which, these colonies have hitherto so amazingly flourished and increased. These are the rights, a profligate Ministry are not striving, by force of arms, to ravish from us, and which we are, with one mind, resolved never to resign but with our lives. . . .

The words of the statute are—that those "laws shall be the rule, until they shall be varied or altered by any ordinances of the Governor and Council." Is the "certainty and lenity of the criminal law of England, and its benefits and advantages," commended in the said statute, and said to "have been sensibly felt by you," secured to you and your descendants? No. They too are subjected to arbitrary "alterations" by the Governor and Council; and a power is expressly reserved of appointing "such courts of criminal, civil, and ecclesiastical jurisdiction, as shall be thought proper." Such is the precarious tenure of mere will, by which you hold your lives and religion. The Crown and its Ministers are impowered, as far as they could be by Parliament, to establish even the Inquisition itself among you. . . . Unhappy people! who are not only injured, but insulted. Nay more!—With such a superlative contempt of your understanding and spirit, has an insolent Ministry presumed to think of you, our respectable fellow-subjects, accouding to the inforemation we have received, as firmly to perswade themselves that your gratitude, for the injuries and insults they have recently offered to you, will engage you to take up arms, and render yourselves the ridicule and detestation of the world, by becoming tools, in their hands, to assist them in taking that freedom from us, which they have treacherously denied to you; the unavoidable consequence of which attempt, if successful, would be the extinction of all hopes of you or your posterity being ever restored to freedom; For idiocy itself cannot believe, that, when their drudgery is performed, they will treat you with less cruelty than they have us, who are of the same blood with themselves. . . .

We do not ask you, by this address, to commence acts of hostility against the government of our common Sovereign. We only invite you to consult your own glory and welfare, and not to suffer yourselves to be inveigled or intimidated by infamous ministers so far, as to become the instruments of their cruelty and despotism, but to unite with us in one social compact, formed on the generous principles of equal liberty, and cemented by such an exchange of beneficial and endearing offices as to render it perpetual. In order to complete this highly desirable union, we submit it to your consideration, whether it may not be expedient for you to meet together in your several towns and districts, and elect Deputies, who afterwards meeting in a provincial Congress, may chuse Delegates, to represent your province in the continental Congress to be held at Philadelphia on the tenth day of May 1775.

In this present Congress, beginning on the fifth of the last month, and continued to this day, it has been, with universal pleasure and unanimous vote, resolved, That we should consider the violation of your rights, by the act for altering the government of your province, as a violation of our own, and that you should be invited to accede to our confederation, which has no other objects than the perfect security of the natural and civil rights of all the constituent members, according to their respective circumstances, and the preservation of a happy and lasting connection with Great-Britain, on the salutary and constitutional principles herein before mentioned. For effecting these purposes, we have addressed an humble and loyal petition to his Majesty, praying relief of our and your grievances; and have associated to stop all importations from Great-Britain and Ireland, after the first day of December, and all exportations to those Kingdoms and the West-Indies, after the tenth day of next September, unless the said grievances are redressed.

That Almight God may incline your minds to approve our equitable and necessary measures, to add yourselves to us, to put your fate, whenever you suffer injuries which you are determined to oppose, not on the small influence of your single province, but on the consolidated powers of North-America, and may grant to our joint exertions an event as happy as our cause is just, is the fervent prayer of us, your sincere and affectionate friends and fellow-subjects.

By order of the Congress,

Henry Middleton, President

Source: Journals of the Continental Congress, 1774–1789. Vol. 1, 105–13. Washington, D.C.: Government Printing Office, 1910.

DOCUMENT 10: Virginia Declaration of Rights (1776)

As the movement for revolution against England grew in intensity, Virginia, the largest and oldest colony, produced the first constitutional bill of rights adopted by elected representatives of the people. The governor had dissolved the House of Burgesses, so Virginians created in 1774 their own elected representative body, the Virginia Colonial Convention. The fifth and last convention voted on May 15, 1776, to recommend to the Continental Congress that independence should be declared from England. A large committee was then constituted to create a declaration of rights and a plan of government.

Among the members of this committee were George Mason and James Madison. Madison later wrote the federal Bill of Rights. Suspicious of many of the other members of the committee, Mason wrote his own statement of rights and submitted it for consideration on May 27. Edmund Randolph, another delegate, described that when Mason presented his draft, it "swallowed up all the rest, by fixing the grounds and plan, which after great discussion and correction, were finally ratified" (Rutland 1991, 33). On June 12, his draft was unanimously approved with few changes. The Declaration of Rights became the first part of the new state constitution adopted on June 29. Regarding trial rights, Mason included the right to a jury trial in criminal and civil cases; right to a unanimous jury verdict; right against excessive bail and fines and against cruel and unusual punishment; right to a speedy trial; right to be informed of the cause and nature of the charge; right to confront the accuser and witnesses; and right to call evidence in the defendant's favor. Mason also included the right against self-incrimination, the first constitutional statement of what will become a clause in the Fifth Amendment.

The Virginia Declaration of Rights expanded the personal rights of citizens more than any other document officially adopted, and it influenced many that followed.

* * *

Virginia Declaration of Rights, 1776

A Declaration of Rights made by the Representatives of the good people of Virginia, assembled in full and free Convention; which rights do pertain to them and their posterity, as the basis and foundation of Government.

1. That all men are by nature equally free and independent, and have certain inherent rights, of which, when they enter into a state of society, they cannot, by any compact, deprive or divest their posterity; namely, the enjoyment of life and liberty, with the means of acquiring and possessing property, and persuing and obtaining happiness and safety.

2. That all power is vested in, and consequently derived from, the People; that magistrates are their trustees and servants, and at all times amenable to them.

3. That Government is, or ought to be, instituted for the common benefit, protection, and security of the people, nation, or community; of all the various modes and forms of Government that is best which is capable of producing the greatest degree of happiness and safety, and is most effectually secured against the danger of mal-administration; and that, whenever any Government shall be found inadequate or contrary to these purposes, a majority of the community hath an indubitable, unalienable, and indefeasible right, to reform, alter, or abolish it, in such manner as shall be judged most conducive to the publick weal.

4. That no man, or set of men, are entitled to exclusive or separate emoluments and privileges from the community, but in consideration of publick services; which, not being descendible, neither ought the offices of Magistrate, Legislator, or Judge, to be hereditary.

5. That the Legislative and Executive powers of the State should be separate and distinct from the Judicative; and, that the members of the two first may be restrained from oppression, by feeling and participating

the burdens of the people, they should, at fixed periods, be reduced to a private station, return into that body from which they were originally taken, and the vacancies be supplied by frequent, certain, and regular elections, in which all, or any part of the former members, to be again eligible, or ineligible, as the law shall direct.

6. That elections of members to serve as Representatives of the people, in Assembly, ought to be free; and that all men, having sufficient evidence of permanent common interest with, and attachment to, the community, have the right of suffrage, and cannot be taxed or deprived of their property for publick uses without their own consent or that of their Representative so elected, nor bound by any law to which they have not, in like manner, assented, for the publick good.

7. That all power of suspending laws, or the execution of laws, by any authority, without consent of the Representatives of the people, is injurious to their rights, and ought not to be exercised.

8. That in all capital or criminal prosecutions a man hath a right to demand the cause and nature of his accusation, to be confronted with the accusers and witnesses, to call for evidence in his favour, and to a speedy trial by an impartial jury of his vicinage, without whose unanimous consent he cannot be found guilty, nor can he be compelled to give evidence against himself; that no man be deprived of his liberty except by the law of the land, or the judgment of his peers.

9. That excessive bail ought not to be required, nor excessive fines imposed, nor cruel and unusual punishments inflicted.

10. That general warrants, whereby any officer or messenger may be commanded to search suspected places without evidence of a fact committed, or to seize any person or persons not named, or whose offence is not particularly described and supported by evidence, are grievous and oppressive, and ought not to be granted.

11. That in controversies respecting property, and in suits between man and man, the ancient trial by Jury is preferable to any other, and ought to be held sacred.

12. That the freedom of the Press is one of the greatest bulwarks of liberty, and can never be restrained but by despotick Governments.

13. That a well-regulated Militia, composed of the body of the people, trained to arms, is the proper, natural, and safe defence of a free State; that Standing Armies, in time of peace, should be avoided as dangerous to liberty; and that, in all cases, the military should be under strict subordination to, and governed by, the civil power.

14. That the people have a right to uniform Government; and, therefore, that no Government separate from, or independent of, the Government of Virginia, ought to be erected or established within the limits thereof.

15. That no free Government, or the blessing of liberty, can be pre-

served to any people but by a firm adherence to justice, moderation, temperance, frugality, and virtue, and by frequent recurrence to fundamental principles.

16. That Religion, or the duty which we owe to our Creator, and the manner of discharging it, can be directed only by reason and conviction, not by force or violence; and, therefore, all men are equally entitled to the free exercise of religion, according to the dictates of conscience; and that it is the mutual duty of all to practise Christian forbearance, love, and charity, towards each other.

Source: Force, Peter, ed. *American Archieves*. Fourth series (1846). Vol. 6, 1561. n.p.: M. St. Clair Clarke and Peter Force.

DOCUMENT 11: New Jersey Constitution (1776)

Written at the same time as the Virginia Declaration of Rights and approved only a few days later, the New Jersey Constitution was one of the four that incorporated citizen rights in the body of its constitution, instead of as a separate statement. The Constitution of the United States of America would follow this model and include any mention of citizen rights in the body of the document.

The New Jersey Constitution specifically states that it is based on common law and on statute law of New Jersey. This claim to be based on a combination of common law and colonial law is one of its unique contributions.

Regarding criminal rights, this constitution guarantees a trial by jury (Article XXI); further, criminal defendants are entitled to the "same privileges of witnesses and counsel, as their prosecutors" (Article XVI). This statement is phrased exactly as it is in the 1701 Pennsylvania Charter of Privileges. The New Jersey Constitution also states that the right to a jury trial "shall remain confirmed as part of the law of this Colony, without repeal, forever."

* * *

New Jersey Constitution, 1776

Whereas all the constitutional authority ever possessed by the kings of Great Britain over these colonies, or their other dominions, was, by compact derived from the people, and held of them, for the common interest of the whole society; allegiance and protection are, in the nature of things, reciprocal ties, each equally depending upon the other, and liable to be dissolved by the others being refused or withdrawn. And whereas George the Third, king of Great Britain, has refused protection to the good people of these colonies; and, by assenting to sundry acts of the British parliament, attempted to subject them to the absolute domin- ion of that body; and has also made war upon them, in the most cruel and unnatural manner, for no other cause, than asserting their just rights—all civil authority under him is necessarily at an end, and a dis- solution of government in each colony has consequently taken place.

And whereas, in the present deplorable situation of these colonies, exposed to the fury of a cruel and relentless enemy, some form of gov- ernment is absolutely necessary, not only for the preservation of good order, but also the more effectually to unite the people, and enable them to exert their whole force in their own necessary defence; and as the honorable continental congress, the supreme council of the American colonies, has advised such of the colonies as have not yet gone into measures, to adopt for themselves, respectively, such government as shall best conduce to their own happiness and safety, and the well-being of America in general: We, the representatives of the colony of New Jersey, having been elected by all the counties, in the freest manner, and in congress assembled, have, after mature deliberations, agreed upon a set of charter rights and the form of a Constitution, in manner following, viz.

I. That the government of this Province shall be vested in a Governor, Legislative Council. And General Assembly. . . .

VIII. That the Governor, or, in his absence, the Vice-President of the Council, shall have the supreme executive power, be Chancellor of the Colony, and act as captain-general and commander in chief of all the militia . . .

IX. That the Governor and Council, (seven whereof shall be a quorum) be the Court of Appeals, in the last resort, in all clauses of law, as heretofore; and that they possess the power of granting pardons to crim- inals, after condemnation, in all cases of treason, felony, or other offences. . . .

XII. That the Judges of the Supreme Court shall continue in office for seven years; the Judges of the Inferior Court of Common Pleas in the several counties, Justices of the Peace, Clerks of the Supreme Court, Clerks of the Inferior Court of Common Pleas and Quarter Sessions, the Attorney-General, and Provincial Secretary, shall continue in office for five years; and the provincial Treasurer shall continue in office for one year; and that they shall be severally appointed by the Council and As- sembly, in manner aforesaid, and commissioned by the Governor, or, in his absence, the Vice-President of the Council. Provided always, that the said offiers, severally, shall be capable of being re-appointed, at the end of the terms severally before limited; and that any of the said officers shall be liable to be dismissed, when adjudged guilty of misbehaviour, by the Council, on an impeachment of the Assembly.

XIII. That the inhabitants of each county, qualified to vote as aforesaid, shall at the time and place of electing their Representatives, annually elect one Sheriff, and one or more coroners; and that they may re-elect the same person to such offices, until he shall have served three years, but no longer; after which, three years must elapse before the same person is capable of being elected again. When the election is certified to the Governor, or Vice-President, under the hands of six freeholders of the county for which they were elected, they shall be immediately commissioned to serve in their respective offices.

XIV. That the townships, at their annual town meetings for electing other officers, shall choose constables for the districts respectively; and also three or more judicious freeholders of good character, to hear and finally determine all appeals, relative to unjust assessments, in cases of public taxation; which commissioners of appeal shall, for that purpose, sit at some suitable time or times, to be by them appointed, and made known to the people by advertisements. . . .

XVI. That all criminals shall be admitted to the same privileges of witnesses and counsel, as their prosecutors are or shall be entitled to.

XX. That the legislative department of this government may, as much as possible, be preserved from all suspicion of corruption, none of the Judges of the Supreme or other Courts, Sheriffs, or any other person or persons possessed of any post of profit under the government, other than Justices of the Peace, shall be entitled to a seat in the Assembly; but that, on his being elected, and taking his seat, his office or post shall be considered as vacant.

XXI. That the common law of England, as well as so much of the statute law, as have been heretofore practised in the Colony, shall still remain in force, until they shall be altered by a future law of the Legislature; such parts only excepted, as are repugnant to the rights and privileges contained in this Charter; and that the inestimable right of trial by jury shall remain confirmed as a part of the law of this Colony, without repeal, forever. . . .

Provided always, and it is the true intent and meaning of this Congress, that if a reconciliation between Great-Britain and these Colonies should take place, and the latter be taken again under the protection and government of the crown of Britain, this Charter shall be null and void—otherwise to remain firm and inviolable.

In Provincial Congress, New Jersey,
Burlington, July 2, 1776
By order of Congress
Samuel Tucker, Pres.
William Paterson, Secretary

Source: Poore, Benjamin P., ed. *The Federal and State Constitutions, Colonial Charters and Other Organic Laws of the United States.* Vol. 2, 1310–14. Washington, D.C.: Government Printing Office, 1878.

DOCUMENT 12: Massachusetts Declaration of Rights (1780)

Massachusetts was one of the last colonies to have a constitution. Its first proposed constitution was rejected 5 to 1 by the people. Their primary objection was the absence of a bill of rights. Only two rights were mentioned, the right to a jury trial and the right to freedom of religion for Protestants.

A convention was chosen in 1779 to draft a new constitution. At its first session, the delegates approved a resolution calling for the preparation of a declaration of rights before dealing with the frame of government. The appointed committee created a subcommittee that included John Adams. He wrote the Massachusetts Declaration of Rights, and, like George Mason's Virginia Declaration of Rights, it was accepted by the convention with very few modifications on March 2, 1779, and approved by the people in 1780.

The Massachusetts Declaration repeats the trial right of prior rights statements. It is largely based on the Virginia Declaration of Rights. Included are the right to legal process, no deprivation of "life, liberty, or estate, but by the judgment of his peers, or the law of the land." Also included are the rights to know the charges, against self-incrimination, to produce evidence, to confront witnesses, to counsel, to trial by jury in criminal and civil cases, to judgment of peers, to trial in the jurisdiction where the crime was committed, and to protection against unreasonable searches and seizures. The absence of any new trial rights testifies that the colonists had reached general agreement on what trial rights should be guaranteed.

The Massachusetts Declaration presents a clear summation of the rights Americans expected just seven years before the writing of the U.S. Constitution. The history of its creation promotes the idea that a bill of rights should be written before the frame of government.

* * *

Massachusetts Declaration of Rights, 1780

A Constitution or Frame of Government, Agreed upon by the Delegates of the People of the State of Massachusetts-Bay,—In Convention,— Began and held at Cambridge, on the First of September, 1779, and continued by Adjournments to the Second of March, 1780.

Preamble

The end of the institution, maintenance and administration of government, is to secure the existence of the body-politic; to protect it; and to furnish the individuals who compose it, with the power of enjoying, in safety and tranquility, their natural rights, and the blessings of life; And whenever these great objects are not obtained, the people have a right to alter the government, and to take measures necessary for their safety, prosperity and happiness. . . .

We, therefore, the people of Massachusetts, acknowledging, with grateful hearts, the goodness of the Great Legislator of the Universe, in affording us, in the course of His providence, an opportunity, deliberately and peaceably without fraud, violence or surprise, of entering into an original, explicit, and solemn compact with each other; and of forming a new Constitution of Civil Government, for ourselves and posterity; and devoutly imploring His direction in so interesting a design. Do agree upon, ordain and establish, the following Declaration of Rights, and Frame of Government, as the Constitution of the Commonwealth of Massachusetts.

Part the First
A Declaration of the Rights of the Inhabitants of the Commonwealth of Massachusetts

I. All men are born free and equal, and have certain natural, essential, and unalienable rights; among which may be reckoned the right of enjoying and defending their lives and liberties; that of acquiring, possessing, and protecting property; in fine, that of seeking and obtaining their safety and happinesss.

II. It is the right as well as the duty of all men in society, publicly, and at stated seasons, to worship the Supreme Being. . . .

And every denomination of christians, demeaning themselves peaceably, and as good subjects of the Commonwealth, shall be equally under the protection of the law; And no subordination of any one sect or denomination to another shall ever be established by law.

IV. The people of this Commonwealth have the sole and exclusive right of governing themselves as a free, sovereign, and independent state; . . .

VIII. In order to prevent those, who are vested with authority, from becoming oppressors, the people have a right, at such periods and in such manner as they shall establish by their frame of government, to cause their public officers to return to private life; and to fill up vacant places by certain and regular elections and appointments.

IX. All elections ought to be free; . . .

X. Each individual of the society has a right to be protected by it in the enjoyment of his life, liberty and property, according to standing laws. He is obliged, consequently, to contribute his share to the expense of this protection; to give his personal service, or an equivalent, when necessary; But no part of the property of any individual, can, with justice, be taken from him, or applied to public uses without his own consent, or that of the representative body of the people; In fine, the people of this commonwealth are not controlable by any other laws, than those to which their constitutional representative body have given their consent. And whenever the public exigencies require, that the property of any individual should be appropriated to public uses, he shall receive a reasonable compensation therefor.

XI. Every subject of the Commonwealth ought to find a certain remedy, by having recourse to the laws, for all injuries or wrongs which he may receive in his person, property or character. He ought to obtain right and justice freely, and without being obliged to purchase it; completely, and without any denial; promptly, and without delay; conformably to the laws.

XII. No subject shall be held to answer for any crime or offence, until the same is fully and plainly, substantially and formally, described to him; or be compelled to accuse, or furnish evidence against himself. And every subject shall have a right to produce all proofs, that may be favorable to him; to meet the witnesses against him face to face, and to be fully heard in his defence by himself, or his council, at his election. And no subject shall be arrested, imprisoned, despoiled, or deprived of his property, immunities, or privileges, put out of the protection of the law, exiled, or deprived of his life, liberty, or estate; but by the judgement of his peers, or the law of the land.

And the legislature shall not make any law, that shall subject any person to capital or infamous punishment, excepting for the government of the army and navy, without trial by jury.

XIII. In criminal prosecutions, the verification of facts in the vicinity where they happen, is one of the greatest securities of the life, liberty, and property of the citizen.

XIV. Every subject has a right to be secure from all unreasonable searches, and seizures of his person, his houses, his papers, and all his possessions. . . .

XV. In all controversies concerning property, and in all suits between two or more persons, except in cases in which it has heretofore been otherways used and practised, the parties have a right to a trial by jury; and this method of procedure shall be held sacred, unless, in causes arising on the high-seas, and such as relate to mariners wages, the legislature shall hereafter find it necessary to alter it.

XVI. The liberty of the press is essential to the security of freedom in a state; it ought not, therefore, to be restrained in this Commonwealth. . . .

XIX. The people have a right, in an orderly and peaceable manner, to assemble to consult upon the common good; give instructions to their representatives; and to request of the legislative body, by the way of addresses, petitions, or remonstrances, redress of the wrongs done them, and of the grievances they suffer. . . .

XXV. No subject ought, in any case, or in any time, to be declared guilty of treason or felony by the legislature.

XXVI. No magistrate or court of law shall demand excessive bail or sureties, impose excessive fines, or inflict cruel or unusual punishments. . . .

XXIX. It is essential to the preservation of the rights of every individual, his life, liberty, property and character, that there be an impartial interpretation of the laws, and administration of justice. It is the right of every citizen to be tried by judges as free, impartial and independent as the lot of humanity will admit. It is therefore not only the best policy, but for the security of the rights of the people, and of every citizen, that the judges of the supreme judicial court should hold their offices as long as they behave themselves well; and that they should have honorable salaries ascertained and established by standing laws.

XXX. In the government of this Commonwealth, the legislative department shall never exercise the executive and judicial powers, or either of them; The executive shall never exercise the legislative and judicial powers, or either of them; The judicial shall never exercise the legislative and executive powers, or either of them; to the end it may be a government of laws and not of men.

Source: Journal of the Convention for Framing a Constitution of Government for the State of Massachusetts Bay, 1779–1780, 222–27. Boston: Dutton & Westworth Printers, 1832.

DOCUMENT 13: Northwest Ordinance (1787)

The first constitution for the newly independent colonies, the Articles of Confederation, did not have a bill of rights or any provisions guaranteeing fundamental rights. That was left to the state constitutions. However, Congress did create a list of rights in 1787 for the Northwest Territory.

State claims to land in the largely unsettled western portions of the new country were ceded to the central government. Some plan of government was needed. After several attempts, Congress created the Northwest Ordinance. It applied to the land north of the Ohio River and west of settled regions. No fewer than three states nor more than five states were to be created from this territory. The Northwest Ordinance's statement of rights was the first enacted by the new federal government.

The first draft contained a very short provision dealing with personal rights, guaranteeing trial by jury and the right of habeas corpus. By the time the ordinance was passed on July 13, 1787, that brief passage had been expanded considerably. The statement of rights is in Article II. It is modeled on state bills of rights. The ordinance also declares that the bill of rights constitutes "articles of compact between the original States and the people . . . [and shall] forever remain unalterable, unless by common consent."

The Northwest Ordinance is also memorable because in Article VI, slavery is outlawed forever in the region.

* * *

An Ordinance for the government of the territory of the United States northwest of the river Ohio (1787)

Section 1. *Be it ordained by the United States in Congress assembled,* That the said Territory, for the purpose of temporary government, be one district, subject, however, to be divided into two districts, as future circumstances may, in the opinion of Congress, make it expedient. . . .

Sec. 3. *Be it ordained by the authority aforesaid,* That there shall be appointed, from time to time, by Congress, a governor, whose commission shall continue in force for the term of three years, unless sooner revoked by Congress; he shall reside in the district, and have a freehold estate therein, in one thousand acres of land, while in the exercise of his office. . . .

Sec. 5. The governor and judges, or a majority of them, shall adopt and publish in the district such laws of the original States, criminal and civil, as may be necessary, and best suited to the circumstances of the district, and report them to Congress from time to time, which laws shall be in force in the district until the organization of the general assembly therein, unless disapproved of by Congress; but afterwards the legislature shall have authority to alter them as they shall think fit. . . .

Sec. 13. And for extending the fundamental principles of civil and religious liberty, which form the basis whereon these republics, their laws and constitutions, are erected; to fix and establish those principles as the basis of all laws, constitutions, and governments, which forever hereafter shall be formed in the said territory; to provide, also, for the establishment of States, and permanent government therein, and for their admission to a share in the Federal councils on an equal footing with the original States, at as early periods as they may be consistent with the general interest:

Sec. 14. It is hereby ordained and declared, by the authority aforesaid, that the following articles shall be considered as articles of compact, between the original States and the people and States in the said territory, and forever remain unalterable, unless by common consent, to wit:

Article I

No person, demeaning himself in a peaceable and orderly manner, shall ever be molested on account of his mode of worship, or religious sentiments, in the said territory.

Article II

The inhabitants of the said territory shall always be entitled to the benefits of the writs of *habeas corpus*, and of the trial by jury; of a proportionate representation of the people in the legislature, and of judicial proceedings according to the course of the common law. All persons shall be bailable, unless for capital offences, where the proof shall be evident, or the presumption great. All fines shall be moderate; and no cruel or unusual punishment shall be inflicted. No man shall be deprived of his liberty or property, but by the judgment of his peers, or the law of the land, and should the public exigencies make it necessary, for the common preservation, to take any person's property, or to demand his particular services, full compensation shall be made for the same. And in the just preservation of rights and property, it is understood and declared, that no law ought ever to be made or have force in the said territory, that shall, in any manner whatever, interfere with or affect private contracts, or engagements, *bona fide*, and without fraud previously formed. . . .

Article VI

There shall be neither slavery nor involuntary servitude in the said territory, otherwise than in the punishment of crimes, whereof the party shall have been duly convicted: *Provided always*, That any person escaping into the same, from whom labor or service is lawfully claimed in any one of the original States, such fugitive may be lawfully reclaimed, and conveyed to the person claiming his or her labor or service as aforesaid. . . .

Done by the United States, in Congress assembled, the 13th day of July, in the year of our Lord 1787, and of their sovereignty and independence the twelfth.

Source: Ford, Worthington C., ed. *Journals of the Continental Congress, 1774–1789*, Vol. 32, 334–43. Washington, D.C.: Government Printing Office, 1910.

DOCUMENT 14: U.S. Constitution, Article III, Section 2 (1787)

The Constitution produced by the Federal Constitutional Convention in 1787 was indeed a remarkable document, a concise framework for government contained in only seven articles. The famous opening line "We, the People of the United States, in Order to form . . ." clearly shows that the people granted the government its powers. This was the reverse of the traditional relationship of governments and their subjects. When approved, the Constitution became the supreme law of the country. Those powers not granted to the federal government, by implication, were reserved for state governments, thus establishing federalism. Governmental powers were also divided between three distinctive branches—legislative, executive, and judicial—creating checks and balances on each branch. Each of these features was designed to control the power of the new government.

The goals of the Constitution were stated in the preamble. The twin principles of republican government (representatives elected by the people) and popular sovereignty (consent of the governed) run through the Constitution, but no bill of rights was included and only a few rights are guaranteed. Those rights dealing with trial rights are in Article 3, Section 2.

* * *

U.S. Constitution, Article III, Section 2

Trial of all crimes, except in cases of impeachment, shall be by jury; and such trial shall be held in the State where the said crimes shall have been committed; but when not committed within any State, the trial shall be at such place or places as the Congress may by law have directed.

DOCUMENT 15: The Federalist No. 83 (1788)

The great debate among the colonists about the relationship of subject to ruler, of citizen to government, of rights and obligations of citizens and governors, now had to be resolved in the proposed Constitution. Every state had the right to accept or reject the new government, and citizens were not shy about voicing their opinions. They divided into two great camps: the Federalists, who favored the Constitution, and the Anti-Federalists, who opposed it. A series of pamphlets written by both camps known as the Federalist and Anti-Federalist papers aired these debates.

The Federalist No. 83, written by Alexander Hamilton, explores the charge by Anti-Federalists that the jury trial was eliminated for civil cases under the Constitution. The Anti-Federalists argued that since a jury trial for civil cases was not mentioned in the Constitution, it was forbidden. The Constitution does specifically call for a jury trial in criminal cases. Some argued, however, that if a jury trial was not required in civil cases, then it could be eliminated for criminal trials. Hamilton dismisses this argument as unworthy of discussion. He argues that jury trials are not eliminated for civil cases, just not mentioned. The new government is free to establish how civil cases are to be tried.

Hamilton also argues that despotism by government is carried out, not in civil cases, but in criminal cases. He further argues that there are difficulties in requiring a jury trial in civil cases, since the states differ greatly in how they deal with various civil cases. Finally, he argues that the best judges would not want a constitutional requirement for jury trials in all civil cases. They would prefer to be more flexible, establishing procedures over time, in some cases using jury trials and in other cases not. Hamilton ends by pointing out that Connecticut has no constitutional provision for a jury trial in civil or criminal cases. Yet it is widely regarded as a state in which the rights of citizens are protected.

* * *

The Federalist No. 83

THE objection to the plan of the convention (Constitution), which has met with most success in this State, and perhaps in several of the other States, is that relative to the want of a constitutional provision for the trial by jury in civil cases. The disingenuous form in which this objection is usually stated has been repeatedly adverted to and exposed, but continues to be pursued in all the conversations and writings of the opponents of the plan. The mere silence of the Constitution in regard to civil causes, is represented as an abolition of the trial by jury, and the declamations to which it has afforded a pretext are artfully calculated to induce a persuasion that this pretended abolition is complete and universal, extending not only to every species of civil, but even to criminal, causes. To argue with respect to the latter would, however, be as vain and fruitless as to attempt the serious proof of the existence of matter, or to demonstrate any of those propositions which, by their own internal evidence, force conviction, when expressed in language adapted to convey their meaning.

With regard to civil causes, subtleties almost too contemptible for refutation have been employed to countenance the surmise that a thing which is only not provided for, is entirely abolished. Every man of discernment must at once perceive the wide difference between silence and abolition. . . .

The maxims on which they rely are of this nature: "A specification of particulars is an exclusion of generals"; or, "The expression of one thing is the exclusion of another." Hence, say they, as the Constitution has established the trial by jury in criminal cases, and is silent in respect to civil, this silence is an implied prohibition of trial by jury in regard to the latter. . . .

A power to constitute courts is a power to prescribe the mode of trial; and consequently, if nothing was said in the Constitution on the subject of juries, the legislature would be at liberty either to adopt that institution or to let it alone. This discretion, in regard to criminal causes, is abridged by the express injunction of trial by jury in all such cases; but it is, of course, left at large in relation to civil causes, there being a total silence on this head. The specification of an obligation to try all criminal causes in a particular mode, excludes indeed the obligation or necessity of employing the same mode in civil causes, but does not abridge the power of the legislature to exercise that mode if it should be thought proper. The pretence, therefore, that the national legislature would not be at full liberty to submit all the civil causes of federal cognizance to the determination of juries, is a pretence destitute of all just foundation.

From these observations this conclusion results: that the trial by jury in civil cases would not be abolished; and that the use attempted to be made of the maxims which have been quoted, is contrary to reason and common-sense, and therefore not admissible. . . .

The friends and adversaries of the plan of the convention, if they agree in nothing else, concur at least in the value they set upon the trial by jury; or if there is any difference between them it consists in this: the former regard it as a valuable safeguard to liberty; the latter represent it as the very palladium of free government. For my own part, the more the operation of the institution has fallen under my observation, the more reason I have discovered for holding it in high estimation; and it would be altogether superfluous to examine to what extent it deserves to be esteemed useful or essential in a representative republic, or how much more merit it may be entitled to, as a defence against the oppressions of an hereditary monarch, than as a barrier to the tyranny of popular magistrates in a popular government. Discussions of this kind would be more curious than beneficial, as all are satisfied of the utility of the institution, and of its friendly aspect to liberty. But I must acknowledge that I cannot readily discern the inseparable connection between the existence of liberty, and the trial by jury in civil cases. Arbitrary impeachments, arbitrary methods of prosecuting pretended offences, and arbitrary punishments upon arbitrary convictions, have ever appeared to me to be the great engines of judicial despotism; and these have all relation to criminal proceedings. The trial by jury in criminal cases, aided by the habeas corpus act, seems therefore to be alone concerned in the question. And both of these are provided for, in the most ample manner, in the plan of the convention. . . .

It certainly sounds not a little harsh and extraordinary to affirm that there is no security for liberty in a Constitution which expressly establishes the trial by jury in criminal cases, because it does not do it in civil also; while it is a notorious fact that Connecticut, which has been always regarded as the most popular State in the Union, can boast of no constitutional provision for either.

PUBLIUS

Source: See Cooke, Jacob E., ed. *The Federalist*. Middletown, Conn.: Wesleyan University Press, 1961.

DOCUMENT 16: U.S. Constitution, Amendments Five and Six (1791)

In many ways, the framers of the Constitution attempted to control the power of the new government. Federalism, division of power between three branches, sovereignty of the people, all were limits; nonetheless, the new government was stronger than the Articles of Confederation, and many were afraid of its strength. To secure approval of the new government, supporters had to agree that amendments would be added to guarantee the rights and liberties of the people.

In the fall, winter, and spring of 1788–1789, the new government came into existence. Washington convened the new government; the first laws and taxes were enacted; and James Madison introduced in Congress a proposed bill of rights with seventeen articles on June 8, 1789. After debate, the list was reduced and reconciled with one passed by the Senate, and in September Congress officially proposed twelve articles as amendments to the Constitution. To be approved, each amendment needed to be ratified by three-fourths of the states. By December 15, 1791, ten amendments had been ratified.

The Fifth and Sixth Amendments contain our basic trial rights. Each amendment lists several. There is nothing new or original in this list of trial rights. These rights were earlier expressed in state constitutions and have their roots in the history of England and the colonies.

* * *

Amendment Five (1791)

No person shall be held to answer for a capital, or otherwise infamous crime, unless on a presentment or indictment of a Grand Jury, except in cases arising in the land or naval forces, or in the militia, when in actual service in time of war or public danger; nor shall any person be subject for the same offence to be twice put in jeopardy of life or limb; nor shall be compelled in any criminal case to be a witness against himself, nor be deprived of life, liberty, or property, without due process of law; nor shall private property be taken for public use, without just compensation.

Amendment Six (1791)

In all criminal prosecutions, the accused shall enjoy the right to a speedy and public trial, by an impartial jury of the State and district wherein the crime shall have been committed, which district shall have been previously ascertained by law, and to be informed of the nature and cause of the accusation; to be confronted with the witnesses against him; to have compulsory process for obtaining witnesses in his favor, and to have the assistance of counsel for his defence.

Part II

Early Nineteenth-Century Trial Rights

DOCUMENT 17: *Barron v. Mayor & City Council of Baltimore* (1833)

The Bill of Rights clearly protects citizens from the national government. But what about actions of state governments that violate the Bill of Rights? Does the Bill of Rights in the Constitution apply to the states? Chief Justice John Marshall answered this question in *Barron v. Mayor & City of Baltimore.* The City of Baltimore paved streets and thereby diverted several streams from their natural course. The result was growing deposits of sand and gravel near Barron's Wharf, rendering the water too shallow for boat traffic and the wharf useless. Barron argued that the city had taken his property without just compensation in violation of the Fifth Amendment. The Baltimore county court decided for Barron on all counts and ordered that he be paid $4,500. The city appealed the decision and it was reversed. Barron then appealed the case to the Supreme Court.

John Marshall's decision declared that the Fifth Amendment applied only to the national government and not to the states. Marshall reasoned that the Constitution was established for the national government and not for the individual states. This decision was stated in broad terms and was interpreted as barring the application of any part of the Bill of Rights to the states. Each state was free to establish its own rights. The precedent set by this decision lasted throughout the nineteenth century.

* * *

Barron v. Mayor & City Council of Baltimore, 7 Peters 243

Mr. Chief Justice Marshall delivered the opinion of the court.

The judgment brought up by this writ of error having been rendered by the court of a State, this tribunal can exercise no jurisdiction over it unless it be shown to come within the provisions of the 25th section of the Judiciary Act. The plaintiff in error contends that it comes within that clause in the Fifth Amendment to the Constitution which inhibits the taking of private property for public use without just compensation. He insists that this amendment, being in favor of the liberty of the citizen, ought to be so construed as to restrain the legislative power of a state, as well as that of the United States. If this proposition be untrue, the court can take no jurisdiction of the cause.

The question thus presented is, we think, of great importance, but not of much difficulty. The Constitution was ordained and established by the people of the United States for themselves, for their own government, and not for the government of the individual States. Each State established a constitution for itself, and in that constitution provided such limitations and restrictions on the powers of its particular government as its judgment dictated. The people of the United States framed such a government for the United States as they supposed best adapted to their situation and best calculated to promote their interests. The powers they conferred on this government were to be exercised by itself, and the limitations on power, if expressed in general terms, are naturally, and we think necessarily, applicable to the government created by the instrument. They are limitations of power granted in the instrument itself, not of distinct governments framed by different persons and for different purposes.

If these propositions be correct, the fifth amendment must be understood as restraining the power of the General Government, not as applicable to the States. In their several Constitutions, they have imposed such restrictions on their respective governments, as their own wisdom suggested, such as they deemed most proper for themselves. It is a subject on which they judge exclusively, and with which others interfere no further than they are supposed to have a common interest.

The counsel for the plaintiff in error insists that the Constitution was intended to secure the people of the several States against the undue exercise of power by their respective State governments, as well as against that which might be attempted by their General Government. In support of this argument he relies on the inhibitions contained in the tenth section of the first article. We think that section affords a strong, if not a conclusive, argument in support of the opinion already indicated by the court. The preceding section contains restrictions which are obviously intended for the exclusive purpose of restraining the exercise of power by the departments of the General Government. Some of them use language applicable only to Congress, others are expressed in general terms. The third clause, for example, declares, that "no bill of attainder or ex post facto law shall be passed." No language can be more general, yet the demonstration is complete that it applies solely to the Government of the United States. In addition to the general arguments furnished by the instrument itself, some of which have been already suggested, the succeeding section, the avowed purpose of which is to restrain State legislation, contains in terms the very prohibition. It declares, that "no State shall pass any bill of attainder or ex post facto law." This provision, then, of the ninth section, however comprehensive its language, contains no restriction on State legislation.

The ninth section having enumerated, in the nature of a bill of rights, the limitations intended to be imposed on the powers of the General Government, the tenth proceeds to enumerate those which were to operate on the State legislatures. These restrictions are brought together in the same section, and are by express words applied to the States. "No State shall enter into any treaty," &c. Perceiving, that in a constitution framed by the people of the United States, for the government of all, no limitation of the action of government on the people would apply to the State government, unless expressed in terms, the restrictions contained in the tenth section are in direct words so applied to the States. . . .

Had the framers of these amendments intended them to be limitations on the powers of the State governments, they would have imitated the framers of the original Constitution, and have expressed that intention. Had Congress engaged in the extraordinary occupation of improving the Constitutions of the several States by affording the people additional protection from the exercise of power by their own governments in matters which concerned themselves alone, they would have declared this purpose in plain and intelligible language.

But it is universally understood, it is a part of the history of the day, that the great revolution which established the Constitution of the United States was not effected without immense opposition. Serious fears were extensively entertained that those powers which the patriot statesmen who then watched over the interests of our country deemed essential to union, and to the attainment of those invaluable objects for which union was sought, might be exercised in a manner dangerous to liberty. In almost every convention by which the Constitution was adopted, amendments to guard against the abuse of power were recommended. These amendments demanded security against the apprehended encroachments of the General Government—not against those of the local governments. In compliance with a sentiment thus generally expressed, to quiet fears thus extensively entertained, amendments were proposed by the required majority in Congress and adopted by the States. These amendments contain no expression indicating an intention to apply them to the State governments. This court cannot so apply them.

We are of opinion that the provision in the Fifth Amendment to the Constitution declaring that private property shall not be taken for public use without just compensation is intended solely as a limitation on the exercise of power by the Government of the United States, and is not applicable to the legislation of the States. We are therefore of opinion that there is no repugnancy between the several acts of the general assembly of Maryland, given in evidence by the defendants at the trial of this cause, in the court of that State, and the Constitution of the United States. This court, therefore, has no jurisdiction of the cause, and it is dismissed.

This cause came on to be heard on the transcript of the record from the Court of Appeals for the Western Shore of the State of Maryland, and was argued by counsel. On consideration whereof, it is the opinion of this Court that there is no repugnancy between the several acts of the General Assembly of Maryland given in evidence by the defendants at the trial of this cause in the court of that State and the Constitution of the United States; whereupon it is ordered and adjudged by this court that this writ of error be, and the same is hereby, dismissed for the want of jurisdiction.

Source: United States Supreme Court Reports. Lawyers Edition, Book 8, 672–75. Rochester, N.Y.: Lawyers Cooperative Publishing Company, 1918.

DOCUMENT 18: An Act Relating to Habeas Corpus, and Regulating Judicial Proceedings in Certain Cases (1863)

On April 12, 1861, the Civil War began. Quickly hostilities drove Virginia, Arkansas, Tennessee, and North Carolina into the Confederacy. The Civil War presented President Lincoln with unprecedented challenges. The young country was tearing apart. Lincoln felt compelled to do whatever was necessary to contain the rebellion and maintain the union.

To control the pro-Confederacy forces in states still part of the Union, such as slave-owning Maryland, President Lincoln ordered his military commanders to arrest those who promoted secession. He empowered them to suspend the writ of habeas corpus. The writ of habeas corpus is an order that a prisoner can request that requires the authorities to bring the prisoner to trial. By suspending it, those suspected of supporting the Confederacy could be arrested and held in jail without charges. With the writ suspended, the accused had no trial rights and could be jailed indefinitely.

The Constitution provides that the writ of habeas corpus can be suspended in cases of "rebellion or invasion" when required for public safety. Who has the authority to suspend the writ is not stated. President Lincoln claimed he could; Supreme Court Chief Justice Taney and others thought only Congress could. The prospect of armed soldiers seizing citizens from their homes at night brought terror to many. The writ of habeas corpus was ultimately suspended throughout the country by Lincoln's order; this action was one of his most controversial policies.

On March 3, 1863, Congress passed legislation asserting its control over habeas corpus but authorizing the president to suspend it when needed. The legislation provided procedures to be followed. Within a few weeks, those arrested needed to be indicted by a grand jury or let go, providing they were willing to take an oath of allegiance to the government of the United States and to support the Constitution. The law also provided protections for those conducting arrests when the writ of habeas corpus was suspended.

* * *

An Act Relating to Habeas Corpus, and Regulating Judicial Proceedings in Certain Cases. (1863)

Be it enacted by the Senate and House of Representatives of the United States of America in Congress assembled, That, during the present rebellion, the President of the United States, whenever, in his judgment, the public safety may require it, is authorized to suspend the privilege of the writ of habeas corpus in any case throughout the United States, or any part thereof. And whenever and wherever the said privilege shall be suspended, as aforesaid, no military or other officer shall be compelled, in answer to any writ of habeas corpus, to return the body of any person or persons detained by him by authority of the President; but upon the certificate, under oath, of the officer having charge of any one so detained that such person is detained by him as a prisoner under authority of the President, further proceedings under the writ of habeas corpus shall be suspended by the judge or court having issued the said writ, so long as said suspension by the President shall remain in force, and said rebellion continue.

Sec. 2. *And be it further enacted,* That the Secretary of State and the Secretary of War be, and they are hereby, directed, as soon as may be practicable, to furnish to the judges of the circuit and district courts of the United States and of the District of Columbia a list of the names of all persons, citizens of states in which the administration of the laws has continued unimpaired in the said Federal courts, who are now, or may hereafter be, held as prisoners of the United States, by order of authority of the President of the United States or either of said Secretaries, in any fort, arsenal, or other place, as state or political prisoners, or otherwise than as prisoners of war; the said list to contain the names of all those who reside in the respective jurisdictions of said judges, or who may be deemed by the said Secretaries, or either of them, to have violated any law of the United States in any of said jurisdictions, and also the date of each arrest; the Secretary of State to furnish a list of such persons as are imprisoned by the order or authority of the President, acting through the State Department, and the Department of War a list of such as are imprisoned by the order or authority of the President, acting through the Department of War. And in all cases where a grand jury, having attended any of said courts having jurisdiction in the premises, after the passage of this act, and after the furnishing of said list, as aforesaid, has terminated its session without finding an indictment or presentment, or other proceeding against any such person, it shall be the duty of the judge of said court forthwith to make an order that any such prisoner desiring a discharge from said imprisonment be brought before him to be discharged; and every officer of the Untied States having custody of such prisoner is hereby directed immediately to obey and execute said judge's order; and in case he shall delay or refuse so to do, he shall be subject to indictment for a misdemeanor, and be punished by a fine of not less than five hundred dollars and imprisonment in the common jail for a period not less than six months, in the discretion of the court: *Provided, however*, That no person shall be discharged by virtue of the provisions of this act until after he or she shall have taken an oath of allegiance to the Government of the United States, and to support the Constitution thereof; and that he or she will not hereafter in any way encourage or give aid and comfort to the present rebellion, or the supporters thereof: *And provided, also*, That the judge or court before whom such person may be brought, before discharging him or her from imprisonment, shall have power, on examination of the case, and, if the public safety shall require it, shall be required to cause him or her to enter into recognizance, with or without surety, in a sum to be fixed by said judge or court, to keep the peace and be of good behavior towards the United States and its citizens, and from time to time, and at such times as such judge or court may direct, appear before said judge or court to be further dealt with, according to law, as the circumstances may require. And it shall be the duty of the district attorney for the United States to attend such examination before the judge.

Sec. 3. *And be it further enacted*, That in case any of such prisoners shall be under indictment or presentment for any offence against the laws of the United States, and by existing laws bail or a recognizance may be taken for the appearance for trial of such person, it shall be the duty of said judge at once to discharge such person upon bail or recognizance for trial as aforesaid. And in case the said Secretaries of State and War shall for any reason refuse or omit to furnish the said list of persons held as prisoners as aforesaid at the time of the passage of this act within twenty days thereafter, and of such persons as hereafter may be arrested within twenty days from the time of the arrest, any citizen may, after a grand jury shall have terminated its session without finding an indictment or presentment, as provided in the second section of this act, by a petition alleging the facts aforesaid touching any of the persons so as aforesaid imprisoned, supported by the oath of such petitioner or any other credible person, obtain and be entitled to have the said judge's order to discharge such prisoner on the same terms and conditions prescribed in the second section of this act: *Provided, however*, That the said judge shall be satisfied such allegations are true.

Sec. 4. *And be it further enacted*, That any order of the President, or under his authority, made at any time during the existence of the present rebellion, shall be a defense in all courts to any action or prosecution, civil or criminal, pending, or to be commenced, for any search, seizure, arrest, or imprisonment, made, done, or committed, or acts omitted to be done, under any by virtue of such order, or under color of any law of Congress, and such defense may be made by special plea, or under the general issue.

Sec. 5. *And be it further enacted*, That if any suit or prosecution, civil or criminal, has been or shall be commenced in any state court against any officer, civil or military, or against any other person, for any arrest or imprisonment made, or other trespasses or wrongs done or committed, or any act omitted to be done, at any time during the present rebellion, by virtue or under color of any authority derived from or exercised by or under the President of the United States, or any act of Congress, and the defendant shall, at the time of entering his appearance in such court, or if such appearance shall have been entered before the passage of this act, then at the next session of the court in which such suit or prosecution is pending, file a petition, stating the facts and verified by affidavit, for the removal of the cause for trial at the next circuit court of the United States, to be holden in the district where the suit is pending, and offer good and sufficient surety for his filing in such court, on the first day of its session, copies of such process and other proceedings against him, and also for his appearing in such court and entering special bail in the cause, if special bail was originally required therein.

Sec. 6. *And be it further enacted*, That any suit or prosecution described in this act, in which final judgment may be rendered in the circuit court, may be carried by writ of error to the supreme court, whatever may be the amount of said judgment.

Sec. 7. *And be it further enacted*, That no suit or prosecution, civil or criminal, shall be maintained for any arrest or imprisonment made, or other trespasses or wrongs done or committed, or act omitted to be done, at any time during the present rebellion, by virtue or under color of any authority derived from or exercised by or under the President of the United States, or by or under any act of congress, unless the same shall have been commenced within two years next after such arrest, imprisonment, trespass, or wrong may have been done or committed or act may have been omitted to be done: *Provided*, That in no case shall the limitation herein provided commence to run until the passage of this act, so that no party shall, by virtue of this act, be debarred of his remedy by suit or prosecution until two years from and after the passage of this act.

Source: United States Statutes at Large and Treaties, 36th and 37th Congress, 1859–1863. Vol. 12. Washington, D.C.: Government Printing Office, 1864.

DOCUMENT 19: *Ex Parte Milligan* (1866)

During the Civil War, Lambden P. Milligan had been sentenced to death by an army court in Indiana for allegedly disloyal activities. His lawyer appealed for his release under the 1863 Habeas Corpus Act (see Document 18). His case went before the Supreme Court.

The Supreme Court ruled that his trial before a military court was improper, since the civilian courts were operating effectively in Indiana. The military courts had no jurisdiction over a civilian. This case further clarified the limits of federal authority during times of crisis and helped assured trial rights as guaranteed in the Constitution.

* * *

Ex Parte Milligan, S.C. 4 Wall. 2

Justice Davis delivered the opinion of the Court:

On the 10th day of May, 1865, Lambden P. Milligan presented a petition to the Circuit Court of the United States for the District of Indiana, to be discharged from an alleged unlawful imprisonment. . . .

Milligan insists that said military commission had no jurisdiction to try him upon the charges preferred, or upon any charges whatever; because he was a citizen of the United States and the State of Indiana, and had not been, since the commencement of the late Rebellion, a resident of any of the States whose citizens were arrayed against the government, and that the right of trial by jury was guaranteed to him by the Constitution of the United States. . . .

The importance of the main question presented by this record cannot be overstated; for it involves the very framework of the government and the fundamental principles of American liberty. . . .

The controlling question in the case is this: Upon the *facts* stated in Milligan's petition, and the exhibits filed, had the military commission mentioned in it *jurisdiction*, legally, to try and sentence him? Milligan, not a resident of one of the rebellious states, or a prisoner of war, but a citizen of Indiana for twenty years past and never in the military or naval service, is, while at his home, arrested by the military power of the United States, imprisoned, and, on certain criminal charges preferred against him, tried, convicted, and sentenced to be hanged by a military commission, organized under the direction of the military commander of the military district of Indiana. Had this tribunal the *legal* power and authority to try and punish this man?

No graver question was ever considered by this court, nor one which more nearly concerns the rights of the whole people; for it is the birthright of every American citizen when charged with crime, to be tried and punished according to law. The power of punishment is, alone through the means which the laws have provided for that purpose, and if they are ineffectual, there is an immunity from punishment, no matter how great an offender the individual may be, or how much his crimes may have shocked the sense of justice of the country, or endangered its safety. By the protection of the law human rights are secured; withdraw that protection, and they are at the mercy of wicked rulers, or the clamor of an excited people. If there was law to justify this military trial, it is not our province to interfere; if there was not, it is our duty to declare the nullity of the whole proceedings. The decision of this question does not depend on argument or judicial precedents, numerous and highly illustrative as they are. These precedents inform us of the extent of the struggle to preserve liberty and to relieve those in civil life from military trials. The founders of our government were familiar with the history of that struggle; and secured in a written constitution every right which the people had wrested from power during a contest of ages. By that Constitution and the laws authorized by it this question must be determined. The provisions of that instrument on the administration of criminal justice are too plain and direct, to leave room for misconstruction or doubt of their true meaning. Those applicable to this case are found in that clause of the original Constitution which says, "That the trial of all crimes, except in case of impeachment, shall be by jury"; and in the fourth, fifth, and sixth articles of the amendments. . . .

Have any of the rights guaranteed by the Constitution been violated in the case of Milligan? and if so, what are they?

Every trial involves the exercise of judicial power; and from what source did the military commission that tried him derive their authority? Certainly no part of the judicial power of the country was conferred on them; because the Constitution expressly vests it "in one supreme court and such inferior courts as the Congress may from time to time ordain and establish," and it is not pretended that the commission was a court ordained and established by Congress. They cannot justify on the mandate of the President; because he is controlled by law, and has his appropriate sphere of duty, which is to execute, not to make, the laws; and there is "no unwritten criminal code to which resort can be had as a source of jurisdiction."

But it is said that the jurisdiction is complete under the "laws and usages of war." It can serve no useful purpose to inquire what those laws and usages are, whence they originated, where found, and on whom they operate; they can never be applied to citizens in states which have upheld the authority of the government, and where the courts are open and their process unobstructed. This court has judicial knowledge that in Indiana the Federal authority was always unopposed, and its courts always open to hear criminal accusations and redress grievances; and no usage of war could sanction a military trial there for any offence whatever of a citizen in civil life, in nowise connected with the military service. Congress could grant no such power; and to the honor of our national legislature be it said, it has never been provoked by the state of the country even to attempt its exercise. One of the plainest constitutional provisions was, therefore, infringed when Milligan was tried by a court not ordained and established by Congress, and not composed of judges appointed during good behavior. . . .

It is claimed that martial law covers with its broad mantle the proceedings of this military commission. The proposition is this: that in a time of war the commander of an armed force (if in his opinion the exigencies of the country demand it, and of which he is to judge), has the power, within the lines of his military district, to suspend all civil rights and their remedies, and subject citizens as well as soldiers to the rule of *his will*; and in the exercise of his lawful authority cannot be restrained, except by his superior officer or the President of the United States.

If this position is sound to the extent claimed, then when war exists, foreign or domestic, and the country is subdivided into military departments for mere convenience, the commander of one of them can, if he chooses, within his limits, on the plea of necessity, with the approval of the Executive, substitute military force for and to the exclusion of the laws, and punish all persons, as he thinks right and proper, without fixed or certain rules.

The statement of this proposition shows its importance; for, if true, republican government is a failure, and there is an end of liberty regulated by law. Martial law, established on such a basis, destroys every guarantee of the Constitution, and effectually renders the "military independent of and superior to the civil power"—the attempt to do which by the King of Great Britain was deemed by our fathers such an offence, that they assigned it to the world as one of the causes which impelled them to declare their independence. Civil liberty and this kind of martial law cannot endure together; the antagonism is irreconcilable; and, in the conflict, one or the other must perish. . . .

It is essential to the safety of every government that, in a great crisis, like the one we have just passed through, there should be a power somewhere of suspending the writ of *habeas corpus*. In every war, there are men of previously good character, wicked enough to counsel their fellow-citizens to resist the measures deemed necessary by a good government to sustain its just authority and overthrow its enemies; and their influence may lead to dangerous combinations. In the emergency of the times, an immediate public investigation according to law may not be possible; and yet, the peril to the country may be too imminent to suffer such persons to go at large. Unquestionably, there is then an exigency which demands that the government, if it should see fit in the exercise of a proper discretion to make arrests, should not be required to produce the persons arrested in answer to a writ of *habeas corpus*. The Constitution goes no further. It does not say after a writ of *habeas corpus* is denied a citizen, that he shall be tried otherwise than by the course of the common law; if it had intended this result, it was easy by the use of direct words to have accomplished it. The illustrious men who framed that instrument were guarding the foundations of civil liberty against the abuses of unlimited power; they were full of wisdom, and the lessons of history informed them that a trial by an established court, assisted by an impartial jury, was the only sure way of protecting the citizen against oppression and wrong. Knowing this, they limited the suspension to one great right, and left the rest to remain forever inviolable. But, it is insisted that the safety of the country in time of war demands that this broad claim for martial law shall be sustained. If this were true, it could be well said that a country, preserved at the sacrifice of all the cardinal principles of liberty, is not worth the cost of preservation. Happily, it is not so.

It is difficult to see how the *safety* of the country required martial law in Indiana. If any of her citizens were plotting treason, the power of arrest could secure them, until the government was prepared for their trial, when the courts were open and ready to try them. It was as easy to protect witnesses before a civil as a military tribunal; and as there could be no wish to convict, except on sufficient legal evidence, surely an ordained and established court was better able to judge of this than a military tribunal composed of gentlemen not trained to the profession of the law.

It follows, from what has been said on this subject, that there are occasions when martial rule can be properly applied. If, in foreign invasion or civil war, the courts are actually closed, and it is impossible to administer criminal justice according to law, then, on the theatre of active military operations, where war really prevails, there is a necessity to furnish a substitute for the civil authority, thus overthrown, to preserve the safety of the army and society; and as no power is left but the military, it is allowed to govern by martial rule until the laws can have their free course. As necessity creates the rule, so it limits its duration; for, if this government is continued after the courts are reinstated, it is a gross usurpation of power. Martial rule can never exist where the courts are open, and in the proper and unobstructed exercise of their jurisdiction. It is also confined to the locality of actual war.

Source: United States Supreme Court Reports. Lawyers Edition, Book 8, 281–303. Rochester, N.Y.: Lawyers Cooperative Publishing Company, 1918.

DOCUMENT 20: Amendment Fourteen to the U.S. Constitution (1868)

After the Civil War, legal actions were taken to help assure that the newly freed slaves would be guaranteed their legal rights. Congress passed the Civil Rights Act of 1866, which declared that "all persons born in the United States and not subject to any foreign power, excluding Indians not taxed, are hereby declared to be citizens of the United States." The law guaranteed regardless of "race and color, without regard to any previous condition of slavery or involuntary servitude . . . full and equal benefit of all laws and proceedings for the security of person and property, as is enjoyed by white citizens." Additional provisions provided punishment for anyone who breaks the law and requires state courts to help enforce it.

President Andrew Johnson vetoed the law. Among his reasons was his belief that it violated the rights of the states by requiring them to apply a federal standard in their state courts. Congress promptly passed the legislation over the president's veto. Concern over the constitutionality of the law, however, led Congress within two months to propose the Fourteenth Amendment. An amendment to the Constitution, since it becomes part of the Constitution, cannot be unconstitutional.

The language of the amendment mirrored that of the Civil Rights Act of 1866. The amendment was ratified July 28, 1868. One condition of former Confederate states rejoining the Union was their ratification of this amendment. The first section is the most important. It not only guarantees that former slaves are citizens but stops any state from depriving them of "life, liberty, or property, without due process of law." The meaning of "due process of law" is critical and evolves through a number of Supreme Court decisions over the next century.

* * *

Amendment Fourteen (1868)

Section 1. All persons born or naturalized in the United States, and subject to the jurisdiction thereof, are citizens of the United States and of the State wherein they reside. No State shall make or enforce any law which shall abridge the privileges or immunities of citizens of the United States; nor shall any State deprive any person of life, liberty, or property, without due process of law; nor deny to any person within its jurisdiction the equal protection of the laws.

Section 2. Representatives shall be apportioned among the several States according to their respective numbers, counting the whole number of persons in each State, excluding Indians not taxed. But when the right to vote at any election for the choice of Electors for President and Vice-President of the United States, Representatives in Congress, the executive and judicial officers of a State, or the members of the Legislature thereof, is denied to any of the male inhabitants of such State, being twenty-one years of age, and citizens of the United States, or in any way abridged, except for participation in rebellion, or other crime, the basis of representation therein shall be reduced in the proportion which the number of such male citizens shall bear to the whole number of male citizens twenty-one years of age in such State.

Section 3. No person shall be a Senator or Representative in Congress, or elector of President and Vice-President, or hold any office, civil or military, under the United States, or under any State, who, having previously taken an oath, as a member of Congress, or as an officer of the United States, or as a member of any State legislature, or as an executive or judicial officer of any State, to support the Constitution of the United States, shall have engaged in insurrection or rebellion against the same, or given aid or comfort to the enemies thereof. But Congress may by a vote of two-thirds of each House, remove such disability.

Section 4. The validity of the public debt of the United States, authorized by law, including debts incurred for payment of pensions and bounties for services in suppressing insurrection or rebellion, shall not be questioned. But neither the United States nor any State shall assume or pay any debt or obligation incurred in aid of insurrection or rebellion against the United States, or any claim for the loss or emancipation of any slave; but all such debts, obligations and claims shall be held illegal and void.

Section 5. The Congress shall have power to enforce, by appropriate legislation, the provisions of this Amendment.

Part III

The Fourteenth Amendment, Due Process, and Trial Rights

DOCUMENT 21: *Hurtado v. California* (1884)

After the passage of the Fourteenth Amendment (see Document 20), some argued that the amendment's granting of citizenship meant that all the rights guaranteed in the Bill of Rights now applied to the states. The Court, in a long series of cases over many decades, revisited this debate many times.

Joseph Hurtado had been tried and convicted of murder in the California state courts and sentenced to be executed. His case was appealed to the Supreme Court arguing that he had been denied due process. His lawyers reasoned that the Fourteenth Amendment requirement of due process meant that states are bound by the due process procedures listed in the Bill of Rights. Hurtado had been indicted not by a grand jury but by another process known as "information," which had, under English Common Law, been used only for misdemeanors.

The Supreme Court denied his claim. The Court reasoned that the due process procedures outlined in the Constitution are only one form of due process, and the procedures can be different in state courts. The Fourteenth Amendment does not require the states to adhere to the rights granted in the Bill of Rights. Justice Harlan argued in his dissent that the Fourteenth Amendment did indeed require states to follow the due process procedures listed in the Constitution. These two views will continue to compete with each other for decades to come.

* * *

Hurtado v. California, 110 U.S. 516

Mr. Justice Matthews delivered the opinion of the court.

. . . The proposition of law we are asked to affirm is that an indictment or presentment by a grand jury, as known to the common law of England, is essential to that "due process of law," when applied to prosecutions for felonies, which is secured and guaranteed by this provision of the Constitution of the United States, and which, accordingly, it is forbidden to the States respectively to dispense with in the administration of criminal law.

The question . . . involves a consideration of what additional restrictions upon the legislative policy of the States has been imposed by the Fourteenth Amendment to the Constitution of the United States.

The Constitution of the United States was ordained, it is true, by descendants of Englishmen, who inherited the traditions of English law and history; but it was made for an undefined and expanding future, and for a people gathered and to be gathered from many nations and of may tongues. And while we take just pride in the principles and institutions of the common law, we are not to forget that, in lands where other systems of jurisprudence prevail, the ideas and processes of civil justice are also not unknown. . . .

We are to construe this phrase in the Fourteenth Amendment by the *usus loquendi* of the Constitution itself. The same words are contained in the Fifth Amendment. That article makes specific and express provision for perpetuating the institution of the grand jury so far as relates to prosecutions for the more aggravated crimes under the laws of the United States. . . . It then immediately adds: or be deprived of life, liberty, or property, without due process of law.

According to a recognized canon of interpretation especially applicable to formal and solemn instruments of constitutional law, we are forbidden to assume, without clear reason to the contrary, that any part of this most important amendment is superfluous. The natural and obvious inference is that, in the sense of the Constitution, "due process of law" was not meant or intended to include, ex vi termini, the institution and procedure of a grand jury in any case. The conclusion is equally irresistible that, when the same phrase was employed in the Fourteenth Amendment to restrain the action of the States, it was used in the same sense and with no greater extent, and that, if in the adoption of that amendment it had been part of its purpose to perpetuate the institution of the grand jury in all the States, it would have embodied, as did the Fifth Amendment, express declarations to that effect. Due process of law in the latter refers to that law of the land which derives its authority from the legislative powers conferred upon Congress by the Constitution of the United States, exercised within the limits therein prescribed and interpreted according to the principles of the common law. In the Fourteenth Amendment, by parity of reason, it refers to that law of the land in each State which derives its authority from the inherent and reserved powers of the State, exerted within the limits of those fundamental principles of liberty and justice which lie at the base of all our civil and political institutions, and the greatest security for which resides in the right of the people to make their own laws, and alter them at their pleasure. . . .

It follows that any legal proceeding enforced by public authority, whether sanctioned by age and custom, or newly devised in the discretion of the legislative power, in furtherance of the general public good, which regards and preserves these principles of liberty and justice, must be held to be due process of law. . . .

Mr. Justice Harlan, dissenting.

"Due process of law," within the meaning of the national Constitution, does not import one thing with reference to the powers of the States and another with reference to the powers of the general government. If particular proceedings conducted under the authority of the general government, and involving life, are prohibited because not constituting that due process of law required by the Fifth Amendment of the Constitution of the United States, similar proceedings, conducted under the authority of a State, must be deemed illegal as not being due process of law within the meaning of the Fourteenth Amendment. . . .

[A]ccording to the settled usages and modes of proceeding existing under the common and statute law of England at the settlement of this country, information in capital cases was not consistent with the "law of the land," or with "due process of law." Such was the understanding of the patriotic men who established free institutions upon this continent. Almost the identical words of Magna Charta were incorporated into most of the State Constitutions before the adoption of our national Constitution. When they declared, in substance, that no person should be deprived of life, liberty, or property except by the judgment of his peers or the law of the land, they intended to assert his right to the same guaranties that were given in the mother country by the great charter and the laws passed in furtherance of its fundamental principles. . . .

If the presence in the Fifth Amendment of a specific provision for grand juries in capital cases, alongside the provision for due process of law in proceedings involving life, liberty, or property, is held to prove that "due process of law" did not, in the judgment of the framers of the Constitution, necessarily require a grand jury in capital cases, inexorable logic would require it to be, likewise, held that the right not to be put twice in jeopardy of life and limb for the same offence, nor compelled in a criminal case to testify against one's self—rights and immunities also specifically recognized in the Fifth Amendment—were not protected by that due process of law required by the settled usages and proceedings existing under the common and statute law of England at the settlement of this country. . . .

So that the court, in this case, while conceding that the requirement of due process of law protects the fundamental principles of liberty and justice, adjudges, in effect, that an immunity or right, recognized at the common law to be essential to personal security, jealously guarded by our national Constitution against violation by any tribunal or body exercising authority under the general government, and expressly or impliedly recognized, when the Fourteenth Amendment was adopted in the Bill of Rights or Constitution of every State in the Union, is, yet, not a fundamental principle in governments established, as those of the States of the Union are, to secure to the citizen liberty and justice, and, therefore, is not involved in that due process of law required in proceedings conducted under the sanction of a State. My sense of duty constrains me to dissent from this interpretation of the supreme law of the land.

Source: United States Reports. Vol. 110, 16–558. Washington, D.C.: Government Printing Office, 1884.

DOCUMENT 22: *Ex Parte Wilson* (1885)

Wilson was charged and convicted in federal court of having in his possession and intending to sell counterfeit government bonds. He was sentenced to a fine of $5,000 and fifteen years' imprisonment at hard labor. His case was appealed for several reasons, but the Court felt only one was worthy of consideration.

Wilson had not had the benefit of a grand jury indictment. Instead, prosecutors had used the process of "information," which replaces a grand jury with a simpler process. The use of the procedure of information had grown considerably and was being used by circuit and district courts for any crime.

The Court held that the Constitution requires a grand jury indictment for an "infamous crime" and defined any crime punishable by up to fifteen years' imprisonment at hard labor as an "infamous crime." The Court held that the Sixth Amendment requirement of a grand jury indictment could not be replaced with any other process for "infamous crimes." Therefore, Wilson's conviction was overturned. This decision applied only to cases in federal courts; state court cases were not affected by the decision.

* * *

Ex Parte Wilson, 114 U.S. 417

The first provision of this [Sixth] amendment, which is all that relates to this subject, is in these words: "No person shall be held to answer for a capital or otherwise infamous crime, unless on a presentment or indictment of a grand jury, except in cases arising in the land or naval forces, or in the militia, when in actual service in time of war or public danger. . . ."

. . . [N]o person can be held to answer, without presentment or indictment by a grand jury, for any crime for which an infamous punishment may be imposed by the court. The question is whether the crime is one for which the statutes authorize the court to award an infamous punishment not whether the punishment ultimately awarded is an infamous one. When the accused is in danger of being subjected to an infamous punishment if convicted, he has the right to insist that he shall not be put upon his trial, except on the accusation of a grand jury. . . .

The remaining question to be considered is whether imprisonment at hard labor for a term of years is an infamous punishment. . . .

What punishments shall be considered as infamous may be affected by the changes of public opinion from one age to another. In former times, being put in the stocks was not considered as necessarily infamous. And by the first judiciary act of the United States, whipping was classed with moderate fines and short terms of imprisonment in limiting the criminal jurisdiction of the district courts to cases "where no other punishment than whipping, not exceeding thirty stripes, a fine not exceeding one hundred dollars, or a term of imprisonment not exceeding six months, is to be inflicted." Act September 24, 1789, c. 20, 9, (1 St. 77.) But at the present day either stocks or whipping might be thought an infamous punishment.

For more than a century, imprisonment at hard labor in the state prison or penitentiary or other similar institution has been considered an infamous punishment in England and America. . . .

The same view has been forcibly expressed by Chief Justice Shaw. Speaking of imprisonment in the state prison, which by the statutes of Massachusetts was required to be at hard labor, he said: "Whether we consider the words 'infamous punishment' in their popular meaning, or as they are understood by the constitution and laws, a sentence to the state prison, for any term of time, must be considered as falling within them. The convict is placed in a public place of punishment, common to the whole state, subject to solitary imprisonment, to have his hair cropped, to be clothed in conspicuous prison dress, subjected to hard labor without pay, to hard fare, coarse and meager food, and to severe discipline. . . . Besides, the state prison, for any term of time, is now by law substituted for all the ignominious punishments formerly in use; and, unless this is infamous, then there is now no infamous punishment other than capital." Jones v. Robbins. In the same case, Mr. Justice Merrick, while dissenting from the rest of the court upon the question whether under the words 'the law of the land' in the constitution of Massachusetts an indictment by a grand jury was essential to a prosecution for a crime punishable by imprisonment in the state prison, and taking a position upon that question more accordant with the recent judgment of this court in Hurtado v. California yet concurred with the other judges in holding that such imprisonment at hard labor was an infamous punishment.

Imprisonment at hard labor, compulsory and unpaid, is, in the strongest sense of the words, "involuntary servitude for crime," spoken of in the provision of the Ordinance of 1787, and of the Thirteenth Amendment of the Constitution, by which all other slavery was abolished.

Deciding nothing beyond what is required by the facts of the case before us, our judgment is that a crime punishable by imprisonment for a term of years at hard labor is an infamous crime, within the meaning of the fifth amendment of the constitution; and that the district court, in holding the petitioner to answer for such a crime, and sentencing him to such imprisonment, without indictment or presentment by a grand jury, exceeded its jurisdiction, and he is therefore entitled to be discharged.

Writ of habeas corpus to issue.

Source: United States Reports. Vol. 114, 417–29. Washington, D.C.: Government Printing Office, 1885.

DOCUMENT 23: *Ball v. United States* (1896)

It may seem simple to say that a person cannot be put in jeopardy twice for the same crime, but legal cases are filled with subtlties that the Court needs to sort through to give meaning to this constitutional protection. This case is an example showing how the Court deals with the many variations real-life situations present.

Millard Ball and two other defendants were arrested and charged with murder. They pleaded not guilty and were tried. Ball was acquitted and released, but the other two defendants were found guilty of murder and sentenced to death. Upon appeal, the Supreme Court found that the original indictment from the grand jury was faulty and ordered a retrial. All three men were indicted again and retried. Ball objected claiming he had been acquitted and was thus being placed in double jeopardy. His plea was to no avail. The jury found all three guilty of murder and sentenced them to death.

Ball appealed his case to the Supreme Court. His lawyers argued that he was subjected to double jeopardy. Having been once acquitted, he should not have been retried. The state argued that since the first indictment was defective, the trial had been set aside and so no double jeopardy was involved. The Court found that Ball was indeed a victim of double jeopardy. The Court reasoned that his first trial had been fair, since there was no objection to its fairness. The second trial had put him in jeopardy a second time. His conviction was reversed.

* * *

Ball v. United States, 163 U.S. 662

Mr. Justice Gray delivered the opinion of the court.

After the full consideration which the importance of the question demands . . . and, the question being now for the first time presented to this court, we are unable to resist the conclusion that a general verdict of acquittal upon the issue of not guilty to an indictment undertaking to charge murder, and not objected to before the verdict as insufficient in that respect, is a bar to a second indictment for the same killing.

The constitution of the United States, in the fifth amendment, declares, 'nor shall any person be subject to be twice put in jeopardy of life or limb.' The prohibition is not against being twice punished, but against being twice put in jeopardy; and the accused, whether convicted or acquitted, is equally put in jeopardy at the first trial. An acquittal before a court having no jurisdiction is, of course, like all the proceedings in the case, absolutely void, and therefore no bar to subsequent indictment and trial in a court which has jurisdiction of the offense. . . . But, although the indictment was fatally defective, yet, if the court had jurisdiction of the cause and of the party, its judgment is not void, but only voidable by writ of error, and until so avoided cannot be collaterally impeached. If the judgment is upon a verdict of guilty, and unreversed, it stands good, and warrants the punishment of the defendant accordingly, and he could not be discharged by writ of habeas corpus. If the judgment is upon an acquittal, the defendant, indeed, will not seek to have it reversed, and the government cannot. . . . But the fact that the judgment of a court having jurisdiction of the case is practically final affords no reason for allowing its validity and conclusiveness to be impugned in another case.

The former indictment set forth a charge of murder, although lacking the requisite fullness and precision. The verdict of the jury, after a trial upon the issue of guilty or not guilty, acquitted Millard F. Ball of the whole charge, of murder, as well as of any less offense included therein. That he was thereupon discharged by the circuit court by reason of his acquittal by the jury, and not by reason of any insufficiency in the indictment, is clearly shown by the fact that the court, by the same order which discharged him, committed the other defendants, found guilty by the same verdict to custody to await sentence, and afterwards adjudged them guilty and sentenced them to death upon that indictment. Millard F. Ball's acquittal by the verdict of the jury could not be deprived of its legitimate effect by the subsequent reversal by this court of the judgment against the other defendants upon the writ of error sued out by them only. . . .

As to the defendant who had been acquitted by the verdict duly returned and received, the court could take no other action than to order his discharge. The verdict of acquittal was final, and could not be reviewed, on error or otherwise, without putting him twice in jeopardy, and thereby violating the constitution. However it may be in England, in this country a verdict of acquittal, although not followed by any judgment, is a bar to a subsequent prosecution for the same offense.

For these reasons the verdict of acquittal was conclusive in favor of Millard F. Ball, and as to him the judgment must be reversed, and judgment rendered for him upon his plea of former acquittal. . . .

Source: United States Reports. Vol. 163, 662–74. Washington, D.C.: Government Printing Office, 1896.

DOCUMENT 24: *Chicago, B. & Q. R. Co. v. City of Chicago* (1897)

This case is significant because it uses the Fourteenth Amendment to require that private property cannot be taken by states for public use without just compensation. This is also a guarantee in the Fifth Amendment.

The City of Chicago decided to lengthen and widen a street, causing it to cross the railroad line of the Chicago, Burlington & Quincy Railroad Company. The railroad was awarded $1 as just compensation. It objected to that valuation for its loss and appealed the verdict through the Illinois courts with no success.

The case was then appealed to the Supreme Court, claiming that the Fourteenth Amendment required due process and that was taken to mean just compensation for the usurped property, as guaranteed in the Fifth Amendment. The Court agreed. But after careful consideration of the loss incurred by the railroad, the Court ruled that $1 was just compensation.

Although the Fifth Amendment was not mentioned in the case, the Court's decision was generally believed to mean that its requirement for just compensation was applied to the states through the Fourteenth Amendment. This case established that under the right circumstances the Court was willing to use the Fourteenth Amendment to apply specific rights from the Bill of Rights to the states.

* * *

Chicago, B.& Q. R. Co. v. City of Chicago, 166 U.S. 226

Mr. Justice Harlan delivered the opinion of the court.

The questions presented on this writ of error relate to the jurisdiction of this court to re-examine the final judgment of the supreme court of Illinois, and to certain rulings of the state court, which, it is alleged, were in disregard of that part of the fourteenth amendment declaring that no state shall deprive any person of his property without due process of law, or deny the equal protection of the laws to any person within its jurisdiction. . . .

By an ordinance of the city council of Chicago approved October 9, 1880, it was ordained that Rockwell street, in that city, be opened and widened from West Eighteenth street to West Nineteenth street by condemning therefore, in accordance with the above act of April 10, 1872, certain parcels of land owned by individuals, and also certain parts of the right of way in that city of the Chicago, Burlington & Quincy Railroad Company, a corporation of Illinois.

In execution of that ordinance a petition was filed by the city, November 12, 1890, in the circuit court of Cook county, Ill., for the condemnation of the lots, pieces, or parcels of land and property proposed to be taken or damaged for the proposed improvement, and praying that the just compensation required for private property taken or damaged be ascertained by a jury.

The parties interested in the property described in the petition, including the Chicago, Burlington & Quincy Railroad Company, were admitted as defendants in the proceeding. In their verdict the jury fixed the just compensation to be paid to the respective individual owners of the lots, pieces, and parcels of land and property sought to be taken or damaged by the proposed improvements, and fixed one dollar as just compensation to the railroad company in respect of those parts of its right of way described in the city's petition as necessary to be used for the purposes of the proposed street.

Thereupon the railroad company moved for a new trial. The motion was overruled, and a final judgment was rendered in execution of the award by the jury. That judgment was affirmed by the supreme court of the state. . . .

It is true that the supreme court of Illinois did not, in its opinion, expressly refer to the constitution of the United States. But that circumstance is not conclusive against the jurisdiction of this court to reexamine the final judgment of the state court. The judgment of affirmance necessarily denied the federal rights thus specially set up by the defendant, for that judgment could not have been rendered without deciding adversely to such claims of right. Those claims went to the very foundation of the whole proceeding so far as it related to the railroad company, and the legal effect of the judgment of the supreme court of the state was to deny them. . . .

The general contentions of the railroad company are:

That the judgment of the state court whereby a public street is opened across its land used for railroad purposes, and whereby compensation to the extent of one dollar only is awarded, deprives it of its property without due process of law, contrary to the prohibitions of the fourteenth amendment; and That the railroad company was entitled, by reason of the opening of the street, to recover as compensation a sum equal to the difference between the value of the fee of the land sought to be crossed, without any restrictions on its right to use the land for any lawful purpose, and the value of the land burdened with a perpetual right in the public to use it for the purpose of a street subject to the right of the company or those acquiring title under it to use it only for railroad tracks, or any purpose for which the same could be used without interfering with its use by the public. . . .

It is therefore necessary to inquire at the outset whether 'due process of law' requires compensation to be made or secured to the owner of private property taken for public use, and also as to the circumstances under which the final judgment of the highest court of a state in a proceeding instituted to condemn such property for public use may be reviewed by this court. . . .

It is proper now to inquire whether the due process of law enjoined by the fourteenth amendment requires compensation to be made or adequately secured to the owner of private property taken for public use under the authority of a state. . . .

But if, as this court has adjudged, a legislative enactment, assuming arbitrarily to take the property of one individual and give it to another individual, would not be due process of law, as enjoined by the fourteenth amendment, it must be that the requirement of due process of law in that amendment is applicable to the direct appropriation by the state to public use, and without compensation, of the private property of the citizen. The legislature may prescribe a form of procedure to be observed in the taking of private property for public use, but it is not due process of law if provision be not made for compensation. Notice to the owner to appear in some judicial tribunal and show cause why his property shall not be taken for public use without compensation would be a mockery of justice. Due process of law, as applied to judicial proceedings instituted for the taking of private property for public use means, therefore, such process as recognizes the right of the owner to be compensated if his property be wrested from him and transferred to the public. The mere form of the proceeding instituted against the owner, even if he be admitted to defend, cannot convert the process used into due process of law, if the necessary result be to deprive him of his property without compensation. . . .

The contention of the railroad company is that the verdict and judgment for one dollar as the amount to be paid to it was, in effect, an appropriation of its property rights without any compensation whatever; that the judgment should be read as if, in form as well as in fact, it made no provision whatever for compensation for the property so appropriated.

Undoubtedly the verdict may not unreasonably be taken as meaning that in the judgment of the jury the company's property, proposed to be taken, was not materially damaged; that is, looking at the nature of the property, and the purposes for which it was obtained and was being used, that which was taken from the company was not, in the judgment of the jury, of any substantial value in money. The owner of private property taken under the right of eminent domain obtains just compensation if he is awarded such sum as, under all the circumstances, is a fair and full equivalent for the thing taken from him by the public.

If the opening of the street across the railroad tracks did not unduly interfere with the company's use of the right of way for legitimate railroad purposes, then its compensation would be nominal. But whether there was such an interference, what was its extent, and what was the value of that lost by the company as the direct result of such interference, were questions of fact, which the state committed to the jury under such instructions touching the law as were proper and necessary. It was for the jury to determine the facts, but it belonged to the court to determine the legal principles by which they were to be governed in fixing the amount of compensation to the owner.

Whatever may have been the power of the trial court to set aside the

verdict as not awarding just compensation . . . can this court go behind
the final judgment of the state court for the purpose of re-examining and
weighing the evidence, and of determining whether, upon the facts, the
jury erred in not returning a verdict in favor of the railroad company
for a larger sum than one dollar? This question may be considered in
two aspects: First, with reference to the seventh amendment of the constitution, providing that "in suits at common law, where the value in
controversy shall exceed twenty dollars, the right of trial by jury shall
be preserved, and no fact tried by a jury shall be otherwise re-examined
in any court of the United States, than according to the rules of the
common law"; second, with reference to the statute (Rev. St. 709) which
provides that the final judgment of the highest court of a state in certain
named cases may be re-examined in this court upon writ of error. . . .

Even if we were of opinion, in view of the evidence, that the jury erred
in finding that no property right, of substantial value in money, had been
taken from the railroad company, by reason of the opening of a street
across its right of way, we cannot, on that ground, re-examine the final
judgment of the state court. We are permitted only to inquire whether
the trial court prescribed any rule of law for the guidance of the jury
that was in absolute disregard of the company's right to just compensation.

We say, "in absolute disregard of the company's right to just compensation," because we do not wish to be understood as holding that every
order or ruling of the state court in a case like this may be reviewed
here, notwithstanding our jurisdiction, for some purposes, is beyond
question. Many matters may occur in the progress of such cases that do
not necessarily involve, in any substantial sense, the federal right alleged
to have been denied; and, in respect of such matters, that which is done
or omitted to be done by the state court may constitute only error in the
administration of the law under which the proceedings were instituted. . . .

We have examined all the questions of law arising on the record of
which this court may take cognizance, and which, in our opinion, are of
sufficient importance to require notice at our hands; and, finding no error, the judgment is affirmed.

Source: United States Reports. Vol. 166, 226–41. Washington, D.C.: Government
Printing Office, 1897.

DOCUMENT 25: *Bram v. United States* (1897)

Bram was the first officer on the U.S. ship *Herbert Fuller* bound from
Boston to South America. On the high seas, the captain, his wife, and

the second mate were found murdered in their cabins. The ship returned to port. There was no evidence regarding who had committed the crimes, but suspicion centered on seaman Brown. He was placed in irons by his shipmates until port was reached. After several days in irons and as the ship neared port, Brown said he had seen Bram commit the murders. At that, the sailors put Bram in irons too.

In port, Bram was brought to a detective's office, stripped naked, and questioned. The detective said he was sure Bram had committed the crimes and that Brown had provided testimony. Bram made statements that were taken as a confession. He was tried and convicted. The confession was the major evidence against him.

The Supreme Court found that Bram's confession was not freely given. The situation in which Bram had been questioned, faced with a detective and naked, could be taken as intimidating. Thus the confession should not have been entered as evidence. The Court reinforced a strict interpretation of voluntary confessions. A new trial was ordered for Bram.

* * *

Bram v. United States, 168 U.S. 532

Mr. Justice White delivered the opinion of the court.

This writ of error is prosecuted to a verdict and sentence thereon, by which the plaintiff was found guilty of murder, and condemned to suffer death. . . .

We first examine the error relied on which seems to us deserving of the most serious consideration. During the trial, a detective, by whom the accused was questioned while at Halifax, was placed upon the stand as a witness for the prosecution, for the purpose of testifying to the conversation had between himself and the accused. . . .

In this court the general rule that the confession must be free and voluntary—that is, not produced by inducements engendering either hope or fear—is settled. . . . In this court also it has been settled that the mere fact that the confession is made to a police officer, while the accused was under arrest in or out of prison, or was drawn out by his questions, does not necessarily render the confession involuntary; but, as one of the circumstances, such imprisonment or interrogation may be taken into account in determining whether or not the statements of the prisoner were voluntary. . . .

In the following cases the language in each mentioned was held to be an inducement sufficient to exclude a confession or statement made in consequence thereof: In Kelly v. State (1882), saying to the prisoner: 'You have got your foot in it, and somebody else was with you. Now, if you did break open the door, the best thing you can do is to tell all about it, and to tell who was with you, and to tell the truth, the whole truth, and nothing but the truth.' In People v. Barrie, saying to the accused: 'It will be better for you to make a full disclosure.' In People v. Thompson (1890), saying to the accused: 'I don't think the truth will hurt anybody. It will be better for you to come out and tell all you know about it, if you feel that way.' In Berry v. U.S. (1893), advising the prisoner to make full restitution, and saying: 'If you do so, it will go easy with you. It will be better for you to confess. The door of mercy is open, and that of justice closed;' and threatening to arrest the accused and expose his family if he did not confess. In State v. Bostick (1845), saying to one suspected of crime: 'The suspicion is general against you, and you had as well tell all about it. The prosecution will be no greater. I don't expect to do anything with you. I am going to send you home to your mother.' . . .

We come, then, to a consideration of the circumstances surrounding, and the facts established to exist, in reference to the confession, in order to determine whether it was shown to have been voluntarily made. . . . [T]he police detective caused Bram to be brought from jail to his private office; and, when there alone with the detective, he was stripped of his clothing, and . . . the conversation offered as a confession took place. The detective repeats what he said to the prisoner, whom he had thus stripped, as follows:

"When Mr. Bram came into my office, I said to him: 'Bram, we are trying to unravel this horrible mystery.' I said: 'Your position is rather an awkward one. I have had Brown in this office, and he made a statement that he saw you do the murder.' He said: 'He could not have seen me. Where was he?' I said: 'He states he was at the wheel.' 'Well,' he said, 'he could not see me from there.'" . . .

But the situation of the accused, and the nature of the communication made to him by the detective, necessarily overthrow any possible implication that his reply to the detective could have been the result of a purely voluntary mental action; that is to say, when all the surrounding circumstances are considered in their true relations, not only is the claim that the statement was voluntary overthrown, but the impression is irresistibly produced that it must necessarily have been the result of either hope or fear, or both, operating on the mind.

It cannot be doubted that, placed in the position in which the accused was when the statement was made to him that the other suspected person had charged him with crime, the result was to produce upon his mind the fear that, if he remained silent, it would be considered an admission of guilt, and therefore render certain his being committed for trial as the guilty person; and it cannot be conceived that the converse impression would not also have naturally arisen that, by denying, there was hope of removing the suspicion from himself. . . . A plainer violation as well of the letter as of the spirit and purpose of the constitutional immunity could scarcely be conceived of.

Moreover, aside from the natural result arising from the situation of the accused and the communication made to him by the detective, the conversation conveyed an express intimation rendering the confession involuntary. . . .

In the case before us we find that an influence was exerted, and, as any doubt as to whether the confession was voluntary must be determined in favor of the accused, we cannot escape the conclusion that error was committed by the trial court in admitting the confession under the circumstances disclosed by the record. . . .

The judgment is reversed, and the cause remanded, with directions to set aside the verdict and to order a new trial.

Source: United States Reports. Vol. 168, 532–41. Washington, D.C.: Government Printing Office, 1897.

DOCUMENT 26: *Twining v. State of New Jersey* (1908)

Twining and his partner were charged and convicted of misrepresentation. During the trial, neither one testified. The judge commented to the jury that their refusal to testify should not be held against them, though the jury could "consider the fact that he does not go upon the stand where a direct accusation is made against him." New Jersey was only one of two states that did not have a provision in its state constitution protecting individuals from being forced to give testimony incriminating themselves.

Twining's lawyers argued that his refusal to testify was used against him and that was a violation of the Fifth Amendment as applied to the states through the Fourteenth Amendment. His lawyers knew the court would probably reject that argument, since it had consistently done so in many similar cases. So they also argued that protection from self-incrimination is so fundamental that a refusal to the right is denial of the due process promised in the Fourteenth Amendment.

The Court decided against Twining. As expected, it rejected the proposition that the Fourteenth Amendment required states to honor every right in the Bill of Rights. The Court also rejected the claim that protection from self-incrimination is necessary for due process. It did, however, make the important concession that the Fourteenth Amendment might safeguard some of the personal rights in the Bill of Rights in state action, not because they are enumerated in the Bill of Rights, but because a denial of them would be a denial of due process of law. This was not enough for Justice Harlan, who again dissented, arguing that protection against self-incrimination is an essential right that states should uphold.

* * *

Twining v. State of New Jersey, 211 U.S. 78

Mr. Justice Moody . . . delivered the opinion of the court. . . .

The defendants contend, in the first place, that the exemption from self-incrimination is one of the privileges and immunities of citizens of the United States which the 14th Amendment forbids the states to abridge. It is not argued that the defendants are protected by that part of the 5th Amendment which provides that 'no person . . . shall be compelled in any criminal case to be a witness against himself,' for it is recognized by counsel that, by a long line of decisions, the first ten Amendments are not operative on the states. . . . But it is argued that this privilege is one of the fundamental rights of national citizenship, placed under national protection by the 14th Amendment, and it is specifically argued that the 'privileges and immunities of citizens of the United States,' protected against state action by that Amendment, include those fundamental personal rights which were protected against national action by the first eight Amendments; that this was the intention of the framers of the 14th Amendment, and that this part of it would otherwise have little or no meaning and effect. . . .

We conclude, therefore, that the exemption from compulsory self-incrimination is not a privilege or immunity of National citizenship guaranteed by this clause of the Fourteenth Amendment against abridgment by the States.

The defendants, however, do not stop here. They appeal to another clause of the 14th Amendment, and insist that the self-incrimination which they allege the instruction to the jury compelled was a denial of due process of law. This contention requires separate consideration, for it is possible that some of the personal rights safeguarded by the first eight Amendments against national action may also be safeguarded against state action, because a denial of them would be a denial of due process of law. . . . If this is so, it is not because those rights are enumerated in the first eight Amendments, but because they are of such a nature that they are included in the conception of due process of law. Few phrases of the law are so elusive of exact apprehension as this. Doubtless the difficulties of ascertaining its connotation have been increased in American jurisprudence, where it has been embodied in constitutions and put to new uses as a limit on legislative power. This court has always declined to give a comprehensive definition of it, and has preferred that its full meaning should be gradually ascertained by the process of inclusion and exclusion in the course of the decisions of cases as they arise. . . .

First. What is due process of law may be ascertained by an examination of those settled usages and modes of proceedings existing in the common and statute law of England before the emigration of our ancestors, and shown not to have been unsuited to their civil and political condition by having been acted on by them after the settlement of this country. . . .

Second. It does not follow, however, that a procedure settled in English law at the time of the emigration, and brought to this country and practiced by our ancestors, is an essential element of due process of law. If that were so, the procedure of the first half of the seventeenth century would be fastened upon the American jurisprudence like a straight jacket, only to be unloosed by constitutional amendment. . . .

Third. But, consistently with the requirements of due process, no change in ancient procedure can be made which disregards those fundamental principles, to be ascertained from time to time by judicial action, which have relation to process of law, and protect the citizen in his private right, and guard him against the arbitrary action of government. This idea has been many times expressed in differing words by this court, and it seems well to cite some expressions of it. The words 'due process of law' 'were intended to secure the individual from the arbitrary exercise of the powers of government, unrestrained by the established principles of private rights and distributive justice. . . .'

[W]e prefer to rest our decision on broader grounds, and inquire whether the exemption from self-incrimination is of such a nature that it must be included in the conception of due process. Is it a fundamental principle of liberty and justice which inheres in the very idea of free government and is the inalienable right of a citizen of such a government? If it is, and if it is of a nature that pertains to process of law, this court has declared it to be essential to due process of law. . . . The question before us is the meaning of a constitutional provision which forbids the states to deny to any person due process of law. In the decision of this question we have the authority to take into account only those fundamental rights which are expressed in that provision; not the rights fundamental in citizenship, state or national, for they are secured otherwise; but the rights fundamental in due process, and therefore an essential part of it. We have to consider whether the right is so fundamental in due process that a refusal of the right is a denial of due process. . . .

Salutary as the principle may seem to the great majority, it cannot be ranked with the right to hearing before condemnation, the immunity from arbitrary power not acting by general laws, and the inviolability of private property. . . . There seems to be no reason whatever, however, for straining the meaning of due process of law to include this privilege within it, because, perhaps, we may think it of great value. The states had guarded the privilege to the satisfaction of their own people up to the adoption of the 14th Amendment. No reason is perceived why they cannot continue to do so. The power of their people ought not to be fettered, their sense of responsibility lessened, and their capacity for sober and restrained self-government weakened, by forced construction of the Federal Constitution. If the people of New Jersey are not content with the law as declared in repeated decisions of their courts, the remedy is in their own hands. They may, if they choose, alter it by legislation, as the people of Maine did when the courts of that state made the same ruling.

Judgment affirmed.

Mr. Justice Harlan, dissenting:

I feel constrained by a sense of duty to express my nonconcurrence in the action of the court in this present case. . . .

The court, in its consideration of the relative rights of the United States and of the several states, holds, in this case, that, without violating the Constitution of the United States, a state can *compel* a person accused of crime to testify against himself. In my judgment, immunity from self-incrimination is protected against hostile state action, not only by that clause in the 14th Amendment declaring that 'no state shall make or enforce any law which shall abridge the privileges or immunities of citizens of the United States,' but by the clause, in the same Amendment, 'nor shall any state deprive any person of life, liberty, or property, without due process of law.' No argument is needed to support the proposition that, whether manifested by statute or by the final judgment of a court, state action, if liable to the objection that it abridges the privileges or immunities of national citizenship, must also be regarded as wanting in the due process of law enjoined by the 14th Amendment, when such state action substantially affects life, liberty, or property.

At the time of the adoption of the 14th Amendment immunity from self-incrimination was one of the privileges or immunities belonging to citizens, for the reason that the 5th Amendment, speaking in the name of the people of the United States, had declared, in terms, that no person 'shall be compelled, in any criminal case, to be a witness against himself; nor be deprived of life, liberty, or property, without due process of law.' That Amendment, it was long ago decided, operated as a restriction on the exercise of powers by the United States or by Federal tribunals and agencies, but did not impose any restraint upon a state or upon a state tribunal or agency. . . .

Can there be any doubt that, at the opening of the War of Independence, the people of the colonies claimed as one of their birthrights the privilege of immunity from self-incrimination? This question can be answered in but one way. If, at the beginning of the Revolutionary War, any lawyer had claimed that one accused of crime could lawfully be compelled to testify against himself, he would have been laughed at by his brethren of the bar, both in England and America. . . .

What, then, were the privileges and immunities of citizens of the United States which the 14th Amendment guarded against encroachment by the states? Whatever they were, that Amendment placed them beyond the power of any state to abridge. And what were the rights of life and liberty which the Amendment protected? Whatever they were, that Amendment guarded them against any hostile state action that was wanting in due process of law.

I will not attempt to enumerate all the privileges and immunities which at that time belonged to citizens of the United States. But I confidently assert that among such privileges was the privilege of immunity from self-incrimination which the people of the United States, by adopting the 5th Amendment, had placed beyond Federal encroachment. Can such a view be deemed unreasonable in the face of the fact, frankly conceded in the opinion of the court, that, at common law, as well at the time of the formation of the Union and when the 14th Amendment was adopted, immunity from self-incrimination was a privilege 'universal in American law,' was everywhere deemed 'of great value, a protection to the innocent, though a shelter to the guilty, and a safeguard against heedless, unfounded, or tyrannical prosecutions?' . . . The 14th Amendment would have been disapproved by every state in the Union if it had saved or recognized the right of a state to compel one accused of crime, in its courts, to be a witness against himself. We state the matter in this way because it is common knowledge that the compelling of a person to criminate himself shocks or ought to shock the sense of right and justice to everyone who loves liberty. . . .

I am of opinion that, as immunity from self-incrimination was recognized in the 5th Amendment of the Constitution, and placed beyond violation by any Federal agency, it should be deemed one of the immunities of citizens of the United States which the 14th Amendment, in express terms, forbids any state from abridging,—as much so, for instance, as the right of free speech (1st Amend.) or the exemption from cruel or unusual punishments (8th Amend.), or the exemption from being put twice in jeopardy of life or limb for the same offense (5th Amend.), or the exemption from unreasonable searches and seizures of one's person, house, papers, or effects (4th Amend.). Even if I were anxious or willing to cripple the operation of the 14th Amendment by strained or narrow interpretations, I should feel obliged to hold that, when that Amendment was adopted, all these last-mentioned exemptions were among the immunities belonging to citizens of the United States, which, after the adoption of the 14th Amendment, no state could impair or destroy. . . .

It is my opinion, also, that the right to immunity from self-incrimination cannot be taken away by any state consistently with the clause of the 14th Amendment that relates to the deprivation by the state of life or liberty without due process of law. . . .

Source: United States Reports. Vol. 211, 78–92. Washington, D.C.: Government Printing Office, 1908.

DOCUMENT 27: *Powell v. Alabama* (1932)

Ozzie Powell and six other African American young men were convicted in Scottsboro, Alabama, in 1931 for the rape of two white girls. Ozzie and the others came from neighboring states and were traveling through Alabama. The crime so outraged the white community that within six days of the arrest, the youth were put on trial. The trial lasted one day and they were sentenced to death.

The trial occurred so quickly that the young men did not have time to contact their families and were too poor to afford a lawyer. The judge vaguely appointed all members of the Alabama bar to represent them. Their conviction was appealed to the Alabama Supreme Court, which upheld the conviction. The chief justice, however, dissented strongly, stating they had not received a fair trial.

Powell's lawyers argued that their client had been denied a fair trial and that a fair trial should be guaranteed in every state because the Fourteenth Amendment promises due process. The lawyers built their hope on a series of Supreme Court decisions that required states to honor the First Amendment rights of freedom of speech, press, religion, and assembly. Each right was ruled as necessary for due process. Thus, through the due process clause of the Fourteenth Amendment, states were required to honor the First Amendment rights. Should not a fair trial also be assured under the due process clause of the Fourteenth Amendment?

The Supreme Court agreed. It ruled that the youth indeed did not have a fair trial. The Court recognized the hostile atmosphere in which the trial occurred, the quickness of the trial, and the systematic exclusion of African Americans from juries. But the Court focused its decision on the absence of counsel for an adequate defense. The Court stated that the trial court has an obligation to make sure defendants are adequately represented by counsel. The Court limited its decision to capital cases that involved those who cannot afford an attorney or are unlikely to be able to defend themselves. For the first time, the Court applied the due process clause of the Fourteenth Amendment to a trial rights case.

* * *

Powell v. Alabama, 287 U.S. 45

Mr. Justice Sutherland delivered the opinion of the Court.

In this court, the judgments are assailed upon the grounds that the defendants, and each of them, were denied due process of law and the equal protection of the laws in contravention of the Fourteenth Amendment, specifically as follows: (1) they were not given a fair, impartial and deliberate trial; (2) they were denied the right of counsel, with the accustomed incidents of consultation and opportunity of preparation for trial, and (3) they were tried before juries from which qualified members of their own race were systematically excluded. These questions were properly raised and saved in the courts below.

The only one of the assignments which we shall consider is the second, in respect of the denial of counsel, and it becomes unnecessary to discuss the facts of the case or the circumstances surrounding the prosecution except insofar as they reflect light upon that question. . . .

. . . The record shows that, immediately upon the return of the indictment, defendants were arraigned, and pleaded not guilty. Apparently they were not asked whether they had, or were able to, employ counsel, or wished to have counsel appointed, or whether they had friends or relatives who might assist in that regard if communicated with. That it would not have been an idle ceremony to have given the defendants reasonable opportunity to communicate with their families and endeavor to obtain counsel is demonstrated by the fact that, very soon after conviction, able counsel appeared in their behalf. This was pointed out by Chief Justice Anderson in the course of his dissenting opinion. "They were nonresidents," he said, and had little time or opportunity to get in touch with their families and friends who were scattered throughout two other states, and time has demonstrated that they could or would have been represented by able counsel had a better opportunity been given by a reasonable delay in the trial of the cases, judging from the number and activity of counsel that appeared immediately or shortly after their conviction. . . .

It is hardly necessary to say that, the right to counsel being conceded, a defendant should be afforded a fair opportunity to secure counsel of his own choice. Not only was that not done here, but such designation of counsel as was attempted was either so indefinite or so close upon the trial as to amount to a denial of effective and substantial aid in that regard. . . .

. . . [U]ntil the very morning of the trial, no lawyer had been named or definitely designated to represent the defendants. Prior to that time, the trial judge had "appointed all the members of the bar" for the limited "purpose of arraigning the defendants." Whether they would represent the defendants thereafter if no counsel appeared in their behalf was a matter of speculation only, or, as the judge indicated, of mere anticipation on the part of the court. Such a designation, even if made for all purposes, would, in our opinion, have fallen far short of meeting, in any proper sense, a requirement for the appointment of counsel. How many lawyers were members of the bar does not appear, but, in the very nature of things, whether many or few, they would not, thus collectively named, have been given that clear appreciation of responsibility or impressed with that individual sense of duty which should and naturally would accompany the appointment of a selected member of the bar, specifically named and assigned. . . .

. . . The Constitution of Alabama provides that, in all criminal prosecutions the accused shall enjoy the right to have the assistance of counsel, and a state statute requires the court in a capital case where the defendant is unable to employ counsel to appoint counsel for him. The state supreme court held that these provisions had not been infringed, and with that holding we are powerless to interfere. The question, however, which it is our duty, and within our power, to decide is whether the denial of the assistance of counsel contravenes the due process clause of the Fourteenth Amendment to the federal Constitution. . . .

One test which has been applied to determine whether due process of law has been accorded in given instances is to ascertain what were the settled usages and modes of proceeding under the common and statute law of England before the Declaration of Independence, subject, however, to the qualification that they be shown not to have been unsuited to the civil and political conditions of our ancestors by having been followed in this country after it became a nation. . . . Plainly, as appears from the foregoing, this test, as thus qualified, has not been met in the present case. . . .

It never has been doubted by this court, or any other, so far as we know, that notice and hearing are preliminary steps essential to the passing of an enforceable judgment, and that they, together with a legally competent tribunal having jurisdiction of the case, constitute basic elements of the constitutional requirement of due process of law. . . .

What, then, does a hearing include? Historically and in practice, in our own country, at least, it has always included the right to the aid of counsel when desired and provided by the party asserting the right. The right

to be heard would be, in many cases, of little avail if it did not compre-
hend the right to be heard by counsel. Even the intelligent and educated
layman has small and sometimes no skill in the science of law. If charged
with crime, he is incapable, generally, of determining for himself whether
the indictment is good or bad. He is unfamiliar with the rules of evidence. Left without the aid of counsel, he may be put on trial without a
proper charge, and convicted upon incompetent evidence, or evidence
irrelevant to the issue or otherwise inadmissible. He lacks both the skill
and knowledge adequately to prepare his defense, even though he have
a perfect one. He requires the guiding hand of counsel at every step in
the proceedings against him. Without it, though he be not guilty, he faces
the danger of conviction because he does not know how to establish his
innocence. If that be true of men of intelligence, how much more true is
it of the ignorant and illiterate, or those of feeble intellect. If in any case,
civil or criminal, a state or federal court were arbitrarily to refuse to hear
a party by counsel, employed by and appearing for him, it reasonably
may not be doubted that such a refusal would be a denial of a hearing,
and, therefore, of due process in the constitutional sense. . . .

In the light of the facts outlined in the forepart of this opinion—the
ignorance and illiteracy of the defendants, their youth, the circumstances
of public hostility, the imprisonment and the close surveillance of the
defendants by the military forces, the fact that their friends and families
were all in other states and communication with them necessarily difficult, and, above all, that they stood in deadly peril of their lives—we
think the failure of the trial court to give them reasonable time and opportunity to secure counsel was a clear denial of due process.

But passing that, and assuming their inability, even if opportunity had
been given, to employ counsel, as the trial court evidently did assume,
we are of opinion that, under the circumstances just stated, the necessity
of counsel was so vital and imperative that the failure of the trial court
to make an effective appointment of counsel was likewise a denial of
due process within the meaning of the Fourteenth Amendment. Whether
this would be so in other criminal prosecutions, or under other circumstances, we need not determine. All that it is necessary now to decide,
as we do decide, is that, in a capital case, where the defendant is unable
to employ counsel and is incapable adequately of making his own defense because of ignorance, feeble mindedness, illiteracy, or the like, it
is the duty of the court, whether requested or not, to assign counsel for
him as a necessary requisite of due process of law, and that duty is not
discharged by an assignment at such a time or under such circumstances
as to preclude the giving of effective aid in the preparation and trial of
the case. To hold otherwise would be to ignore the fundamental postu-
late, already adverted to, "that there are certain immutable principles of
justice which inhere in the very idea of free government which no mem-

ber of the Union may disregard." . . . In a case such as this, whatever may be the rule in other cases, the right to have counsel appointed, when necessary, is a logical corollary from the constitutional right to be heard by counsel. . . .

The judgments must be reversed, and the causes remanded for further proceedings not inconsistent with this opinion.

Source: United States Reports. Vol. 287, 45–77. Washington, D.C.: Government Printing Office, 1933.

DOCUMENT 28: *Norris v. Alabama* (1935)

Clarence Norris was another of the youths arrested in Scottsboro, Alabama, charged with rape, convicted, and sentenced to death. This is a companion case to *Powell v. Alabama* (see Document 27). Norris's lawyers appealed his conviction, claiming he had been deprived of due process guaranteed under the Fourteenth Amendment since there had been no African Americans on the jury.

The state claimed that race or color of prospective jurors was not taken into consideration in selecting the jury. No one had been excluded or included because of race or color.

The Supreme Court disagreed and found a systematic exclusion of African Americans from juries in two counties of Alabama solely because of their race and color. Note that the Court decision uses the term "Negroes," which was the polite terminology at the time, and the local officials used the older term "colored." The exclusion of African Americans denied Norris a jury of his peers and thus a fair trial.

* * *

Norris v. Alabama, 294 U.S. 587

Mr. Chief Justice Hughes delivered the opinion of the Court.

There is no controversy as to the constitutional principle involved. That principle, long since declared, was not challenged, but was expressly recognized, by the Supreme Court of the State. . . .

And although the state statute defining the qualifications of jurors may be fair on its face, the constitutional provision affords protection against action of the State through its administrative officers in effecting the prohibited discrimination.

The question is of the application of this established principle to the facts disclosed by the record. That the question is one of fact does not relieve us of the duty to determine whether, in truth, a federal right has been denied. When a federal right has been specially set up and claimed in a state court, it is our province to inquire not merely whether it was denied in express terms, but also whether it was denied in substance and effect. If this requires an examination of evidence, that examination must be made. Otherwise, review by this Court would fail of its purpose in safeguarding constitutional rights. . . .

. . . In 1930, the total population of Jackson County, where the indictment was found, was 36,881, of whom 2,688 were negroes. The male population over twenty-one years of age numbered 8,801, and of these, 666 were negroes.

Defendant adduced evidence to support the charge of unconstitutional discrimination in the actual administration of the statute in Jackson County. The testimony, as the state court said, tended to show that, "in a long number of years, no negro had been called for jury service in that county." It appeared that no negro had served on any grand or petit jury in that county within the memory of witnesses who had lived there all their lives. . . .

That testimony, in itself, made out a prima facie case of the denial of the equal protection which the Constitution guarantees. The case thus made was supplemented by direct testimony that specified negroes, thirty or more in number, were qualified for jury service. Among these were negroes who were members of school boards, or trustees, of colored schools, and property owners and householders. It also appeared that negroes from that county had been called for jury service in the federal court. Several of those who were thus described as qualified were witnesses. While there was testimony which cast doubt upon the qualifications of some of the negroes who had been named, and there was also general testimony by the editor of a local newspaper who gave his opinion as to the lack of "sound judgment" of the "good negroes" in Jackson County, we think that the definite testimony as to the actual qualifications of individual negroes, which was not met by any testimony equally direct, showed that there were negroes in Jackson County qualified for jury service.

The question arose whether names of negroes were, in fact, on the jury roll. The books containing the jury roll for Jackson County for the year 1930–31 were produced. They were produced from the custody of a member of the jury commission which, in 1931, had succeeded the commission which had made up the jury roll from which the grand jury in question had been drawn. On the pages of this roll appeared the names of six negroes. They were entered, respectively, at the end of the precinct lists, which were alphabetically arranged. The genuineness of these entries was disputed. It appeared that, after the jury roll in question had been made up, and after the new jury commission had taken office, one of the new commissioners directed the new clerk to draw lines after the names which had been placed on the roll by the preceding commission. These lines, on the pages under consideration, were red lines, and the clerk of the old commission testified that they were not put in by him. The entries made by the new clerk for the new jury roll were below these lines.

The names of the six negroes were in each instance written immediately above the red lines. An expert of long experience testified that these names were superimposed upon the red lines, that is, that they were written after the lines had been drawn. The expert was not cross-examined, and no testimony was introduced to contradict him. . . .

The state court rested its decision upon the ground that, even if it were assumed that there was no name of a negro on the jury roll, it was not established that race or color caused the omission. The court pointed out that the statute fixed a high standard of qualifications for jurors, and that the jury commission was vested with a wide discretion. . . .

The testimony showed the practice of the jury commission. . . . It was shown that the clerk, under the direction of the commissioners, made up a preliminary list which was based on the registration list of voters, the polling list and the tax list, and apparently also upon the telephone directory. The clerk testified that he made up a list of all male citizens between the ages of twenty-one and sixty-five years without regard to their status or qualifications. The commissioner testified that the designation "col." was placed after the names of those who were colored. . . . And the commissioner testified that, in the selections for the jury roll, no one was "automatically or systematically" excluded, or excluded on account of race or color; that he "did not inquire as to color, that was not discussed."

But, in appraising the action of the commissioners, these statements cannot be divorced from other testimony. As we have seen, there was testimony, not overborne or discredited, that there were, in fact, negroes in the county qualified for jury service. . . . The fact that the testimony as to these persons, fully identified, was not challenged by evidence appropriately direct, cannot be brushed aside. There is no ground for an assumption that the names of these negroes were not on the preliminary list. The inference to be drawn from the testimony is that they were on that preliminary list, and were designated on that list as the names of negroes, and that they were not placed on the jury roll. There was thus presented a test of the practice of the commissioners. Something more than mere general asseverations was required. Why were these names excluded from the jury roll? . . .

The testimony of the commissioner on this crucial question puts the case in a strong light. That testimony leads to the conclusion that these or other negroes were not excluded on account of age, or lack of esteem in the community for integrity and judgment, or because of disease or want of any other qualification. The commissioner's answer to specific inquiry upon this point was that negroes were "never discussed." . . .

. . . We think that the evidence that, for a generation or longer, no negro had been called for service on any jury in Jackson County, that there were negroes qualified for jury service, that, according to the practice of the jury commission, their names would normally appear on the preliminary list of male citizens of the requisite age, but that no names of negroes were placed on the jury roll, and the testimony with respect to the lack of appropriate consideration of the qualifications of negroes established the discrimination which the Constitution forbids. . . .

For this long-continued, unvarying, and wholesale exclusion of negroes from jury service, we find no justification consistent with the constitutional mandate. . . .

. . . And, upon the proof contained in the record now before us, a conclusion that their [African Americans] continuous and total exclusion from juries was because there were none possessing the requisite qualifications cannot be sustained.

We are concerned only with the federal question which we have discussed, and, in view of the denial of the federal right suitably asserted, the judgment must be reversed and the cause remanded for further proceedings not inconsistent with this opinion.

Reversed.

Source: United States Reports. Vol. 294, 587–99. Washington, D.C.: Government Printing Office, 1935.

DOCUMENT 29: *Brown v. Mississippi* (1936)

Common law and constitutional law has long condemned the use of torture or brutality to force confessions. In federal courts, such confessions cannot be admitted as evidence. *Brown v. Mississippi* gave the Court the opportunity to rule on the use of torture in state and local cases. The Court decided that torture of defendants is a violation of the due process clause of the Fourteenth Amendment.

Brown, and later two co-defendants, were convicted of murder and sentenced to death in a two-day trial. A court-appointed lawyer represented them. They pled not guilty even though the state produced signed confessions from all three. The confessions were clearly not freely given. Brown had been hanged from a tree several times and whipped on two occasions before he signed a confession. The others were whipped. Evidence of the torture was obvious. Brown still had rope burns on his neck during the trial. The only evidence against them was their own confessions. The trial court convicted them and the appeals courts upheld the conviction, though they had ample evidence that the confessions were forced.

The Supreme Court did not agree. Although not willing to declare that states were bound through the due process clause of the Fourteenth Amendment in all the federally guaranteed trial rights, it did declare the treatment of the defendants "a wrong so fundamental that it made the whole proceeding a mere pretense of a trial, and rendered the conviction and sentence wholly void."

* * *

Brown v. Mississippi, 297 U.S. 278

Mr. Chief Justice Hughes delivered the opinion of the Court.

The question in this case is whether convictions which rest solely upon confessions shown to have been extorted by officers of the State by brutality and violence are consistent with the due process of law required by the Fourteenth Amendment of the Constitution of the United States. . . .

Aside from the confessions, there was no evidence sufficient to warrant the submission of the case to the jury. After a preliminary inquiry, testimony as to the confessions was received over the objection of defendants' counsel. Defendants then testified that the confessions were false, and had been procured by physical torture. The case went to the jury with instructions, upon the request of defendants' counsel, that, if the jury had reasonable doubt as to the confessions' having resulted from coercion, and that they were not true, they were not to be considered as evidence. On their appeal to the Supreme Court of the State, defendants assigned as error the inadmissibility of the confessions. The judgment was affirmed.

Defendants then moved in the Supreme Court of the State to arrest the judgment and for a new trial on the ground that all the evidence against them was obtained by coercion and brutality known to the court and to the district attorney, and that defendants had been denied the benefit of counsel or opportunity to confer with counsel in a reasonable manner. . . .

. . . There is no dispute as to the facts upon this point [coerced confessions], and, as they are clearly and adequately stated . . . —showing both the extreme brutality of the measures to extort the confessions and the participation of the state authorities—we quote this part of his opinion in full, as follows:

"The crime with which these defendants, all ignorant negroes, are charged was discovered about one o'clock P.M. on Friday, March 30, 1934. On that night, one Dial, a deputy sheriff, accompanied by others, came to the home of Ellington, one of the defendants, and requested him to accompany them to the house of the deceased, and there a number of white men were gathered who began to accuse the defendant of the crime. Upon his denial, they seized him and, with the participation of the deputy, they hanged him by a rope to the limb of a tree, and, having let him down, they hung him again, and when he was let down the second time, and he still protested his innocence, he was tied to a tree and whipped, and still declining to accede to the demands that he confess, he was finally released and he returned with some difficulty to his home, suffering intense pain and agony. The record of the testimony shows that the signs of the rope on his neck were plainly visible during the so-called trial. A day or two thereafter, the said deputy, accompanied by another, returned to the home of the said defendant and arrested him, and departed with the prisoner towards the jail in an adjoining county, but went by a route which led into the State of Alabama, and while on the way, in that State, the deputy stopped and again severely whipped the defendant, declaring that he would continue the whipping [297 U.S. 282] until he confessed, and the defendant then agreed to confess to such a statement as the deputy would dictate, and he did so, after which he was delivered to jail."

The other two defendants, Ed Brown and Henry Shields, were also arrested and taken to the same jail. . . . [T]he same deputy, accompanied by a number of white men, one of whom was also an officer, and by the jailer, came to the jail, and the two last named defendants were made to strip, and they were laid over chairs and their backs were cut to pieces with a leather strap with buckles on it, and they were likewise made by the said deputy definitely to understand that the whipping would be continued unless and until they confessed, and not only confessed, but confessed in every matter of detail as demanded by those present. . . .

. . . There was thus enough before the court when these confessions were first offered to make known to the court that they were not, beyond all reasonable doubt, free and voluntary, and the failure of the court then to exclude the confessions is sufficient to reverse the judgment under every rule of procedure that has heretofore been prescribed, and hence it was not necessary subsequently to renew the objections by motion or otherwise. . . .

1. The State stresses the statement in Twining v. New Jersey, that "exemption from compulsory self-incrimination in the courts of the States is not secured by any part of the Federal Constitution," and the statement in Snyder v. Massachusetts, that "the privilege against self-incrimination may be withdrawn, and the accused put upon the stand as a witness for the State." But the question of the right of the State to withdraw the

privilege against self-incrimination is not here involved. The compulsion to which the quoted statements refer is that of the processes of justice by which the accused may be called as a witness and required to testify. Compulsion by torture to extort a confession is a different matter.

The State is free to regulate the procedure of its courts in accordance with its own conceptions of policy unless, in so doing, it "offends some principle of justice so rooted in the traditions and conscience of our people as to be ranked as fundamental." Snyder v. Massachusetts. The State may abolish trial by jury. It may dispense with indictment by a grand jury and substitute complaint or information. But the freedom of the State in establishing its policy is the freedom of constitutional government, and is limited by the requirement of due process of law. Because a State may dispense with a jury trial, it does not follow that it may substitute trial by ordeal. The rack and torture chamber may not be substituted for the witness stand. The State may not permit an accused to be hurried to conviction under mob domination—where the whole proceeding is but a mask—without supplying corrective process. The State may not deny to the accused the aid of counsel. Nor may a State, through the action of its officers, contrive a conviction through the pretense of a trial which, in truth, is but used as a means of depriving a defendant of liberty through a deliberate deception of court and jury by the presentation of testimony known to be perjured. And the trial equally is a mere pretense where the state authorities have contrived a conviction resting solely upon confessions obtained by violence. The due process clause requires that state action, whether through one agency or another, shall be consistent with the fundamental principles of liberty and justice which lie at the base of all our civil and political institutions. It would be difficult to conceive of methods more revolting to the sense of justice than those taken to procure the confessions of these petitioners, and the use of the confessions thus obtained as the basis for conviction and sentence was a clear denial of due process.

2. It is in this view that the further contention of the State must be considered. That contention rests upon the failure of counsel for the accused, who had objected to the admissibility of the confessions, to move for their exclusion after they had been introduced and the fact of coercion had been proved. It is a contention which proceeds upon a misconception of the nature of petitioners' complaint. That complaint is not of the commission of mere error, but of a wrong so fundamental that it made the whole proceeding a mere pretense of a trial, and rendered the conviction and sentence wholly void. We are not concerned with a mere question of state practice, or whether counsel assigned to petitioners were competent or mistakenly assumed that their first objections were sufficient. In an earlier case, the Supreme Court of the State had recog-

nized the duty of the court to supply corrective process where due process of law had been denied. In Fisher v. State, . . . the court said:

"Coercing the supposed state's criminals into confessions and using such confessions so coerced from them against them in trials has been the curse of all countries. It was the chief inequity, the crowning infamy, of the Star Chamber and the Inquisition, and other similar institutions. The constitution recognized the evils that lay behind these practices, and prohibited them in this country. . . . The duty of maintaining constitutional rights of a person on trial for his life rises above mere rules of procedure, and wherever the court is clearly satisfied that such violations exist, it will refuse to sanction such violations and will apply the corrective."

In the instant case, the trial court was fully advised by the undisputed evidence of the way in which the confessions had been procured. The trial court knew that there was no other evidence upon which conviction and sentence could be based. Yet it proceeded to permit conviction, and to pronounce sentence. The conviction and sentence were void for want of the essential elements of due process, and the proceeding thus vitiated could be challenged in any appropriate manner. . . . The court thus denied a federal right fully established and specially set up and claimed, and the judgment must be
Reversed.

Source: United States Reports. Vol. 297, 278–87. Washington, D.C.: Government Printing Office, 1936.

DOCUMENT 30: *Palko v. Connecticut* (1937)

With *Powell v. Alabama* (see Document 27), the Court had ruled that some of the trial rights in the Bill of Rights applied in state courts. The Court had already ruled that other parts of the Bill of Rights (free speech, press, religion, and assembly) were also protected in state courts because of the due process clause in the Fourteenth Amendment. *Palko v. Connecticut* is a significant case because in its ruling, the court clarifies why the rights to counsel and free speech are absorbed into due process, whereas others, like grand jury indictment and jury trial, are not.

The Court reasoned that only the federal government is limited by the Bill of Rights, though the Fourteenth Amendment requires that states respect due process. As individual cases have come to it, the Court explained that it has ruled which parts of the Bill of Rights are essential to due process and are therefore required of the states through the Fourteenth Amendment. In this decision, the Court summarizes which rights are fundamental for due process and which are not.

In *Palko v. Connecticut*, the Court remains unwilling to reverse decisions made in *Hurtado* (see Document 21) and *Twining* (see Document 26). Frank Palko had been indicted for the crime of first-degree murder. The jury found him guilty of second-degree murder and sentenced him to life imprisonment. The state of Connecticut appealed the conviction claiming errors in the trial. A new trial was ordered and Palko was found guilty of first-degree murder and sentenced to death. His lawyers argued that he was tried twice for the same crime in violation of the Fifth Amendment. The Court ruled that Connecticut was not bound by the double jeopardy clause in the Bill of Rights. The second trial was a trial to correct errors made in the first trial, not a separate case.

* * *

Palko v. Connecticut, 302 U.S. 319

Mr. Justice Cardozo delivered the opinion of the Court. . . .

Appellant was indicted . . . for the crime of murder in the first degree. A jury found him guilty of murder in the second degree, and he was sentenced to confinement in the state prison for life. Thereafter, the State of Connecticut, with the permission of the judge presiding at the trial, gave notice of appeal to the Supreme Court of Errors. This it did pursuant to an act adopted in 1886. . . . Upon such appeal, the Supreme Court of Errors reversed the judgment and ordered a new trial. It found that there had been error of law to the prejudice of the state. . . .

. . . [T]he defendant was brought to trial again. Before a jury was impaneled and also at later stages of the case, he made the objection that the effect of the new trial was to place him twice in jeopardy for the same offense, and, in so doing, to violate the Fourteenth Amendment of the Constitution of the United States. Upon the overruling of the objection, the trial proceeded. The jury returned a verdict of murder in the first degree, and the court sentenced the defendant to the punishment of death. . . . The case is here upon appeal.

1. The execution of the sentence will not deprive appellant of his life without the process of law assured to him by the Fourteenth Amendment of the Federal Constitution.

The argument for appellant is that whatever is forbidden by the Fifth Amendment is forbidden by the Fourteenth also. The Fifth Amendment, which is not directed to the states, but solely to the federal government, creates immunity from double jeopardy. No person shall be "subject for the same offense to be twice put in jeopardy of life or limb." The Fourteenth Amendment ordains, "nor shall any State deprive any person of life, liberty, or property, without due process of law." To retry a defendant, though under one indictment and only one, subjects him, it is said, to double jeopardy in violation of the Fifth Amendment if the prosecution is one on behalf of the United States. From this the consequence is said to follow that there is a denial of life or liberty without due process of law, if the prosecution is one on behalf of the People of a State. . . .

We have said that, in appellant's view, the Fourteenth Amendment is to be taken as embodying the prohibitions of the Fifth. His thesis is even broader. Whatever would be a violation of the original bill of rights (Amendments I to VIII) if done by the federal government is now equally unlawful by force of the Fourteenth Amendment if done by a state. There is no such general rule.

The Fifth Amendment provides, among other things, that no person shall be held to answer for a capital or otherwise infamous crime unless on presentment or indictment of a grand jury. This court has held that, in prosecutions by a state, presentment or indictment by a grand jury may give way to informations at the instance of a public officer. The Fifth Amendment provides also that no person shall be compelled in any criminal case to be a witness against himself. This court has said that, in prosecutions by a state, the exemption will fail if the state elects to end it. The Sixth Amendment calls for a jury trial in criminal cases, and the Seventh for a jury trial in civil cases at common law where the value in controversy shall exceed twenty dollars. This court has ruled that consistently with those amendments trial by jury may be modified by a state or abolished altogether. . . .

On the other hand, the due process clause of the Fourteenth Amendment may make it unlawful for a state to abridge by its statutes the freedom of speech which the First Amendment safeguards against encroachment by the Congress; or the like freedom of the press; or the free exercise of religion; or the right of peaceable assembly, without which speech would be unduly trammeled; or the right of one accused of crime to the benefit of counsel. In these and other situations, immunities that are valid as against the federal government by force of the specific pledges of particular amendments have been found to be implicit in the concept of ordered liberty, and thus, through the Fourteenth Amendment, become valid as against the states.

The line of division may seem to be wavering and broken if there is a hasty catalogue of the cases on the one side and the other. Reflection and analysis will induce a different view. There emerges the perception of a rationalizing principle which gives to discrete instances a proper order and coherence. The right to trial by jury and the immunity from prosecution except as the result of an indictment may have value and importance. Even so, they are not of the very essence of a scheme of ordered liberty. To abolish them is not to violate a "principle of justice so rooted in the traditions and conscience of our people as to be ranked as fundamental." Snyder v. Massachusetts. Few would be so narrow or provincial as to maintain that a fair and enlightened system of justice would be impossible without them. What is true of jury trials and indictments is true also, as the cases show, of the immunity from compulsory self-incrimination. Twining v. New Jersey, supra. This too might be lost, and justice still be done. Indeed, today, as in the past, there are students of our penal system who look upon the immunity as a mischief, rather than a benefit, and who would limit its scope, or destroy it altogether. No doubt there would remain the need to give protection against torture, physical or mental. Brown v. Mississippi, supra. Justice, however, would not perish if the accused were subject to a duty to respond to orderly inquiry. The exclusion of these immunities and privileges from the privileges and immunities protected against the action of the states has not been arbitrary or casual. It has been dictated by a study and appreciation of the meaning, the essential implications, of liberty itself.

We reach a different plane of social and moral values when we pass to the privileges and immunities that have been taken over from the earlier articles of the federal bill of rights and brought within the Fourteenth Amendment by a process of absorption. These, in their origin, were effective against the federal government alone. If the Fourteenth Amendment has absorbed them, the process of absorption has had its source in the belief that neither liberty nor Justice would exist if they were sacrificed. Twining v. New Jersey. This is true, for illustration, of freedom of thought, and speech. Of that freedom one may say that it is the matrix, the indispensable condition, of nearly every other form of freedom. With rare aberrations, a pervasive recognition of that truth can be traced in our history, political and legal. So it has come about that the domain of liberty, withdrawn by the Fourteenth Amendment from encroachment by the states, has been enlarged by latter-day judgments to include liberty of the mind as well as liberty of action. . . . Fundamental too in the concept of due process, and so in that of liberty, is the thought that condemnation shall be rendered only after trial. The hearing, moreover, must be a real one, not a sham or a pretense. For that reason, ignorant defendants in a capital case were held to have been condemned unlawfully when in truth, though not in form, they were refused the aid of counsel. Powell v. Alabama. The decision did not turn upon the fact that the benefit of counsel would have been guaranteed to the defendants by the provisions of the Sixth Amendment if they had been prosecuted in a federal court. The decision turned upon the fact that, in the particular situation laid before us in the evidence, the benefit of counsel was essential to the substance of a hearing.

Our survey of the cases serves, we think, to justify the statement that the dividing line between them, if not unfaltering throughout its course, has been true for the most part to a unifying principle. On which side of the line the case made out by the appellant has appropriate location must be the next inquiry, and the final one. Is that kind of double jeopardy to which the statute has subjected him a hardship so acute and shocking that our polity will not endure it? Does it violate those "fundamental principles of liberty and justice which lie at the base of all our civil and political institutions"? Hebert v. Louisiana. The answer surely must be "no." What the answer would have to be if the state were permitted after a trial free from error to try the accused over again or to bring another case against him, we have no occasion to consider. We deal with the statute before us, and no other. The state is not attempting to wear the accused out by a multitude of cases with accumulated trials. It asks no more than this, that the case against him shall go on until there shall be a trial free from the corrosion of substantial legal error. This is not cruelty at all, nor even vexation in any immoderate degree. If the trial had been infected with error adverse to the accused, there might have been review at his instance, and as often as necessary to purge the vicious taint. A reciprocal privilege, subject at all times to the discretion of the presiding judge, has now been granted to the state. There is here no seismic innovation. The edifice of justice stands, its symmetry, to many, greater than before.

2. The conviction of appellant is not in derogation of any privileges or immunities that belong to him as a citizen of the United States. . . .

There is argument in his behalf that the privileges and immunities clause of the Fourteenth Amendment as well as the due process clause has been flouted by the judgment.

The judgment is affirmed.

Source: United States Reports. Vol. 302, 319–29. Washington, D.C.: Government Printing Office, 1938.

DOCUMENT 31: *Betts v. Brady* (1942)

Court decisions had left confusion regarding which rights the due process clause of the Fourteenth Amendment made binding on the states. The significance of *Betts v. Brady* is the Court's clarification that not all Sixth Amendment rights are automatically included in the due process clause. The Court explains under what circumstances the Sixth Amendment rights are incorporated.

Betts was arrested and tried for robbery in the state of Maryland.

He could not afford an attorney and requested that one be appointed. The judge refused, saying that counsel was not appointed, except for cases of murder and rape. He was convicted in a trial by judge without a jury and sentenced to eight years. Betts appealed to the Supreme Court claiming his denial of an attorney violated the due process guaranteed him by the Fourteenth Amendment.

The Supreme Court determined that Betts was not denied due process. The Court reasoned that the due process clause does not bind states by the specific rights contained in the Sixth Amendment. Due process is violated in state courts when the proceedings constitute a denial of fundamental fairness shocking to a civilized county's sense of justice. Thus the circumstances of the particular case will determine whether due process is violated.

In their dissent, Justices Black, Douglas, and Murphy disagreed. They argued that any procedure "which subjects innocent men to increased dangers of conviction merely because of their poverty" was unfair. They preferred an unequivocal application, rather than the Court's case-by-case process.

* * *

Betts v. Brady, 316 U.S. 455

Mr. Justice Roberts delivered the opinion of the Court. . . .

Was the petitioner's conviction and sentence a deprivation of his liberty without due process of law, in violation of the Fourteenth Amendment, because of the court's refusal to appoint counsel at his request?

The Sixth Amendment of the national Constitution applies only to trials in federal courts. The due process clause of the Fourteenth Amendment does not incorporate, as such, the specific guarantees found in the Sixth Amendment, although a denial by a State of rights or privileges specifically embodied in that and others of the first eight amendments may, in certain circumstances, or in connection with other elements, operate, in a given case, to deprive a litigant of due process of law in violation of the Fourteenth. Due process of law is secured against invasion by the federal Government by the Fifth Amendment, and is safeguarded against state action in identical words by the Fourteenth. The phrase formulates a concept less rigid and more fluid than those envisaged in other specific and particular provisions of the Bill of Rights. Its application is less a matter of rule. Asserted denial is to be tested by an appraisal of the totality of facts in a given case. . . .

The petitioner, in this instance, asks us, in effect, to apply a rule in the enforcement of the due process clause. He says the rule to be deduced from our former decisions is that, in every case, whatever the circumstances, one charged with crime who is unable to obtain counsel must be furnished counsel by the State. Expressions in the opinions of this court lend color to the argument, but, as the petitioner admits, none of our decisions squarely adjudicates the question now presented. . . .

. . . The question we are now to decide is whether due process of law demands that, in every criminal case, whatever the circumstances, a State must furnish counsel to an indigent defendant. Is the furnishing of counsel in all cases whatever dictated by natural, inherent, and fundamental principles of fairness? . . . By the Sixth Amendment, the people ordained that, in all criminal prosecutions, the accused should "enjoy the right . . . to have the assistance of counsel for his defense." We have construed the provision to require appointment of counsel in all cases where a defendant is unable to procure the services of an attorney, and where the right has not been intentionally and competently waived. Though, as we have noted, the Amendment lays down no rule for the conduct of the States, the question recurs whether the constraint laid by the Amendment upon the national courts expresses a rule so fundamental and essential to a fair trial, and so to due process of law, that it is made obligatory upon the States by the Fourteenth Amendment. . . .

In the light of this common law practice, it is evident that the constitutional provisions to the effect that a defendant should be "allowed" counsel or should have a right "to be heard by himself and his counsel," or that he might be heard by "either or both," at his election, were intended to do away with the rules which denied representation, in whole or in part, by counsel in criminal prosecutions, but were not aimed to compel the State to provide counsel for a defendant. At the least, such a construction by State courts and legislators cannot be said to lack reasonable basis. . . .

. . . [I]n the great majority of the States, it has been the considered judgment of the people, their representatives, and their courts that appointment of counsel is not a fundamental right, essential to a fair trial. On the contrary, the matter has generally been deemed one of legislative policy. In the light of this evidence, we are unable to say that the concept of due process incorporated in the Fourteenth Amendment obligates the States, whatever may be their own views, to furnish counsel in every such case. Every court has power, if it deems proper, to appoint counsel where that course seems to be required in the interest of fairness.

The practice of the courts of Maryland gives point to the principle that the States should not be straight-jacketed in this respect by a construction of the Fourteenth Amendment. . . .

. . . It is quite clear that, in Maryland, if the situation had been otherwise and it had appeared that the petitioner was, for any reason, at a serious disadvantage by reason of the lack of counsel, a refusal to appoint would have resulted in the reversal of a judgment of conviction.

Only recently, the Court of Appeals has reversed a conviction because it was convinced on the whole record that an accused, tried without counsel, had been handicapped by the lack of representation.

As we have said, the Fourteenth Amendment prohibits the conviction and incarceration of one whose trial is offensive to the common and fundamental ideas of fairness and right, and, while want of counsel in a particular case may result in a conviction lacking in such fundamental fairness, we cannot say that the Amendment embodies an inexorable command that no trial for any offense, or in any court, can be fairly conducted and justice accorded a defendant who is not represented by counsel.

The judgment is affirmed.

Mr. Justice Black, dissenting, with whom Mr. Justice Douglas and Mr. Justice Murphy concur. . . .

If this case had come to us from a federal court, it is clear we should have to reverse it, because the Sixth Amendment makes the right to counsel in criminal cases inviolable by the Federal Government. I believe that the Fourteenth Amendment made the Sixth applicable to the states. But this view, although often urged in dissents, has never been accepted by a majority of this Court and is not accepted today. A statement of the grounds supporting it is, therefore, unnecessary at this time. I believe, however, that, under the prevailing view of due process, as reflected in the opinion just announced, a view which gives this Court such vast supervisory powers that I am not prepared to accept it without grave doubts, the judgment below should be reversed. . . .

A practice cannot be reconciled with "common and fundamental ideas of fairness and right," which subjects innocent men to increased dangers of conviction merely because of their poverty. Whether a man is innocent cannot be determined from a trial in which, as here, denial of counsel has made it impossible to conclude, with any satisfactory degree of certainty, that the defendant's case was adequately presented. . . .

Denial to the poor of the request for counsel in proceedings based on charges of serious crime has long been regarded as shocking to the "universal sense of justice" throughout this country. . . . [M]ost of the other States have shown their agreement by constitutional provisions, statutes, or established practice judicially approved, which assure that no man shall be deprived of counsel merely because of his poverty. Any other practice seems to me to defeat the promise of our democratic society to provide equal justice under the law.

Source: United States Reports. Vol. 316, 455–80. Washington, D.C.: Government Printing Office, 1943.

DOCUMENT 32: *Adamson v. California* (1947)

Admiral Dewey Adamson was charged and tried for first-degree murder in California. He refused to testify at his trial, and his refusal was used to suggest to the jury that he was guilty. He was found guilty of the crime. Adamson's lawyers appealed his conviction claiming that using his refusal to testify against him was a violation of the constitutional provision against self-incrimination.

The Court ruled that there was no basis in California law for the objection on due process or other grounds. Adamson's treatment was not a violation of the due process guaranteed by the Fourteenth Amendment. It was unlikely that the jury's decision was based solely on his refusal to testify.

In a concurring statement, Justice Frankfurter explains his own reasoning about why all the provisions of the Bill of Rights should not be incorporated into the due process clause of the Constitution. In his dissent, Justice Black argues that the entire Fifth Amendment should be incorporated into the meaning of due process in the Fourteenth Amendment. His reasoning is important because it shows an alternative view that will gain acceptance in future Court decisions.

* * *

Adamson v. California, 332 U.S. 46

Mr. Justice Reed delivered the opinion of the Court.

The appellant, Adamson, a citizen of the United States, was convicted, without recommendation for mercy, by a jury in a Superior Court of the State of California of murder in the first degree. After considering the same objections to the conviction that are pressed here, the sentence of death was affirmed by the Supreme Court of the state. . . .

. . . [A]ppellant urges that the provision of the Fifth Amendment that no person "shall be compelled in any criminal case to be a witness against himself" is a fundamental national privilege or immunity protected against state abridgment by the Fourteenth Amendment or a privilege or immunity secured, through the Fourteenth Amendment, against deprivation by state action because it is a personal right, enumerated in the federal Bill of Rights.

. . . It is settled law that the clause of the Fifth Amendment, protecting a person against being compelled to be a witness against himself, is not made effective by the Fourteenth Amendment as a protection against state action on the ground that freedom from testimonial compulsion is a right of national citizenship, or because it is a personal privilege or immunity secured by the Federal Constitution as one of the rights of man that are listed in the Bill of Rights.

The reasoning that leads to those conclusions starts with the unquestioned premise that the Bill of Rights, when adopted, was for the protection of the individual against the federal government, and its provisions were inapplicable to similar actions done by the states. With the adoption of the Fourteenth Amendment, it was suggested that the dual citizenship recognized by its first sentence secured for citizens federal protection for their elemental privileges and immunities of state citizenship. The Slaughter-House Cases decided, contrary to the suggestion, that these rights, as privileges and immunities of state citizenship, remained under the sole protection of the state governments. This Court, without the expression of a contrary view upon that phase of the issues before the Court, has approved this determination. . . . This Court held that the inclusion in the Bill of Rights of this protection against the power of the national government did not make the privilege a federal privilege or immunity secured to citizens by the Constitution against state action. After declaring that state and national citizenship coexist in the same person, the Fourteenth Amendment forbids a state from abridging the privileges and immunities of citizens of the United States. As a matter of words, this leaves a state free to abridge, within the limits of the due process clause, the privileges and immunities flowing from state citizenship. This reading of the Federal Constitution has heretofore found favor with the majority of this Court as a natural and logical interpretation. It accords with the constitutional doctrine of federalism by leaving to the states the responsibility of dealing with the privileges and immunities of their citizens except those inherent in national citizenship. It is the construction placed upon the amendment by justices whose own experience had given them contemporaneous knowledge of the purposes that led to the adoption of the Fourteenth Amendment. This construction has become embedded in our federal system as a functioning element in preserving the balance between national and state power. We reaffirm the conclusion of the Twining and Palko cases that protection against self-incrimination is not a privilege or immunity of national citizenship.

Appellant secondly contends that, if the privilege against self-incrimination is not a right protected by the privileges and immunities clause of the Fourteenth Amendment against state action, this privilege, to its full scope under the Fifth Amendment, inheres in the right to a fair trial. A right to a fair trial is a right admittedly protected by the due process clause of the Fourteenth Amendment. Therefore, appellant argues, the due process clause of the Fourteenth Amendment protects his privilege against self-incrimination. The due process clause of the Fourteenth Amendment, however, does not draw all the rights of the federal Bill of Rights under its protection. . . .

Specifically, the due process clause does not protect, by virtue of its mere existence, the accused's freedom from giving testimony by compulsion in state trials that is secured to him against federal interference by the Fifth Amendment. For a state to require testimony from an accused is not necessarily a breach of a state's obligation to give a fair trial. . . .

We find no other error that gives ground for our intervention in California's administration of criminal justice.

Affirmed.

Mr. Justice Frankfurter, concurring. . . .

Indeed, the suggestion that the Fourteenth Amendment incorporates the first eight Amendments as such is not unambiguously urged. Even the boldest innovator would shrink from suggesting to more than half the States that they may no longer initiate prosecutions without indictment by grand jury, or that, thereafter, all the States of the Union must furnish a jury of twelve for every case involving a claim above twenty dollars. There is suggested merely a selective incorporation of the first eight Amendments into the Fourteenth Amendment. Some are in and some are out, but we are left in the dark as to which are in and which are out. Nor are we given the calculus for determining which go in and which stay out. If the basis of selection is merely that those provisions of the first eight Amendments are incorporated which commend themselves to individual justices as indispensable to the dignity and happiness of a free man, we are thrown back to a merely subjective test. . . . If all that is meant is that due process contains within itself certain minimal standards which are "of the very essence of a scheme of ordered liberty," Palko v. Connecticut, putting upon this Court the duty of applying these standards from time to time, then we have merely arrived at the insight which our predecessors long ago expressed. . . .

It may not be amiss to restate the pervasive function of the Fourteenth Amendment in exacting from the States observance of basic liberties. The Amendment neither comprehends the specific provisions by which the founders deemed it appropriate to restrict the federal government nor is it confined to them. The Due Process Clause of the Fourteenth Amendment has an independent potency, precisely as does the Due Process Clause of the Fifth Amendment in relation to the Federal Government. It ought not to require argument to reject the notion that due process of law meant one thing in the Fifth Amendment and another in the Fourteenth. The Fifth Amendment specifically prohibits prosecution of an "infamous crime" except upon indictment; it forbids double jeopardy; it bars compelling a person to be a witness against himself in any criminal case; it precludes deprivation of "life, liberty, or property, without due process of law. . . ." Are Madison and his contemporaries in the framing of the Bill of Rights to be charged with writing into it a meaningless clause? To consider "due process of law" as merely a shorthand statement of other specific clauses in the same amendment is to attribute to the authors and proponents of this Amendment ignorance of, or indifference to, a historic conception which was one of the great instruments in the arsenal of constitutional freedom which the Bill of Rights was to protect and strengthen.

. . . The relevant question is whether the criminal proceedings which resulted in conviction deprived the accused of the due process of law to which the United States Constitution entitled him. Judicial review of that guaranty of the Fourteenth Amendment inescapably imposes upon this Court an exercise of judgment upon the whole course of the proceedings in order to ascertain whether they offend those canons of decency and fairness which express the notions of justice of English-speaking peoples even toward those charged with the most heinous offenses. These standards of justice are not authoritatively formulated anywhere as though they were prescriptions in a pharmacopoeia. But neither does the application of the Due Process Clause imply that judges are wholly at large. The judicial judgment in applying the Due Process Clause must move within the limits of accepted notions of justice, and is not to be based upon the idiosyncrasies of a merely personal judgment. The fact that judges, among themselves, may differ whether, in a particular case, a trial offends accepted notions of justice is not disproof that general, rather than idiosyncratic, standards are applied. An important safeguard against such merely individual judgment is an alert deference to the judgment of the State court under review.

Mr. Justice Black, dissenting. . . .

This decision reasserts a constitutional theory spelled out in Twining v. New Jersey, 211 U.S. 78, that this Court is endowed by the Constitution with boundless power under "natural law" periodically to expand and contract constitutional standards to conform to the Court's conception of what, at a particular time, constitutes "civilized decency" and "fundamental liberty and justice." Invoking this Twining rule, the Court concludes that, although comment upon testimony in a federal court would violate the Fifth Amendment, identical comment in a state court does not violate today's fashion in civilized decency and fundamentals, and is therefore not prohibited by the Federal Constitution, as amended.

. . . I would not reaffirm the Twining decision. I think that decision and the "natural law" theory of the Constitution upon which it relies degrade the constitutional safeguards of the Bill of Rights, and simultaneously appropriate for this Court a broad power which we are not authorized by the Constitution to exercise. . . . My reasons for believing that the Twining decision should not be revitalized can best be understood by reference to the constitutional, judicial, and general history that preceded and followed the case. That reference must be abbreviated far more than is justified but for the necessary limitations of opinion-writing.

The first ten amendments were proposed and adopted largely because of fear that Government might unduly interfere with prized individual liberties. The people wanted and demanded a Bill of Rights written into their Constitution. The amendments embodying the Bill of Rights were intended to curb all branches of the Federal Government in the fields touched by the amendments—Legislative, Executive, and Judicial. . . .

But these limitations were not expressly imposed upon state court action. In 1833, Barron v. Baltimore, supra, was decided by this Court. It specifically held inapplicable to the states that provision of the Fifth Amendment which declares: "nor shall private property be taken for public use, without just compensation." In deciding the particular point raised, the Court there said that it could not hold that the first eight amendments applied to the states. This was the controlling constitutional rule when the Fourteenth Amendment was proposed in 1866.

My study of the historical events that culminated in the Fourteenth Amendment, and the expressions of those who sponsored and favored, as well as those who opposed, its submission and passage persuades me that one of the chief objects that the provisions of the Amendment's first section, separately and as a whole, were intended to accomplish was to make the Bill of Rights, applicable to the states. With full knowledge of the import of the Barron decision, the framers and backers of the Fourteenth Amendment proclaimed its purpose to be to overturn the constitutional rule that case had announced. . . .

. . . Whether this Court ever will, or whether it now should, in the light of past decisions, give full effect to what the Amendment was intended to accomplish is not necessarily essential to a decision here. However that may be, our prior decisions, including Twining, do not prevent our carrying out that purpose, at least to the extent of making applicable to the states, not a mere part, as the Court has, but the full protection of the Fifth Amendment's provision against compelling evidence from an accused to convict him of crime. And I further contend that the "natural law" formula which the Court uses to reach its conclusion in this case should be abandoned as an incongruous excrescence on our Constitution. I believe that formula to be itself a violation of our Constitution, in that it subtly conveys to courts, at the expense of legislatures, ultimate power over public policies in fields where no specific provision of the Constitution limits legislative power. And my belief seems to be in accord with the views expressed by this Court, at least for the first two decades after the Fourteenth Amendment was adopted. . . .

Conceding the possibility that this Court is now wise enough to improve on the Bill of Rights by substituting natural law concepts for the Bill of Rights, I think the possibility is entirely too speculative to agree to take that course. I would therefore hold in this case that the full protection of the Fifth Amendment's proscription against compelled testimony must be afforded by California. This I would do because of reliance upon the original purpose of the Fourteenth Amendment.

It is an illusory apprehension that literal application of some or all of the provisions of the Bill of Rights to the States would unwisely increase the sum total of the powers of this Court to invalidate state legislation. The Federal Government has not been harmfully burdened by the requirement that enforcement of federal laws affecting civil liberty conform literally to the Bill of Rights. Who would advocate its repeal? It must be conceded, of course, that the natural law–due process formula, which the Court today reaffirms, has been interpreted to limit substantially this Court's power to prevent state violations of the individual civil liberties guaranteed by the Bill of Rights. But this formula also has been used in the past, and can be used in the future, to license this Court, in considering regulatory legislation, to roam at large in the broad expanses of policy and morals and to trespass, all too freely, on the legislative domain of the States as well as the Federal Government.

Mr. Justice Douglas joins in this opinion.

Source: United States Reports. Vol. 332, 46–125. Washington, D.C.: Government Printing Office, 1948.

DOCUMENT 33: *Cole v. Arkansas* (1948)

In this case, the Court determined that due process requires that a defendant in a state court be informed of the crime for which the trial is held. This is a basic right that the due process clause of the Fourteenth Amendment requires of states.

Roy Cole was tried and convicted of violation of Section 2 of an Arkansas state law. When he appealed to the Arkansas Supreme Court, that court ruled as if he had been charged with Section 1 of the same law. He had not been tried for violating that section of the law. Thus the state Supreme Court had ruled in error. The U.S. Supreme Court reversed its decision and sent the case back for reconsideration.

* * *

Cole v. Arkansas, 333 U.S. 196 (1948)

Mr. Justice Black delivered the opinion of the Court.

The petitioners were convicted of a felony in an Arkansas state court and sentenced to serve one year in the state penitentiary. . . . The question is: 'Were the petitioners denied due process of law . . . in violation of the Fourteenth Amendment by the circumstance that their convictions were affirmed under a criminal statute for violation of which they had not been charged'?

The present convictions are under an information. The petitioners urge that the information charged them with a violation of 2 of Act 193 of the 1943 Arkansas Legislature and that they were tried and convicted of violating only 2. The State Supreme Court affirmed their convictions on the ground that the information had charged and the evidence had shown that the petitioners had violated 1 of the Arkansas Act which describes an offense separate and distinct from the offense described in 2.

The information charged: ". . . Walter Ted Campbell, acting in concert with other persons, assembled at the Southern Cotton Oil Company's plant in Pulaski County, Arkansas, where a labor dispute existed, and by force and violence prevented Otha Williams from engaging in a lawful vocation. The said Roy Cole, Louis Jones and Jessie Bean, in the County and State aforesaid, on the 26th day of December, 1945, did unlawfully and feloniously, acting in concert with eath (sic) other, promote, encourage and aid such unlawful assemblage against the peace and dignity of the State of Arkansas."

The foregoing language describing the offense charged in the infor mation is substantially identical with the following language of 2 of the Arkansas Act. That section provides: "It shall be unlawful for any person acting in concert with one or more other persons, to assemble at or near any place where a 'labor dispute' exists and by force or violence prevent . . . any person from engaging in any lawful vocation, or for any person acting . . . in concert with one or more other persons, to promote, encourage or aid any such unlawful assemblage." The record indicates that at the request of the prosecuting attorney, the trial judge read 2 to the jury. He then instructed them that 2 "includes two offenses, first, the concert of action between two or more persons resulting in the prevention of a person by means of force and violence from engaging in lawful vocation. And, second, in promoting, encouraging or aiding of such unlawful assemblage by concert of action among the defendants as is charged in the information here. The latter offense is the one on trial in this case."

The trial court also instructed the jury that they could not convict petitioners unless 'convinced beyond a reasonable doubt that they pro-

moted, encouraged, and aided in an unlawful assemblage at the plant of
the Southern Cotton Oil Company, for the purpose of preventing Otha
Williams from engaging in a lawful vocation.' This instruction, like the
preceding one, told the jury that the trial of petitioners was for violation
of 2, since 2 makes an unlawful assemblage an ingredient of the offense
it defines and 1 does not. Thus the petitioners were clearly tried and
convicted by the jury for promoting an unlawful assemblage made an
offense by 2, and were not tried for the offense of using force and violence as described in 1.

   We therefore have this situation. The petitioners read the information
as charging them with an offense under 2 of the Act, the language of
which the information had used. The trial judge construed the information as charging an offense under 2. He instructed the jury to that
effect. He charged the jury that petitioners were on trial for the offense
of promoting an unlawful assemblage, not for the offense 'of using force
and violence.' Without completely ignoring the judge's charge, the jury
could not have convicted petitioners for having committed the separate,
distinct, and substantially different offense defined in 1. Yet the State
Supreme Court refused to consider the validity of the conviction under
2, for violation of which petitioners were tried and convicted. It affirmed
their convictions as though they had been tried for violating 1, an offense
for which they were neither tried nor convicted. No principle of procedural due process is more clearly established than that notice of the specific charge, and a chance to be heard in a trial of the issues raised by
that charge, if desired, are among the constitutional rights of every accused in a criminal proceeding in all courts, state or federal. In re Oliver,
and cases there cited. If, as the State Supreme Court held, petitioners
were charged with a violation of 1, it is doubtful both that the information fairly informed them of that charge and that they sought to defend themselves against such a charge; it is certain that they were not
tried for or found guilty of it. It is as much a violation of due process to
send an accused to prison following conviction of a charge on which he
was never tried as it would be to convict him upon a charge that was
never made. De Jonge v. State of Oregon.

   Furthermore, since Arkansas provides for an appeal to the State Supreme Court and on that appeal considers questions raised under the
Federal Constitution, the proceedings in that court are a part of the process of law under which the petitioners' convictions must stand or fall.
... That court has not affirmed these convictions on the basis of the trial
petitioners were afforded. The convictions were for a violation of 2. Petitioners urged in the State Supreme Court that the evidence was insufficient to support their conviction of a violation of 2. They also raised
serious objections to the validity of that section under the Fourteenth
Amendment to the Federal Constitution. None of their contentions were

passed upon by the State Supreme Court. It affirmed their conviction as though they had been tried and convicted of a violation of 1 when in truth they had been tried and convicted only of a violation of a single offense charged in 2, an offense which is distinctly and substantially different from the offense charged in 1. To conform to due process of law, petitioners were entitled to have the validity of their convictions appraised on consideration of the case as it was tried and as the issues were determined in the trial court.

We are constrained to hold that the petitioners have been denied safeguards guaranteed by due process of law—safeguards essential to liberty in a government dedicated to justice under law.

In the present state of the record we cannot pass upon those contentions which challenge the validity of 2 of the Arkansas Act. The judgment is reversed and remanded to the State Supreme Court for proceedings not inconsistent with this opinion.

Reversed and remanded.

Source: United States Reports. Vol. 333, 196–202. Washington, D.C.: Government Printing Office, 1948.

DOCUMENT 34: *In Re Oliver* (1948)

Under Michigan law, judges can act as a one-person grand jury. This is a unique arrangement. Oliver was subpoenaed as a witness before a judge investigating official corruption and gambling. The proceeding was done in secret and he was not allowed to have an attorney present. After Oliver gave his testimony, the judge told him his testimony did not "jell." The judge then charged him with contempt, immediately convicted him, and sentenced him to sixty days in jail unless he changed his testimony. He was not given the opportunity to defend himself. The Michigan judge–grand jury law permitted the judge's actions.

Oliver's lawyer filed a petition for habeas corpus claiming that he was sentenced without the ability to confer with his lawyer and he was charged with no crime. The Michigan courts upheld the judge's actions.

The Supreme Court found the action unconstitutional. The secret nature of the proceeding was found to violate the due process guarantee of the Fourteenth Amendment. Due process was also violated by the absence of any opportunity to offer any defense. The Court reasoned that Oliver came before the judge as a witness; then suddenly the proceeding changed into a type of trial and he was found guilty and sentenced. Such a procedure is a clear violation of due process.

* * *

In Re Oliver, 333 U.S. 257

Mr. Justice Black delivered the opinion of the Court.

A Michigan circuit judge summarily sent the petitioner to jail for contempt of court. We must determine whether he was denied the procedural due process guaranteed by the Fourteenth Amendment.

In obedience to a subpoena the petitioner appeared as a witness before a Michigan circuit judge who was then conducting, in accordance with Michigan law, a 'one-man grand jury' investigation into alleged gambling and official corruption. . . . It is certain, however, that the public was excluded—the questioning was secret in accordance with the traditional grand jury method.

After petitioner had given certain testimony, the judge–grand jury, still in secret session, told petitioner that neither he nor his advisors believed petitioner's story—that it did not 'jell.' This belief of the judge–grand jury was not based entirely on what the petitioner had testified. As will later be seen, it rested in part on beliefs or suspicions of the judge-jury derived from the testimony of at least one other witness who had previously given evidence in secret. Petitioner had not been present when that witness testified and so far as appears was not even aware that he had testified. Based on its beliefs thus formed—that petitioner's story did not 'jell'—the judge–grand jury immediately charged him with contempt, immediately convicted him, and immediately sentenced him to sixty days in jail. Under these circumstances of haste and secrecy, petitioner, of course, had no chance to enjoy the benefits of counsel, no chance to prepare his defense, and no opportunity either to cross examine the other grand jury witness or to summon witnesses to refute the charge against him. . . .

The petitioner does not here challenge the constitutional power of Michigan to grant traditional inquisitorial grand jury power to a single judge, and therefore we do not concern ourselves with that question. . . .

. . . [O]ur first question is this: Can an accused be tried and convicted for contempt of court in grand jury secrecy?

First. Counsel have not cited and we have been unable to find a single instance of a criminal trial conducted in camera in any federal, state, or municipal court during the history of this country. Nor have we found any record of even one such secret criminal trial in England since abolition of the Court of Star Chamber in 1641, and whether that court ever convicted people secretly is in dispute. Summary trials for alleged misconduct called contempt of court have not been regarded as an exception to this universal rule against secret trials, unless some other Michigan one-man grand jury case may represent such an exception.

. . . [T]he petitioner was called as a witness to testify in secret before a one-man grand jury conducting a grand jury investigation. In the midst of petitioner's testimony the proceedings abruptly changed. The investigation became a 'trial,' the grand jury became a judge, and the witness became an accused charged with contempt of court—all in secret. . . . In view of this nation's historic distrust of secret proceedings, their inherent dangers to freedom, and the universal requirement of our federal and state governments that criminal trials be public, the Fourteenth Amendment's guarantee that no one shall be deprived of his liberty without due process of law means at least that an accused cannot be thus sentenced to prison.

Second. We further hold that failure to afford the petitioner a reasonable opportunity to defend himself against the charge of false and evasive swearing was a denial of due process of law. A person's right to reasonable notice of a charge against him, and an opportunity to be heard in his defense—a right to his day in court—are basic in our system of jurisprudence; and these rights include, as a minimum, a right to examine the witnesses against him, to offer testimony, and to be represented by counsel. Michigan, not denying the existence of these rights in criminal cases generally, apparently concedes that the summary conviction here would have been a denial of procedural due process but for the nature of the charge, namely, a contempt of court, committed, the State urges, in the court's actual presence. . . .

It is 'the law of the land' that no man's life, liberty or property be forfeited as a punishment until there has been a charge fairly made and fairly tried in a public tribunal. The petitioner was convicted without that kind of trial.

The judgment of the Supreme Court of Michigan is reversed and the cause is remanded to it for disposition not inconsistent with this opinion. Reversed and remanded.

Source: United States Reports. Vol. 333, 257–86. Washington, D.C.: Government Printing Office, 1948.

DOCUMENT 35: *Bute v. People of State of Illinois* (1948)

Bute pleaded guilty to two charges of "taking indecent liberties with a minor" and was sentenced to one to twenty years. He did not have the assistance of an attorney. He did not ask for one, and the court did not inquire if he wanted one. While serving his sentence, he filed motions with the Illinois Supreme Court asking that his trial be reviewed, since he did not have the assistance of an attorney and since he was rushed to trial. He claimed these were violations of the state and federal constitutions. The Illinois Supreme Court decided that he had not been denied due process.

Bute appealed to the U.S. Supreme Court claiming that his lack of an attorney was a denial of due process guaranteed by the Fourteenth Amendment. The Court ruled that the state was not required to appoint an attorney for due process. The Court used this case to explain why the entire Bill of Rights is not applied to the states. The states are responsible for due process in their courts. The Fourteenth Amendment does not guarantee the specific rights listed in the Bill of Rights, but a more general requirement of due process. Due process can consist of different procedures in different states. The different procedures of due process in individual states are not necessarily contrary to the requirements of the Fourteenth Amendment. Each case needs to be decided individually. State procedures that are different from federal procedures are only a violation of the requirement for due process when they are unfair. Just being different is not a violation of due process.

The dissent of Justice Douglas and three other justices is evidence of a shift in the opinion of the court. In his dissent, Justice Douglas argued that due process in state courts should be consistent with due process in federal courts. Bute cannot have a fair trial without the assistance of an attorney especially in as inflamatory a case as sexual abuse of a minor.

* * *

Bute v. People of State of Illinois, 333 U.S. 640 (1948)

Mr. Justice Burton delivered the opinion of the Court. . . .

. . . The issue here is whether or not each state sentence shall be held to have been imposed in violation of the due process clause of the Fourteenth Amendment to the Constitution of the United States because each common law record shows that the petitioner appeared 'in his own proper person' and does not show that the court inquired as to the petitioner's desire to be represented by counsel, or his ability to procure counsel, or his desire to have counsel assigned to him to assist him in his defense, or that such counsel was offered or assigned to him. We hold that such a silence in the respective records does not suffice to invalidate the sentences. We hold further that, in the absence of any showing beyond that in these records, the due process clause of the Fourteenth Amendment did not require the Illinois court to make the inquiries or the offer or assignment of counsel now claimed to have been the right of the petitioner.

The present case . . . illustrates equally well the kind of judgments by a state court that should not be invalidated as lacking in the due process of law required by the Fourteenth Amendment. This is so, although the procedure followed, in 1938, by the state court in the instant cases, as to counsel for the accused might not have satisfied the practice then required of a federal court in the case of comparable federal crimes. The Fourteenth Amendment, however, does not say that no state shall deprive any person of liberty without following the federal process of law as prescribed for the federal courts in comparable federal cases. It says merely "nor shall any State deprive any person of life, liberty, or property, without due process of law. . . ." This due process is not an equivalent for the process of the federal courts or for the process of any particular state. It has reference rather to a standard of process that may cover many varieties of processes that are expressive of differing combinations of historical or modern, local or other juridical standards, provided they do not conflict with the "fundamental principles of liberty and justice which lie at the base of all our civil and political institutions. . . ." Hebert v. Louisiana. . . . This clause in the Fourteenth Amendment leaves room for much of the freedom which, under the Constitution of the United States and in accordance with its purposes, was originally reserved to the states for their exercise of their own police powers and for their control over the procedure to be followed in criminal trials in their respective courts. . . .

. . . In our opinion this limitation is descriptive of a broad regulatory power over each state and not of a major transfer by the states to the United States of the primary and pre-existing power of the states over court procedures in state criminal cases.

Until the taking effect of the Fourteenth Amendment in 1868, there was no question but that the states were free to establish their own court procedures. This freedom included state practice as to the assistance of counsel to be permitted or assigned to the accused for his defense in state criminal cases. Because the Constitution of the United States, during nearly 80 formative years, thus permitted each state to establish, maintain and accustom its people to that state's own forms of 'due process of law,' a substantial presumption arises in favor of, rather than against, the lawfulness of those procedures and in favor of their right to continued recognition by the Federal Government as 'due process of law.' While such a presumption does not arise in favor of any practice against which the Fourteenth Amendment was particularly directed, there is no reason to feel that, in 1868, such Amendment was particularly directed against the practice now before us. . . .

... There is and can be no question raised here but that the procedure in the instant cases conformed to the Illinois Constitution as interpreted by the Supreme Court of that State.

The Constitution of the United States thus left the power to regulate the procedure as to the assistance of counsel for the defense of the accused in state criminal cases to the discretion of the respective states, at least until 1868. The Fourteenth Amendment then was adopted to meet the crying needs of that time. . . .

After exhaustive consideration of the subject, this Court has decided that the Fourteenth Amendment does not, through its due process clause or otherwise, have the effect of requiring the several states to conform the procedure of their state criminal trials to the precise procedure of the federal courts, even to the extent that the procedure of federal courts is prescribed by the Federal Constitution or Bill of Rights. There is nothing in the Fourteenth Amendment specifically stating that the long recognized and then existing power of the states over the procedure of their own courts in criminal cases was to be prohibited or even limited. Unlike the Bill of Rights, the Fourteenth Amendment made no mention of any requirement of grand jury presentments or indictments as a preliminary step in certain criminal prosecutions; any universal prohibition against the accused being compelled, in a criminal case, to be a witness against himself; any jurisdictional requirement of juries in all criminal trials; any guaranty to the accused that he have a right to the assistance of counsel for his defense in all criminal prosecutions; or any need to observe the rules of the common law in the re-examination of all facts tried by a jury. In spite of such omissions, it is claimed here, on behalf of the petitioner, that even though the failure of the state court in these cases to inquire of the accused as to his desire to be represented by counsel, or his ability to procure counsel, or his desire to have counsel assigned to him to assist him in his defense, and even though the failure of the state court in these cases to offer or assign counsel to the accused for his defense may have satisfied the Illinois law and have amounted to 'due process of law' under the Illinois Constitution, yet such practices did not satisfy the 'due process of law' required of the states by the Fourteenth Amendment to the Constitution of the United States.

... We recognize that the Fourteenth Amendment, as part of the supreme law of the land under Article VI of the original Constitution, supersedes "any Thing in the Constitution or Laws of any State to the Contrary notwithstanding." The important question remains, however: what shall be considered to be to the contrary? It is the established policy of both the State and Federal Governments to treat possible conflicts between their powers in such a manner as to produce as little conflict and friction as possible. So here the procedure followed by Illinois should not be held to violate the standard of permissible process of law broadly recognized by the Fourteenth Amendment unless the Illinois procedure violates "the very essence of a scheme of ordered liberty" and that to continue it would "violate a 'principle of justice so rooted in the traditions and conscience of our people as to be ranked as fundamental." . . .

. . . The issue is, therefore, whether, in the absence of any request by the petitioner for counsel and, in the absence of any statement under oath by the petitioner that he was unable to procure counsel, the court violated due process of law under the Fourteenth Amendment by the procedure which it took and which accorded with the procedure approved by Illinois for noncapital cases such as these. This procedure called upon the court to use its own judgment in the light of the nature of the offenses, the age, appearance, conduct and statements of the petitioner in court. These circumstances included the petitioner's plea of guilty, persisted in after the court's admonishment of him and explanation to him of the consequences and penalties involved in his plea. The court thereupon granted leave to the petitioner to enter a plea of guilty and such a plea was entered by the petitioner in each case.

In this view of the two cases before us it is not necessary to consider whether the petitioner, by his plea of guilty or otherwise, affirmatively waived any right to the assistance of counsel in his defense, for, under these circumstances, no constitutional right to such assistance had arisen in his favor. . . . [T]he state statute allowed the petitioner to be represented by counsel if the petitioner desired to be so represented. The state statute and practice, however, did not require that the accused must be so represented or that the trial court must initiate inquiry into the petitioner's desires. . . .

The final question is therefore, whether, even in the absence of any state requirement to that effect, the provision requiring due process of law under the Fourteenth Amendment, in and of itself, required the court in these cases to initiate an inquiry into the desire of the accused to be represented by counsel, to inquire into the ability of the accused to procure counsel or, in the event of the inability of the accused to procure counsel, to assign competent counsel to the accused to conduct his defense. We recognize that, if these charges had been capital charges, the court would have been required, both by the state statute and the decisions of this Court interpreting the Fourteenth Amendment, to take some such steps.

These, however, were not capital charges. . . .

On the other hand, this Court repeatedly has held that failure to appoint counsel to assist a defendant or to give a fair opportunity to the defendant's counsel to assist him in his defense where charged with a capital crime is a violation of due process of law under the Fourteenth Amendment. . . .

For the foregoing reasons, and under the principles previously announced by this Court, the judgment of the Supreme Court of Illinois is affirmed.

Affirmed.

Mr. Justice Douglas, with whom Mr. Justice Black, Mr. Justice Murphy and Mr. Justice Rutledge concur, dissenting.

In considering cases like this and the ill-starred decision in Betts v. Brady, we should ask ourselves this question: Of what value is the constitutional guaranty of a fair trial if an accused does not have counsel to advise and defend him?

The Framers deemed the right of counsel indispensable, for they wrote into the Sixth Amendment that in all criminal prosecutions the accused "shall enjoy the right . . . to have the Assistance of Counsel for his defense." Hence, if this case had been tried in the federal court appointment of counsel would have been mandatory, even though Bute did not request it. . . . I do not think the constitutional standards of fairness depend on what court an accused is in. I think that the Bill of Rights is applicable to all courts at all times. Mr. Justice Black demonstrated in his dissent in Adamson v. California, that a chief purpose of the Fourteenth Amendment was to protect the safeguards of the Bill of Rights against invasion by the states. If due process as defined in the Bill of Rights requires appointment of counsel to represent defendants in federal prosecutions, due process demands that the same be done in state prosecutions. The basic requirements for fair trials are those which the Framers deemed so important to procedural due process that they wrote them into the Bill of Rights and thus made it impossible for either legislatures or courts to tinker with them. I fail to see why it is due process to deny an accused the benefit of counsel in a state court when by constitutional standards that benefit could not be withheld from him in a federal court.

But if we take the view more hostile to the rights of the individual and assume that procedural due process guaranteed by the Fourteenth Amendment provides lesser safeguards than those of the Bill of Rights, the result should be the same. . . .

Bute was charged with a most repulsive crime. It may seem easy to say that it is a simple and uncomplicated one, and therefore that he should know whether he committed it and whether he stood in need of counsel. But it has long been recognized that the charge of taking indecent liberties with a child is, like rape, "an accusation easily to be made and hard to be proved, and harder to be defended by the party accused, the never so innocent." As stated by the Illinois Supreme Court in People v. Freeman, "Public indignation is even more apt to be aroused in prosecutions for crimes of this kind against children than when the charge is brought by an adult." Certainly the appraisal of such imponderables, the weight of the prosecution's case, the character of the defense which is available are all questions which only a skilled lawyer can consider intelligently. A layman might rush to confession where counsel would see advantages in a trial before judge or jury. Counsel might see weakness in the prosecution's case which could be utilized either in standing trial or in pleading guilty to a lesser offense. These are the circumstances of the present case which Bute uses to appeal to our conscience. They without more convince me that we could be sure Bute had a fair trial only if counsel had stood at his side and guided him across the treacherous ground he had to traverse.

Source: United States Reports. Vol. 333, 640–82. Washington, D.C.: Government Printing Office, 1948.

Part IV

Due Process Revolution

DOCUMENT 36: *Griffin v. Illinois* **(1956)**

In Illinois a full direct appellate review can be had only by furnishing the appellate court with a bill of exceptions or report of the trial proceedings, certified by the trial judge, and it is sometimes impossible to prepare such documents without a stenographic transcript of the trial proceedings. These documents are expensive to prepare and are provided free in Illinois only to indigent defendants sentenced to death. Griffin was indigent, but convicted of armed robbery only; he was denied free documents.

The Supreme Court considered whether the Illinois rules violated due process and equal protection. The Court declared, "There can be no equal justice where the kind of trial a man gets depends on the amount of money he has." The Illinois rules were a denial of equal justice and the documents would have to be provided without charge.

* * *

Griffin v. Illinois, 351 U.S. 12

Mr. Justice Black announced the judgment of the court and an opinion in which the Chief Justice, Mr. Justice Douglas, and Mr. Justice Clark join.

Illinois law provides that "Writs of error in all criminal cases are writs of right and shall be issued of course." The question presented here is whether Illinois may, consistent with the Due Process and Equal Protection Clauses of the Fourteenth Amendment, administer this statute so as to deny adequate appellate review to the poor while granting such review to all others.

The petitioners Griffin and Crenshaw were tried together and convicted of armed robbery in the Criminal Court of Cook County, Illinois. Immediately after their conviction they filed a motion in the trial court asking that a certified copy of the entire record, including a stenographic transcript of the proceedings, be furnished them without cost. They alleged that they were "poor persons with no means of paying the necessary fees to acquire the Transcript and Court Records needed to prosecute an appeal. . . ." These allegations were not denied. Under Illinois law in order to get full direct appellate review of alleged errors by a writ of error it is necessary for the defendant to furnish the appellate court with a bill of exceptions or report of proceedings at the trial certified by the trial judge. As Illinois concedes, it is sometimes impossible to prepare such bills of exceptions or reports without a stenographic transcript of the trial proceedings. Indigent defendants sentenced to death are provided with a free transcript at the expense of the county where convicted. In all other criminal cases defendants needing a transcript, whether indigent or not, must themselves buy it. The petitioners contended in their motion before the trial court that failure to provide them with the needed transcript would violate the Due Process and Equal Protection Clauses of the Fourteenth Amendment. The trial court denied the motion without a hearing. . . .

In their Post-Conviction proceeding petitioners alleged that there were manifest nonconstitutional errors in the trial which entitled them to have their convictions set aside on appeal and that the only impediment to full appellate review was their lack of funds to buy a transcript. These allegations have not been denied. Petitioners repeated their charge that refusal to afford full appellate review solely because of poverty was a denial of due process and equal protection. This petition like the first was dismissed without hearing any evidence. The Illinois Supreme Court affirmed the dismissal solely on the ground that the charges raised no substantial state or federal constitutional questions—the only kind of questions which may be raised in Post-Conviction proceedings. We granted certiorari.

Counsel for Illinois concedes that these petitioners needed a transcript in order to get adequate appellate review of their alleged trial errors. There is no contention that petitioners were dilatory in their efforts to get appellate review, or that the Illinois Supreme Court denied review on the ground that the allegations of trial error were insufficient. We must therefore assume for purposes of this decision that errors were committed in the trial which would merit reversal, but that the petitioners could not get appellate review of those errors solely because they were too poor to buy a stenographic transcript. . . . The sole question for us to decide, therefore, is whether due process or equal protection has been violated.

Providing equal justice for poor and rich, weak and powerful alike is an age-old problem. People have never ceased to hope and strive to move closer to that goal. This hope, at least in part, brought about in 1215 the royal concessions of Magna Charta: "To no one will we sell, to no one will we refuse, or delay, right or justice. . . . No free man shall be taken or imprisoned, or disseised, or outlawed, or exiled, or anywise destroyed; nor shall we go upon him nor send upon him, but by the lawful judgment of his peers or by the law of the land." . . . In this tradition, our own constitutional guaranties of due process and equal protection both call for procedures in criminal trials which allow no invidious discriminations between persons and different groups of persons. Both equal protection and due process emphasize the central aim of our entire judicial system—all people charged with crime must, so far as the law is concerned, "stand on an equality before the bar of justice in every American court." Chambers v. Florida. . . .

There is no meaningful distinction between a rule which would deny the poor the right to defend themselves in a trial court and one which effectively denies the poor an adequate appellate review accorded to all who have money enough to pay the costs in advance. . . . Appellate review has now become an integral part of the Illinois trial system for finally adjudicating the guilt or innocence of a defendant. Consequently at all stages of the proceedings the Due Process and Equal Protection Clauses protect persons like petitioners from invidious discriminations. . . .

Statistics show that a substantial proportion of criminal convictions are reversed by state appellate courts. Thus to deny adequate review to the poor means that many of them may lose their life, liberty or property because of unjust convictions which appellate courts would set aside. . . . There can be no equal justice where the kind of trial a man gets depends on the amount of money he has. Destitute defendants must be afforded as adequate appellate review as defendants who have money enough to buy transcripts.

The Illinois Supreme Court denied these petitioners relief under the Post-Conviction Act because of its holding that no constitutional rights were violated. In view of our holding to the contrary the State Supreme Court may decide that petitioners are now entitled to a transcript, as the State's brief suggests. . . . The Illinois Supreme Court appears to have broad power to promulgate rules of procedure and appellate practice. We are confident that the State will provide corrective rules to meet the problem which this case lays bare.

The judgment of the Supreme Court of Illinois is vacated and the cause is remanded to that court for further action not inconsistent with the foregoing paragraph. Mr. Justice Frankfurter joins in this disposition of the case.

Vacated and remanded.

Source: United States Reports. Vol. 351, 12–19. Washington, D.C.: Government Printing Office, 1956.

DOCUMENT 37: *Gideon v. Wainwright* (1963)

Gideon, a Florida indigent, was tried and convicted for breaking into a poolroom with intent to commit a misdemeanor. This crime is a felony in Florida. He requested and was denied counsel since Florida required the appointment of counsel only in capital cases. Gideon acted as his own lawyer, was found guilty, and sentenced to five years. From jail, he appealed his case claiming due process protection of the Fourteenth Amendment.

The Court appointed Abe Fortas, later a justice himself, to represent Gideon before the Supreme Court. In this case, the Court reversed itself, overruled *Betts v. Brady* (see Document 31), and required the state court to appoint a lawyer. The decision was written by Justice Black, who had written dissents earlier. This decision of the Court was consistent with the reasoning of his earlier dissents. The state retried Gideon, and he was found innocent.

This case is an important step in the "nationalization" of the Bill of Rights. Every defendant in state courts has the right to an attorney in capital and noncapital cases. The Court reasoned that having an attorney in our adversary system of criminal justice is "fundamental and essential to a fair trial."

* * *

Gideon v. Wainwright, 372 U.S. 335

Mr. Justice Black delivered the opinion of the Court. . . .

. . . Since 1942, when Betts v. Brady was decided by a divided Court, the problem of a defendant's federal constitutional right to counsel in a state court has been a continuing source of controversy and litigation in both state and federal courts. To give this problem another review here, we granted certiorari. Since Gideon was proceeding in forma pauperis, we appointed counsel to represent him and requested both sides to discuss in their briefs and oral arguments the following: "Should this Court's holding in Betts v. Brady be reconsidered?"

The Sixth Amendment provides, "In all criminal prosecutions, the accused shall enjoy the right . . . to have the Assistance of Counsel for his defence." We have construed this to mean that, in federal courts, counsel must be provided for defendants unable to employ counsel unless the right is competently and intelligently waived. Betts argued that this right is extended to indigent defendants in state courts by the Fourteenth Amendment. . . . [T]he Court concluded that "appointment of counsel is not a fundamental right, essential to a fair trial." It was for this reason the Betts Court refused to accept the contention that the Sixth Amendment's guarantee of counsel for indigent federal defendants was extended to or, in the words of that Court, "made obligatory upon, the States by the Fourteenth Amendment." . . .

. . . We think the Court in Betts was wrong, however, in concluding that the Sixth Amendment's guarantee of counsel is not one of these fundamental rights. Ten years before Betts v. Brady, this Court, after full consideration of all the historical data examined in Betts, had unequivocally declared that "the right to the aid of counsel is of this fundamental character." Powell v. Alabama. While the Court, at the close of its Powell opinion, did, by its language, as this Court frequently does, limit its holding to the particular facts and circumstances of that case, its conclusions about the fundamental nature of the right to counsel are unmistakable. Several years later, in 1936, the Court reemphasized what it had said about the fundamental nature of the right to counsel in this language:

"We concluded that certain fundamental rights, safeguarded by the first eight amendments against federal action, were also safeguarded against state action by the due process of law clause of the Fourteenth Amendment, and among them the fundamental right of the accused to the aid of counsel in a criminal prosecution." Grosjean v. American Press Co. (1936).

And again, in 1938, this Court said:

"[The assistance of counsel] is one of the safeguards of the Sixth Amendment deemed necessary to insure fundamental human rights of life and liberty. . . . The Sixth Amendment stands as a constant admonition that, if the constitutional safeguards it provides be lost, justice will not "still be done." Johnson v. Zerbst . . .

[I]n deciding as it did—that "appointment of counsel is not a fundamental right, essential to a fair trial"—the Court in Betts v. Brady made an abrupt break with its own well considered precedents. In returning to these old precedents, sounder, we believe, than the new, we but restore constitutional principles established to achieve a fair system of justice. Not only these precedents, but also reason and reflection, require us to recognize that, in our adversary system of criminal justice, any person hauled into court, who is too poor to hire a lawyer, cannot be assured a fair trial unless counsel is provided for him. This seems to us to be an obvious truth. Governments, both state and federal, quite properly spend vast sums of money to establish machinery to try defendants accused of crime. Lawyers to prosecute are everywhere deemed essential to protect the public's interest in an orderly society. Similarly, there are few defendants charged with crime, few indeed, who fail to hire the best lawyers they can get to prepare and present their defenses. That government hires lawyers to prosecute and defendants who have the money hire lawyers to defend are the strongest indications of the widespread belief that lawyers in criminal courts are necessities, not luxuries. The right of one charged with crime to counsel may not be deemed fundamental and essential to fair trials in some countries, but it is in ours. From the very beginning, our state and national constitutions and laws have laid great emphasis on procedural and substantive safeguards designed to assure fair trials before impartial tribunals in which every defendant stands equal before the law. This noble ideal cannot be realized if the poor man charged with crime has to face his accusers without a lawyer to assist him. . . .

The judgment is reversed, and the cause is remanded to the Supreme Court of Florida for further action not inconsistent with this opinion.

Reversed.

Source: United States Reports. Vol. 372, 335–52. Washington, D.C.: Government Printing Office, 1963.

DOCUMENT 38: *Douglas v. California* (1963)

The right to counsel for indigent defendants has been treated in many contexts by the Court. In *Douglas v. California,* the Court considered the consequences of a California law on the indigents filing appeals.

California had a law that allowed the District Court of Appeal to review a case to determine if the appointment of counsel for an indigent defendant would serve a good and useful purpose. The intent was to save the state money by appointing counsel only when it really mattered. The ruling was that Douglas was not entitled to counsel to assist with his appeal.

The Supreme Court disagreed. It reasoned that the denial of counsel prevented Griffin from having an effective appeal. Other defendants who could afford an attorney would certainly have one assist them. The question then becomes a matter of wealth. The Court ruled that such treatment was unfair and a violation of the "equality demanded

by the Fourteenth Amerndment." The Court ordered that counsel be
appointed for Griffin and his appeal heard again. This decision also
had the effect of nullifying the California law.

* * *

Douglas v. California, 372 U.S. 353

Mr. Justice Douglas delivered the opinion of the Court.

Although several questions are presented in the petition for certiorari,
we address ourselves to only one of them. The record shows that petitioners requested, and were denied, the assistance of counsel on appeal,
even though it plainly appeared they were indigents. In denying petitioners' requests, the California District Court of Appeal stated that it
had "gone through" the record and had come to the conclusion that "no
good whatever could be served by appointment of counsel." 187 Cal.
App. 2d 802, 812, 10 Cal. Rptr. 188, 195. The District Court of Appeal
was acting in accordance with a California rule of criminal procedure
which provides that state appellate courts, upon the request of an indigent for counsel, may make "an independent investigation of the record
and determine whether it would be of advantage to the defendant or
helpful to the appellate court to have counsel appointed. . . . After such
investigation, appellate courts should appoint counsel if in their opinion
it would be helpful to the defendant or the court, and should deny the
appointment of counsel only if in their judgment such appointment
would be of no value to either the defendant or the court." People v.
Hyde. . . .

In Griffin v. Illinois, we held that a State may not grant appellate
review in such a way as to discriminate against some convicted defendants on account of their poverty. . . . [T]he right to a free transcript on
appeal was in issue. Here the issue is whether or not an indigent shall
be denied the assistance of counsel on appeal. In either case the evil is
the same: discrimination against the indigent. For there can be no equal
justice where the kind of an appeal a man enjoys "depends on the
amount of money he has." Griffin v. Illinois, supra, at p. 19.

In spite of California's forward treatment of indigents, under its present practice the type of an appeal a person is afforded in the District
Court of Appeal hinges upon whether or not he can pay for the assistance of counsel. If he can the appellate court passes on the merits of his
case only after having the full benefit of written briefs and oral argument
by counsel. If he cannot the appellate court is forced to prejudge the
merits before it can even determine whether counsel should be provided.
At this stage in the proceedings only the barren record speaks for the
indigent, and, unless the printed pages show that an injustice has been

committed, he is forced to go without a champion on appeal. Any real chance he may have had of showing that his appeal has hidden merit is deprived him when the court decides on an ex parte examination of the record that the assistance of counsel is not required.

We are not here concerned with problems that might arise from the denial of counsel for the preparation of a petition for discretionary or mandatory review beyond the stage in the appellate process at which the claims have once been presented by a lawyer and passed upon by an appellate court. We are dealing only with the first appeal, granted as a matter of right to rich and poor alike from a criminal conviction. . . . But where the merits of the one and only appeal an indigent has as of right are decided without benefit of counsel, we think an unconstitutional line has been drawn between rich and poor.

When an indigent is forced to run this gauntlet of a preliminary showing of merit, the right to appeal does not comport with fair procedure. . . . The present case, where counsel was denied petitioners on appeal, shows that the discrimination is not between "possibly good and obviously bad cases," but between cases where the rich man can require the court to listen to argument of counsel before deciding on the merits, but a poor man cannot. There is lacking that equality demanded by the Fourteenth Amendment where the rich man, who appeals as of right, enjoys the benefit of counsel's examination into the record, research of the law, and marshalling of arguments on his behalf, while the indigent, already burdened by a preliminary determination that his case is without merit, is forced to shift for himself. The indigent, where the record is unclear or the errors are hidden, has only the right to a meaningless ritual, while the rich man has a meaningful appeal.

We vacate the judgment of the District Court of Appeal and remand the case to that court for further proceedings not inconsistent with this opinion.

It is so ordered.

Source: United States Reports. Vol. 372, 353–59. Washington, D.C.: Government Printing Office, 1963.

DOCUMENT 39: *Massiah v. United States* (1964)

Modern technology poses new situations that require Court clarification. Massiah was free on bail after indictment for narcotics activities. He had retained a lawyer. Government agents secured the help of an associate of Massiah. They placed a radio transmitter in the associate's automobile and were thereby able to listen to incriminating remarks made by Massiah.

The Court ruled that the secretly recorded conversations were not admissible as evidence. They were his own words used against him without the advise of counsel. Therefore, they violated Massiah's right to counsel under the Sixth Amendment.

* * *

Massiah v. United States, 377 U.S. 201

Mr. Justice Stewart delivered the opinion of the Court. . . .

The petitioner, a merchant seaman, was in 1958 a member of the crew of the S.S. Santa Maria. In April of that year federal customs officials in New York received information that he was going to transport a quantity of narcotics aboard that ship from South America to the United States. As a result of this and other information, the agents searched the Santa Maria upon its arrival in New York and found in the afterpeak of the vessel five packages containing about three and a half pounds of cocaine. They also learned of circumstances, not here relevant, tending to connect the petitioner with the cocaine. He was arrested, promptly arraigned, and subsequently indicted for possession of narcotics aboard a United States vessel. In July a superseding indictment was returned, charging the petitioner and a man named Colson with the same substantive offense, and in separate counts charging the petitioner, Colson, and others with having conspired to possess narcotics aboard a United States vessel, and to import, conceal, and facilitate the sale of narcotics. The petitioner, who had retained a lawyer, pleaded not guilty and was released on bail, along with Colson.

A few days later, and quite without the petitioner's knowledge, Colson decided to cooperate with the government agents in their continuing investigation of the narcotics activities in which the petitioner, Colson, and others had allegedly been engaged. Colson permitted an agent named Murphy to install a Schmidt radio transmitter under the front seat of Colson's automobile, by means of which Murphy, equipped with an appropriate receiving device, could overhear from some distance away conversations carried on in Colson's car.

On the evening of November 19, 1959, Colson and the petitioner held a lengthy conversation while sitting in Colson's automobile, parked on a New York street. By prearrangement with Colson, and totally unbeknown to the petitioner, the agent Murphy sat in a car parked out of sight down the street and listened over the radio to the entire conversation. The petitioner made several incriminating statements during the course of this conversation. At the petitioner's trial these incriminating statements were brought before the jury through Murphy's testimony, despite the insistent objection of defense counsel. The jury convicted the petitioner of several related narcotics offenses, and the convictions were affirmed by the Court of Appeals.

The petitioner argues that it was an error of constitutional dimensions to permit the agent Murphy at the trial to testify to the petitioner's incriminating statements which Murphy had overheard under the circumstances disclosed by this record. . . . [I]t is said that the petitioner's Fifth and Sixth Amendment rights were violated by the use in evidence against him of incriminating statements which government agents had deliberately elicited from him after he had been indicted and in the absence of his retained counsel. . . .

Here we deal not with a state court conviction, but with a federal case, where the specific guarantee of the Sixth Amendment directly applies. We hold that the petitioner was denied the basic protections of that guarantee when there was used against him at his trial evidence of his own incriminating words, which federal agents had deliberately elicited from him after he had been indicted and in the absence of his counsel. It is true that in the Spano case the defendant was interrogated in a police station, while here the damaging testimony was elicited from the defendant without his knowledge while he was free on bail. But, as Judge Hays pointed out in his dissent in the Court of Appeals, "if such a rule is to have any efficacy it must apply to indirect and surreptitious interrogations as well as those conducted in the jailhouse. In this case, Massiah was more seriously imposed upon . . . because he did not even know that he was under interrogation by a government agent." 307 F.2d, at 72–73.

The Solicitor General, in his brief and oral argument, has strenuously contended that the federal law enforcement agents had the right, if not indeed the duty, to continue their investigation of the petitioner and his alleged criminal associates even though the petitioner had been indicted. He points out that the Government was continuing its investigation in order to uncover not only the source of narcotics found on the S.S. Santa Maria, but also their intended buyer. He says that the quantity of narcotics involved was such as to suggest that the petitioner was part of a large and well-organized ring, and indeed that the continuing investigation confirmed this suspicion, since it resulted in criminal charges against many defendants. Under these circumstances the Solicitor General concludes that the government agents were completely "justified in making use of Colson's cooperation by having Colson continue his normal associations and by surveilling them."

We may accept and, at least for present purposes, completely approve all that this argument implies, Fourth Amendment problems to one side. We do not question that in this case, as in many cases, it was entirely proper to continue an investigation of the suspected criminal activities of the defendant and his alleged confederates, even though the defendant had already been indicted. All that we hold is that the defendant's own incriminating statements, obtained by federal agents under the circumstances here disclosed, could not constitutionally be used by the prosecution as evidence against him at his trial.

Reversed.

Source: United States Reports. Vol. 377, 201–7. Washington, D.C.: Government Printing Office, 1964.

DOCUMENT 40: *Malloy v. Hogan* (1964)

In 1959, William Malloy was arrested during a gambling raid. He was convicted and given a suspended sentence. Later he was called to answer questions about the circumstances of his arrest and conviction by a state court. He refused on the basis of possible self-incrimination and was held in contempt of court. He was committed to prison until he was willing to answer the questions. On appeal, the state courts held that the Fifth Amendment right against self-incrimination was not applicable to state proceedings.

In a 5 to 4 decision of this case, the Supreme Court overturned *Twining v. New Jersey* (see Document 26). The protection against self-incrimination guaranteed by the Fifth Amendment "is also protected by the Fourteenth Amendment against abridgment by the States." Thus protection against self-incrimination is added to those rights considered fundamental to due process.

Four justices dissented from this decision. Their reasoning varied, but essentially they were concerned about the implications of applying the federal standard in state courts.

* * *

Malloy v. Hogan, 378 U.S. 1

Mr. Justice Brennan delivered the opinion of the Court. . . .

The extent to which the Fourteenth Amendment prevents state invasion of rights enumerated in the first eight Amendments has been considered in numerous cases in this Court since the Amendment's adoption in 1868. Although many Justices have deemed the Amendment to incorporate all eight of the Amendments, the view which has thus far prevailed dates from the decision in 1897 in Chicago, B. & Q. R. Co. v. Chicago which held that the Due Process Clause requires the States to pay just compensation for private property taken for public use. It was on the authority of that decision that the Court said in 1908 in Twining v. New Jersey that "it is possible that some of the personal rights safeguarded by the first eight Amendments against National action may also be safeguarded against state action, because a denial of them would be a denial of due process of law."

The Court has not hesitated to reexamine past decisions according the Fourteenth Amendment a less central role in the preservation of basic liberties than that which was contemplated by its Framers when they added the Amendment to our constitutional scheme. Thus, although the Court, as late as 1922, said that "neither the Fourteenth Amendment nor any other provision of the Constitution of the United States imposes upon the States any restrictions about 'freedom of speech' . . . ," Prudential Ins. Co. v. Cheek, three years later, Gitlow v. New York initiated a series of decisions which today hold immune from state invasion every First Amendment protection for the cherished rights of mind and spirit— the freedoms of speech, press, religion, assembly, association, and petition for redress of grievances.

Similarly, Palko v. Connecticut decided in 1937, suggested that the rights secured by the Fourth Amendment were not protected against state action, citing, 302 U.S. at 24, the statement of the Court in 1914 in Weeks v. United States that "the Fourth Amendment is not directed to individual misconduct of [state] officials." In 1961, however, the Court held that, in the light of later decisions, it was taken as settled that ". . . the Fourth Amendment's right of privacy has been declared enforceable against the States through the Due Process Clause of the Fourteenth. . . ." Mapp v. Ohio. Again, although the Court held in 1942 that, in a state prosecution for a noncapital offense, "appointment of counsel is not a fundamental right," Betts v. Brady only last Term, this decision was reexamined and it was held that provision of counsel in all criminal cases was "a fundamental right, essential to a fair trial," and thus was made obligatory on the States by the Fourteenth Amendment. Gideon v. Wainwright.

We hold today that the Fifth Amendment's exception from compulsory self-incrimination is also protected by the Fourteenth Amendment against abridgment by the States. Decisions of the Court since Twining and Adamson have departed from the contrary view expressed in those cases. . . .

. . . What is accorded is a privilege of refusing to incriminate one's self, and the feared prosecution may be by either federal or state authorities. . . . It would be incongruous to have different standards determine the validity of a claim of privilege based on the same feared prosecution depending on whether the claim was asserted in a state or federal court. Therefore, the same standards must determine whether an accused's silence in either a federal or state proceeding is justified. . . .

What is accorded is a privilege of refusing to incriminate one's self, and the feared prosecution may be by either federal or state authorities. It would be incongruous to have different standards determine the validity of a claim of privilege based on the same feared prosecution, depending on whether the claim was asserted in a state or federal court. Therefore, the same standards must determine whether an accused's silence in either a federal or state proceeding is justified. . . .

The State of Connecticut argues that the Connecticut courts properly applied the federal standards to the facts of this case. We disagree.

The investigation in the course of which petitioner was questioned began when the Superior Court in Hartford County appointed the Honorable Ernest A. Inglis, formerly Chief Justice of Connecticut, to conduct an inquiry into whether there was reasonable cause to believe that crimes, including gambling, were being committed in Hartford County. Petitioner appeared on January 16 and 25, 1961, and in both instances he was asked substantially the same questions about the circumstances surrounding his arrest and conviction for pool selling in late 1959. The questions which petitioner refused to answer may be summarized as follows: (1) for whom did he work on September 11, 1959; (2) who selected and paid his counsel in connection with his arrest on that date and subsequent conviction; (3) who selected and paid his bondsman; (4) who paid his fine; (5) what was the name of the tenant of the apartment in which he was arrested; and (6) did he know John Bergoti. The Connecticut Supreme Court of Errors ruled that the answers to these questions could not tend to incriminate him because the defenses of double jeopardy and the running of the one-year statute of limitations on misdemeanors would defeat any prosecution growing out of his answers to the first five questions. As for the sixth question, the court held that petitioner's failure to explain how a revelation of his relationship with Bergoti would incriminate him vitiated his claim to the protection of the privilege afforded by state law.

The conclusions of the Court of Errors, tested by the federal standard, fail to take sufficient account of the setting in which the questions were asked. The interrogation was part of a wide-ranging inquiry into crime, including gambling, in Hartford. It was admitted on behalf of the State at oral argument—and indeed it is obvious from the questions themselves—that the State desired to elicit from the petitioner the identity of the person who ran the pool selling operation in connection with which he had been arrested in 1959. It was apparent that petitioner might apprehend that if this person were still engaged in unlawful activity, disclosure of his name might furnish a link in a chain of evidence sufficient to connect the petitioner with a more recent crime for which he might still be prosecuted.

Analysis of the sixth question, concerning whether petitioner knew John Bergoti yields a similar conclusion. In the context of the inquiry, it should have been apparent to the referee that Bergoti was suspected by the State to be involved in some way in the subject matter of the investigation. An affirmative answer to the question might well have either connected petitioner with a more recent crime, or at least have operated as a waiver of his privilege with reference to his friendship with a possible criminal. We conclude there that as to each of the questions, it was "evident from the implications of the question, in the setting in which it [was] asked, that a responsive answer to the question or an explanation of why it [could not] be answered might be dangerous because injurious disclosure could result," Hoffman v. United States.

Reversed.

Source: United States Reports. Vol. 378, 1–38. Washington, D.C.: Government Printing Office, 1965.

DOCUMENT 41: *Murphy v. Waterfront Commission* (1964)

The Court had ruled that protection from self-incrimination existed in state courts as well as in federal courts. But what if an individual given immunity from prosecution in a state court and compelled to answer questions would be incriminating himself of a federal crime? Could the state still compel him to answer? Or did protection from self-incrimination in one court extend to other courts?

Murphy presented the Court with the opportunity to rule on this issue. Murphy was subpoenaed to testify at a hearing conducted by the Waterfront Commission of Hoboken, New Jersey, piers. Even though granted immunity from prosecution in New Jersey courts, Murphy refused to answer on grounds that his testimony might tend to incriminate him under federal law, where the New Jersey grant of immunity did not extend.

In previous decisions, the Court had ruled that the protection from self-incrimination did not cross jurisdictions and individuals could be compelled to testify even if that testimony could be used against them in another jurisdiction. The Court overruled these previous decisions and decided that the state could not compel Murphy to give testimony. The privilege against self-incrimination "protects a state witness against incrimination under federal as well as state law and a federal witness against incrimination under state as well as federal law." The Court thus expanded the protection of self-incrimination across various jurisdictions.

* * *

Murphy v. Waterfront Commission, 378 U.S. 52

Mr. Justice Goldberg delivered the opinion of the Court.

We have held today that the Fifth Amendment privilege against self-incrimination must be deemed fully applicable to the States through the Fourteenth Amendment. This case presents a related issue: whether one jurisdiction within our federal structure may compel a witness, whom it has immunized from prosecution under its laws, to give testimony which might then be used to convict him of a crime against another such jurisdiction. . . .

. . . We hold that the constitutional privilege against self-incrimination protects a state witness against incrimination under federal as well as state law and a federal witness against incrimination under state as well as federal law.

We must now decide what effect this holding has on existing state immunity legislation. In Counselman v. Hitchcock, this Court considered a federal statute which provided that no "evidence obtained from a party or witness by means of a judicial proceeding . . . shall be given in evidence, or in any manner used against him . . . in any court of the United States. . . ." Notwithstanding this statute, appellant, claiming his privilege against self-incrimination, refused to answer certain questions before a federal grand jury. The Court said "that legislation cannot abridge a constitutional privilege, and that it cannot replace or supply one, at least unless it is so broad as to have the same extent in scope and effect." Applying this principle to the facts of that case, the Court upheld appellant's refusal to answer on the ground that the statute:

"could not, and would not, prevent the use of his testimony to search out other testimony to be used in evidence against him or his property, in a criminal proceeding in such court . . . ," id., at 564,

that it:

"could not prevent the obtaining and the use of witnesses and evidence which should be attributable directly to the testimony he might give under compulsion, and on which he might be convicted, when otherwise, and if he had refused to answer, he could not possibly have been convicted . . . ," ibid.,

and that it:

"affords no protection against that use of compelled testimony which consists in gaining therefrom a knowledge of the details of a crime, and of sources of information which may supply other means of convicting the witness or party." Id., at 586. . . .

[T]he privilege against self-incrimination protects a state witness against federal prosecution and that "the same standards must determine whether [a witness'] silence in either a federal or state proceeding is justified," Malloy v. Hogan, ante at, we hold the constitutional rule to be that a state witness may not be compelled to give testimony which may be incriminating under federal law unless the compelled testimony and its fruits cannot be used in any manner by federal officials in connection with a criminal prosecution against him. We conclude, moreover, that, in order to implement this constitutional rule and accommodate the interests of the State and Federal Governments in investigating and prosecuting crime, the Federal Government must be prohibited from making any such use of compelled testimony and its fruits. This exclusionary rule, while permitting the States to secure information necessary for effective law enforcement, leaves the witness and the Federal Government in substantially the same position as if the witness had claimed his privilege in the absence of a state grant of immunity.

It follows that petitioners here may now be compelled to answer the questions propounded to them. At the time they refused to answer, however, petitioners had a reasonable fear, based on this Court's decision in Feldman v. United States, supra, that the federal authorities might use the answers against them in connection with a federal prosecution. We have now overruled Feldman and held that the Federal Government may make no such use of the answers. Fairness dictates that petitioners should now be afforded an opportunity, in light of this development, to answer the questions. Accordingly, the judgment of the New Jersey courts ordering petitioners to answer the questions may remain undisturbed. But the judgment of contempt is vacated and the cause remanded to the New Jersey Supreme Court for proceedings not inconsistent with this opinion.

It is so ordered.

Source: United States Reports. Vol. 378, 52–107. Washington, D.C.: Government Printing Office, 1965.

DOCUMENT 42: *Escobedo v. Illinois* (1964)

Escobedo was questioned extensively by police regarding the fatal shooting of his brother-in-law. During the questioning, he asked to speak to his lawyer, but his request was refused. His lawyer, aware of his questioning, went to the police station and requested to see his client. His request was refused. The lawyer persisted, talking to various officers and supervisors, but he was not allowed to see Escobedo. During questioning, Escobedo made incriminating comments that were introduced at his trial. He was convicted of murder.

The Supreme Court decided that the denial of access to his lawyer during questioning was a violation of the Sixth Amendment guarantee to counsel. Previously, that guarantee existed only during the trial. The Court reasoned that when the investigation focused on a person about to be charged with a crime, that person needed the assistance of counsel. To deny counsel when incriminating statements are made, undermined the effectiveness of counsel at trial. The Court also ruled any incriminating statements made without the presence of a lawyer could not be admitted at any subsequent trial. Further, this requirement applied to the states, since right to counsel was applied through the Fourteenth Amendment in *Gideon v. Wainwright* (see Document 37).

This decision was very controversial. Many argued that it was impossible to administer. Just when during an investigation should the lawyer be present? From the first question? Police feared that accused would be advised by lawyers to say nothing during the investigation and make the police job much more difficult. These concerns are stated nicely in the dissent written by Justice White and joined by two other justices.

* * *

Escobedo v. Illinois, 378 U.S. 478

Mr. Justice Goldberg delivered the opinion of the Court.

The critical question in this case is whether, under the circumstances, the refusal by the police to honor petitioner's request to consult with his lawyer during the course of an interrogation constitutes a denial of "the Assistance of Counsel" in violation of the Sixth Amendment to the Constitution as "made obligatory upon the States by the Fourteenth Amendment," Gideon v. Wainwright, and thereby renders inadmissible in a state criminal trial any incriminating statement elicited by the police during the interrogation. . . .

On the night of January 19, 1960, petitioner's brother-in-law was fatally shot. In the early hours of the next morning, at 2:30 A.M., petitioner was arrested without a warrant and interrogated. Petitioner made no statement to the police and was released at 5 that afternoon pursuant to a state court writ of habeas corpus obtained by Mr. Warren Wolfson, a lawyer who had been retained by petitioner. . . .

The interrogation here was conducted before petitioner was formally indicted. But in the context of this case, that fact should make no difference. When petitioner requested, and was denied, an opportunity to consult with his lawyer, the investigation had ceased to be a general investigation of "an unsolved crime." Petitioner had become the accused, and the purpose of the interrogation was to "get him" to confess his guilt despite his constitutional right not to do so. At the time of his arrest and throughout the course of the interrogation, the police told petitioner that they had convincing evidence that he had fired the fatal shots. Without informing him of his absolute right to remain silent in the face of this accusation, the police urged him to make a statement. . . .

Petitioner, a layman, was undoubtedly unaware that under Illinois law an admission of "mere" complicity in the murder plot was legally as damaging as an admission of firing of the fatal shots. Illinois v. Escobedo, 28 Ill. 2d 41, 190 N. E. 2d 825. The "guiding hand of counsel" was essential to advise petitioner of his rights in this delicate situation. . . . It would exalt form over substance to make the right to counsel, under these circumstances, depend on whether at the time of the interrogation, the authorities had secured a formal indictment. Petitioner had, for all practical purposes, already been charged with murder. . . .

In Gideon v. Wainwright, we held that every person accused of a crime, whether state or federal, is entitled to a lawyer at trial. The rule sought by the State here, however, would make the trial no more than an appeal from the interrogation; and the "right to use counsel at the formal trial [would be] a very hollow thing [if], for all practical purposes, the conviction is already assured by pretrial examination." . . .

It is argued that if the right to counsel is afforded prior to indictment, the number of confessions obtained by the police will diminish significantly, because most confessions are obtained during the period between arrest and indictment, and "any lawyer worth his salt will tell the suspect in no uncertain terms to make no statement to police under any circumstances." . . . This argument, of course, cuts two ways. The fact that many confessions are obtained during this period points up its critical nature as a "stage when legal aid and advice" are surely needed. . . . The right to counsel would indeed be hollow if it began at a period when few confessions were obtained. There is necessarily a direct relationship between the importance of a stage to the police in their quest for a confession and the criticalness of that stage to the accused in his need for legal advice. Our Constitution, unlike some others, strikes the balance in favor of the right of the accused to be advised by his lawyer of his privilege against self-incrimination. . . .

This Court also has recognized that "history amply shows that confessions have often been extorted to save law enforcement officials the trouble and effort of obtaining valid and independent evidence. . . ." Haynes v. Washington.

We have also learned the companion lesson of history that no system of criminal justice can, or should, survive if it comes to depend for its continued effectiveness on the citizens' abdication through unawareness of their constitutional rights. No system worth preserving should have to fear that if an accused is permitted to consult with a lawyer, he will become aware of, and exercise, these rights. If the exercise of constitutional rights will thwart the effectiveness of a system of law enforcement, then there is something very wrong with that system.

We hold, therefore, that where, as here, the investigation is no longer a general inquiry into an unsolved crime but has begun to focus on a particular suspect, the suspect has been taken into police custody, the police carry out a process of interrogations that lends itself to eliciting incriminating statements, the suspect has requested and been denied an opportunity to consult with his lawyer, and the police have not effectively warned him of his absolute constitutional right to remain silent, the accused has been denied "the Assistance of Counsel" in violation of the Sixth Amendment to the Constitution as "made obligatory upon the States by the Fourteenth Amendment," Gideon v. Wainwright, and that no statement elicited by the police during the interrogation may be used against him at a criminal trial. . . .

Nothing we have said today affects the powers of the police to investigate "an unsolved crime," Spano v. New York, by gathering information from witnesses and by other "proper investigative efforts." Haynes v. Washington. We hold only that when the process shifts from investigatory to accusatory—when its focus is on the accused and its purpose is to elicit a confession—our adversary system begins to operate, and, under the circumstances here, the accused must be permitted to consult with his lawyer.

The judgment of the Illinois Supreme Court is reversed and the case remanded for proceedings not inconsistent with this opinion.

Reversed and remanded.

Mr. Justice White, with whom Mr. Justice Clark and Mr. Justice Stewart join, dissenting.

In Massiah v. United States, the Court held that as of the date of the indictment the prosecution is disentitled to secure admissions from the accused. The Court now moves that date back to the time when the prosecution begins to "focus" on the accused. Although the opinion purports to be limited to the facts of this case, it would be naive to think that the new constitutional right announced will depend upon whether the accused has retained his own counsel, cf. Gideon v. Wainright, Griffin v. Illinois, Douglas v. California, or has asked to consult with counsel in the course of interrogation. Cf. Carnley v. Cochran. At the very least the Court holds that once the accused becomes a suspect and, presumably, is arrested, any admission made to the police thereafter is inadmissible in evidence unless the accused has waived his right to counsel. The decision is thus another major step in the direction of the goal which the Court seemingly has in mind—to bar from evidence all admissions obtained from an individual suspected of crime, whether involuntarily made or not. . . .

By abandoning the voluntary-involuntary test for admissibility of confessions, the Court seems driven by the notion that it is uncivilized law enforcement to use an accused's own admissions against him at his trial. It attempts to find a home for this new and nebulous rule of due process by attaching it to the right to counsel guaranteed in the federal system by the Sixth Amendment and binding upon the States by virtue of the due process guarantee of the Fourteenth Amendment. Gideon v. Wainwright, supra. The right to counsel now not only entitles the accused to counsel's advice and aid in preparing for trial but stands as an impenetrable barrier to any interrogation once the accused has become a suspect. From that very moment apparently his right to counsel attaches, a rule wholly unworkable and impossible to administer unless police cars are equipped with public defenders and undercover agents and police informants have defense counsel at their side. . . .

This new American judges' rule, which is to be applied in both federal and state courts, is perhaps thought to be a necessary safeguard against the possibility of extorted confessions. To this extent it reflects a deepseated distrust of law enforcement officers everywhere, unsupported by relevant data or current material based upon our own experience. Obviously law enforcement officers can make mistakes and exceed their authority, as today's decision shows that even judges can do, but I have somewhat more faith than the Court evidently has in the ability and desire of prosecutors and of the power of the appellate courts to discern and correct such violations of the law. . . .

I do not suggest for a moment that law enforcement will be destroyed by the rule announced today. The need for peace and order is too insistent for that. But it will be crippled and its task made a great deal more difficult, all in my opinion, for unsound, unstated reasons, which can find no home in any of the provisions of the Constitution. . . .

Source: United States Reports. Vol. 378, 478–99. Washington, D.C.: Government Printing Office, 1965.

DOCUMENT 43: *Pointer v. Texas* (1965)

The march toward incorporating all provisions of the Sixth Amendment in the meaning of due process in the Fourteenth Amendment continued in *Pointer v. Texas*. In this decision, the Court required states to be bound by the guarantee to confront witnesses against the accused.

First arrested, Pointer was then questioned at a preliminary hearing before a state judge on a robbery charge. The only complaining witness testified. Pointer had no counsel and did not cross-examine the witness. Later he was indicted and put on trial for the offense. The complaining witness had moved to another state and refused to return to testify. State lawyers introduced as evidence against Pointer the witnesses' testimony at the hearing. Pointer's lawyer objected arguing that doing so denied Pointer the right to question the witness against him. The testimony was allowed and Pointer was convicted.

The Court ruled that the Fourteenth Amendment guarantees defendants in state court the fundamental right to confront and question witnesses against an accused. Had Pointer cross-examined the witness during the preliminary hearing, the Court stated, that would have satisfied the constitutional requirement.

* * *

Pointer v. Texas, 380 U.S. 400

Mr. Justice Black delivered the opinion of the Court. . . .

The question we find necessary to decide in this case is whether the Amendment's guarantee of a defendant's right "to be confronted with the witnesses against him," which has been held to include the right to cross-examine those witnesses, is also made applicable to the States by the Fourteenth Amendment. We hold today that the Sixth Amendment's right of an accused to confront the witnesses against him is likewise a fundamental right, and is made obligatory on the States by the Fourteenth Amendment.

The petitioner Pointer and one Dillard were arrested in Texas and taken before a state judge for a preliminary hearing (in Texas called the "examining trial") on a charge of having robbed Kenneth W. Phillips of $375 "by assault, or violence, or by putting in fear of life or bodily injury," in violation of Texas Penal Code Art. 1408. At this hearing an Assistant District Attorney conducted the prosecution and examined witnesses, but neither of the defendants, both of whom were laymen, had a lawyer. Phillips as chief witness for the State gave his version of the alleged robbery in detail, identifying petitioner as the man who had robbed him at gunpoint. Apparently Dillard tried to cross-examine Phillips, but Pointer did not, although Pointer was said to have tried to cross-examine some other witnesses at the hearing. Petitioner was subsequently indicted on a charge of having committed the robbery. Some time before the trial was held, Phillips moved to California. After putting in evidence to show that Phillips had moved and did not intend to return to Texas, the State at the trial offered the transcript of Phillips' testimony given at the preliminary hearing as evidence against petitioner. Petitioner's counsel immediately objected to introduction of the transcript, stating, "Your Honor, we will object to that as it is a denial of the confrontment of the witnesses against the Defendant." Similar objections were repeatedly made by petitioner's counsel but were overruled by the trial judge, apparently in part because, as the judge viewed it, petitioner had been present at the preliminary hearing and therefore had been "accorded the opportunity of cross examining the witnesses there against him." The Texas court of Criminal Appeals, the highest state court to which the case could be taken, affirmed petitioner's conviction, rejecting his contention that use of the transcript to convict him denied him rights guaranteed by the Sixth and Fourteenth Amendments. We granted certiorari to consider the important constitutional question the case involves. . . .

It cannot seriously be doubted at this late date that the right of cross-examination is included in the right of an accused in a criminal case to confront the witnesses against him. And probably no one, certainly no one experienced in the trial of lawsuits, would deny the value of cross-examination in exposing falsehood and bringing out the truth in the trial of a criminal case. The fact that this right appears in the Sixth Amendment of our Bill of Rights reflects the belief of the Framers of those liberties and safeguards that confrontation was a fundamental right essential to a fair trial in a criminal prosecution. Moreover, the decisions of this Court and other courts throughout the years have constantly emphasized the necessity for cross-examination as a protection for defendants in criminal cases. . . .

There are few subjects, perhaps, upon which this Court and other courts have been more nearly unanimous than in their expressions of belief that the right of confrontation and cross-examination is an essential and fundamental requirement for the kind of fair trial which is this country's constitutional goal. Indeed, we have expressly declared that to deprive an accused of the right to cross-examine the witnesses against him is a denial of the Fourteenth Amendment's guarantee of due process of law. . . .

In the light of Gideon, Malloy, and other cases cited in those opinions holding various provisions of the Bill of Rights applicable to the States by virtue of the Fourteenth Amendment, the statements made in West and similar cases generally declaring that the Sixth Amendment does not apply to the States can no longer be regarded as the law. We hold that petitioner was entitled to be tried in accordance with the protection of the confrontation guarantee of the Sixth Amendment, and that that guarantee, like the right against compelled self-incrimination, is "to be enforced against the States under the Fourteenth Amendment according to the same standards that protect those personal rights against federal encroachment," Malloy v. Hogan. . . .

Under this Court's prior decisions, the Sixth Amendment's guarantee of confrontation and cross-examination was unquestionably denied petitioner in this case. As has been pointed out, a major reason underlying the constitutional confrontation rule is to give a defendant charged with crime an opportunity to cross-examine the witnesses against him. . . . This court has recognized the admissibility against an accused of dying declarations . . . and of testimony of a deceased witness who has testified at a former trial. Nothing we hold here is to the contrary. The case before us would be quite a different one had Phillips' statement been taken at a full-fledged hearing at which petitioner had been represented by counsel who had been given a complete and adequate opportunity to cross-examine. There are other analogous situations which might not fall within the scope of the constitutional rule requiring confrontation of witnesses. The case before us, however, does not present any situation like those mentioned above or others analogous to them. Because the transcript of Phillips' statement offered against petitioner at his trial had not been taken at a time and under circumstances affording petitioner through counsel an adequate opportunity to cross-examine Phillips, its introduction in a federal court in a criminal case against Pointer would have amounted to denial of the privilege of confrontation guaranteed by the Sixth Amendment. Since we hold that the right of an accused to be confronted with the witnesses against him must be determined by the same standards whether the right is denied in a federal or state proceeding, [380 U.S. 408] it follows that use of the transcript to convict petitioner denied him a constitutional right, and that his conviction must be reversed.

Reversed and remanded.

Source: United States Reports. Vol. 380, 400–408. Washington, D.C.: Government Printing Office, 1965.

DOCUMENT 44: *Griffin v. California* (1965)

Convicted of murder in a California court, Griffin appealed his case claiming his Fifth Amendment right of self-incrimination was violated. He had not given testimony that was used against him. Instead, he refused to answer questions that might incriminate him during the trial. The judge commented to the jury that his failure to give testimony could be interpreted as evidence of guilt. California statute provided that such comments are appropriate.

The Court agreed with Griffin's attorneys and ordered that any comment by the prosecution or the court in state or federal courts that implied a defendant's silence was evidence of guilt violated Fifth Amendment rights.

* * *

Griffin v. California, 380 U.S. 609

Mr. Justice Douglas delivered the opinion of the Court.

Petitioner was convicted of murder in the first degree after a jury trial in a California court. He did not testify at the trial on the issue of guilt, though he did testify at the separate trial on the issue of penalty. The trial court instructed the jury on the issue of guilt, stating that a defendant has a constitutional right not to testify. But it told the jury:

"As to any evidence or facts against him which the defendant can reasonably be expected to deny or explain because of facts within his knowledge, if he does not testify or if, though he does testify, he fails to deny or explain such evidence, the jury may take that failure into consideration as tending to indicate the truth of such evidence and as indicating that among the inferences that may be reasonably drawn therefrom those unfavorable to the defendant are the more probable."

It added, however, that no such inference could be drawn as to evidence respecting which he had no knowledge. It stated that failure of a defendant to deny or explain the evidence of which he had knowledge does not create a presumption of guilt nor by itself warrant an inference of guilt nor relieve the prosecution of any of its burden of proof.

Petitioner had been seen with the deceased the evening of her death, the evidence placing him with her in the alley where her body was found. The prosecutor made much of the failure of petitioner to testify. . . .

The death penalty was imposed and the California Supreme Court affirmed. The case is here on a writ of certiorari which we granted, to consider whether comment on the failure to testify violated the Self-Incrimination Clause of the Fifth Amendment which we made applicable to the States by the Fourteenth in Malloy v. Hogan, decided after the Supreme Court of California had affirmed the present conviction. . . .

The question remains whether, statute or not, the comment rule, approved by California, violates the Fifth Amendment.

We think it does. It is in substance a rule of evidence that allows the State the privilege of tendering to the jury for its consideration the failure of the accused to testify. No formal offer of proof is made as in other situations; but the prosecutor's comment and the court's acquiescence are the equivalent of an offer of evidence and its acceptance. . . .

[C]omment on the refusal to testify is a remnant of the "inquisitorial system of criminal justice," Murphy v. Waterfront Comm'n, which the Fifth Amendment outlaws. It is a penalty imposed by courts for exercising a constitutional privilege. It cuts down on the privilege by making its assertion costly. It is said, however, that the inference of guilt for failure to testify as to facts peculiarly within the accused's knowledge is in any event natural and irresistible, and that comment on the failure does not magnify that inference into a penalty for asserting a constitutional privilege. People v. Modesto. What the jury may infer, given no help from the court, is one thing. What it may infer when the court solemnizes the silence of the accused into evidence against him is quite another. . . .

We said in Malloy v. Hogan, p. 11, that "the same standards must determine whether an accused's silence in either a federal or state proceeding is justified." We take that in its literal sense and hold that the Fifth Amendment, in its direct application to the Federal Government, and in its bearing on the States by reason of the Fourteenth Amendment, forbids either comment by the prosecution on the accused's silence or instructions by the court that such silence is evidence of guilt.

Reversed.

Source: United States Reports. Vol. 380, 609–15. Washington, D.C.: Government Printing Office, 1965.

DOCUMENT 45: *Sheppard v. Maxwell* (1966)

The First Amendment guarantee of freedom of the press and the Sixth Amendment guarantee of public trial can conflict with the right of a defendant to have a fair and unbiased jury trial. With the advent of radio and then television, sensational trials could easily and powerfully be brought into citizens' homes.

The Sheppard case was made for drama. Sheppard was a successful doctor whose pregnant wife was bludgeoned to death while he slept in another room. He claimed that another person had invaded their home and committed the murder, but there was no evidence. And soon it was revealed that Sheppard was having an affair. So dramatic was this murder that it sparked two television series and a movie titled *The Fugitive.* In real life, Sheppard never fled as his character did in those dramas. Prosecutors focused on Sheppard as the likely murderer immediately. The murder drew media attention, first locally and then nationally.

A frenzy of newspaper stories appeared before his arrest showing why he was guilty and demanding his arrest. During the trial, the judge made no attempt to control the media. He reserved most of the seats in the courtroom for media. Sheppard's family had to sit in the back row. The small courtroom was filled with reporters. At times, the commotion was so intrusive that jurors could not hear testimony. Anytime court participants left the courtroom, they were attacked by groups of reporters. A room next to the jury deliberation room was turned into a TV studio. The judge maintained that he could do nothing about the press despite continual objections from the defense. The media focused on every detail that was damaging to Sheppard's case, often reporting "evidence" never introduced at the trial. Could anyone have a fair, unbiased trial in such an atmosphere? He was found guilty.

Sheppard's lawyers appealed the case. The Court ruled that Sheppard did not have a fair trial, but it went further, outlining ways in which the judge could have controlled the media. These suggestions were designed to direct courts how to handle similar trials in the future.

* * *

Sheppard v. Maxwell, 384 U.S. 333

Mr. Justice Clark delivered the opinion of the Court.

This federal habeas corpus application involves the question whether Sheppard was deprived of a fair trial in his state conviction for the second-degree murder of his wife because of the trial judge's failure to protect Sheppard sufficiently from the massive, pervasive and prejudicial publicity that attended his prosecution. . . . We have concluded that Sheppard did not receive a fair trial consistent with the Due Process Clause of the Fourteenth Amendment and, therefore, reverse the judgment.

From the outset officials focused suspicion on Sheppard. After a search of the house and premises on the morning of the tragedy, Dr. Gerber, the Coroner, is reported—and it is undenied—to have told his men, "Well, it is evident the doctor did this, so let's go get the confession out of him." He proceeded to interrogate and examine Sheppard while the latter was under sedation in his hospital room. . . .

On the 20th, the "editorial artillery" opened fire with a front-page charge that somebody is "getting away with murder." The editorial attributed the ineptness of the investigation to "friendships, relationships, hired lawyers, a husband who ought to have been subjected instantly to the same third-degree to which any other person under similar circumstances is subjected. . . ." The following day, July 21, another page-one editorial was headed: "Why No Inquest? Do It Now, Dr. Gerber." The Coroner called an inquest the same day and subpoenaed Sheppard. It was staged the next day in a school gymnasium; the Coroner presided with the County Prosecutor as his advisor and two detectives as bailiffs. In the front of the room was a long table occupied by reporters, television and radio personnel, and broadcasting equipment. The hearing was broadcast with live microphones placed at the Coroner's seat and the witness stand. A swarm of reporters and photographers attended. Sheppard was brought into the room by police who searched him in full view of several hundred spectators. Sheppard's counsel were present during the three-day inquest but were not permitted to participate. When Sheppard's chief counsel attempted to place some documents in the record, he was forcibly ejected from the room by the Coroner, who received cheers, hugs, and kisses from ladies in the audience. Sheppard was questioned for five and one-half hours about his actions on the night of the murder, his married life, and a love affair with Susan Hayes. At the end of the hearing the Coroner announced that he "could" order Sheppard held for the grand jury, but did not do so.

Throughout this period the newspapers emphasized evidence that tended to incriminate Sheppard and pointed out discrepancies in his statements to authorities. . . .

A front-page editorial on July 30 asked: "Why Isn't Sam Sheppard in Jail?" It was later titled "Quit Stalling—Bring Him In." After calling Sheppard "the most unusual murder suspect ever seen around these parts" the article said that "[e]xcept for some superficial questioning during Coroner Sam Gerber's inquest he has been scot-free of any official grilling. . . ." It asserted that he was "surrounded by an iron curtain of protection [and] concealment."

That night at 10 o'clock Sheppard was arrested at his father's home on a charge of murder. He was taken to the Bay Village City Hall where hundreds of people, newscasters, photographers and reporters were awaiting his arrival. . . .

With this background the case came on for trial two weeks before the November general election at which the chief prosecutor was a candidate for common pleas judge and the trial judge, Judge Blythin, was a candidate to succeed himself. Twenty-five days before the case was set, 75 veniremen were called as prospective jurors. All three Cleveland newspapers published the names and addresses of the veniremen. As a consequence, anonymous letters and telephone calls, as well as calls from friends, regarding the impending prosecution were received by all of the prospective jurors. . . .

The courtroom in which the trial was held measured 26 by 48 feet. A long temporary table was set up inside the bar, in back of the single counsel table. It ran the width of the courtroom, parallel to the bar railing, with one end less than three feet from the jury box. Approximately 20 representatives of newspapers and wire services were assigned seats at this table by the court. Behind the bar railing there were four rows of benches. These seats were likewise assigned by the court for the entire trial. . . .

All of these arrangements with the news media and their massive coverage of the trial continued during the entire nine weeks of the trial. The courtroom remained crowded to capacity with representatives of news media. Their movement in and out of the courtroom often caused so much confusion that, despite the loudspeaker system installed in the courtroom, it was difficult for the witnesses and counsel to be heard. . . .

The jurors themselves were constantly exposed to the news media. Every juror, except one, testified at voir dire to reading about the case in the Cleveland papers or to having heard broadcasts about it. Seven of the 12 jurors who rendered the verdict had one or more Cleveland papers delivered in their home; the remaining jurors were not interrogated on the point. . . .

We now reach the conduct of the trial. While the intense publicity continued unabated, it is sufficient to relate only the more flagrant episodes: . . .

2. On the second day of voir dire examination a debate was staged and broadcast live over WHK radio. The participants, newspaper reporters, accused Sheppard's counsel of throwing roadblocks in the way of the prosecution and asserted that Sheppard conceded his guilt by hiring a prominent criminal lawyer. Sheppard's counsel objected to this broadcast and requested a continuance, but the judge denied the motion. . . .

4. [T]he jury viewed the scene of the murder on the first day of the trial. Hundreds of reporters, cameramen and onlookers were there, and one representative of the news media was permitted to accompany the jury while it inspected the Sheppard home. The time of the jury's visit was revealed so far in advance that one of the newspapers was able to rent a helicopter and fly over the house taking pictures of the jurors on their tour. . . .

6. On November 24, a story appeared under an eight-column headline: "Sam Called A 'Jekyll-Hyde' By Marilyn, Cousin To Testify." It related that Marilyn had recently told friends that Sheppard was a "Dr. Jekyll and Mr. Hyde" character. No such testimony was ever produced at the trial. The story went on to announce: "The prosecution has a 'bombshell witness' on tap who will testify to Dr. Sam's display of fiery temper—countering the defense claim that the defendant is a gentle phy-

sician with an even disposition." Defense counsel made motions for change of venue, continuance and mistrial, but they were denied. No action was taken by the court. . . .

9. After the case was submitted to the jury, it was sequestered for its deliberations, which took five days and four nights. After the verdict, defense counsel ascertained that the jurors had been allowed to make telephone calls to their homes every day while they were sequestered at the hotel. Although the telephones had been removed from the jurors' rooms, the jurors were permitted to use the phones in the bailiffs' rooms. The calls were placed by the jurors themselves; no record was kept of the jurors who made calls, the telephone numbers or the parties called. The bailiffs sat in the room where they could hear only the jurors' end of the conversation. The court had not instructed the bailiffs to prevent such calls. By a subsequent motion, defense counsel urged that this ground alone warranted a new trial, but the motion was overruled and no evidence was taken on the question.

The principle that justice cannot survive behind walls of silence has long been reflected in the "Anglo-American distrust for secret trials." A responsible press has always been regarded as the handmaiden of effective judicial administration, especially in the criminal field. Its function in this regard is documented by an impressive record of service over several centuries.

But the Court has also pointed out that "[l]egal trials are not like elections, to be won through the use of the meeting-hall, the radio, and the newspaper." Bridges v. California, supra, at 271. And the Court has insisted that no one be punished for a crime without "a charge fairly made and fairly tried in a public tribunal free of prejudice, passion, excitement, and tyrannical power." Chambers v. Florida (1940). But it must not be allowed to divert the trial from the "very purpose of a court system . . . to adjudicate controversies, both criminal and civil, in the calmness and solemnity of the courtroom according to legal procedures." Cox v. Louisiana (1965) (BLACK, J., dissenting). Among these "legal procedures" is the requirement that the jury's verdict be based on evidence received in open court, not from outside sources. . . .

For months the virulent publicity about Sheppard and the murder had made the case notorious. Charges and countercharges were aired in the news media besides those for which Sheppard was called to trial. . . . Furthermore, the trial began two weeks before a hotly contested election at which both Chief Prosecutor Mahon and Judge Blythin were candidates for judgeships.

In light of this background, we believe that the arrangements made by the judge with the news media caused Sheppard to be deprived of that "judicial serenity and calm to which [he] was entitled." Estes v. Texas, supra, at 536. The fact is that bedlam reigned at the courthouse during the trial and newsmen took over practically the entire courtroom, hounding most of the participants in the trial, especially Sheppard. . . .

Much of the material printed or broadcast during the trial was never heard from the witness stand, such as the charges that Sheppard had purposely impeded the murder investigation and must be guilty since he had hired a prominent criminal lawyer; that Sheppard was a perjurer; that he had sexual relations with numerous women; that his slain wife had characterized him as a "Jekyll-Hyde"; that he was "a bare-faced liar" because of his testimony as to police treatment; and, finally, that a woman convict claimed Sheppard to be the father of her illegitimate child. . . .

Nor is there doubt that this deluge of publicity reached at least some of the jury. On the only occasion that the jury was queried, two jurors admitted in open court to hearing the highly inflammatory charge that a prison inmate claimed Sheppard as the father of her illegitimate child. . . .

The court's fundamental error is compounded by the holding that it lacked power to control the publicity about the trial. From the very inception of the proceedings the judge announced that neither he nor anyone else could restrict prejudicial news accounts. . . .

The carnival atmosphere at trial could easily have been avoided since the courtroom and courthouse premises are subject to the control of the court. . . . [T]he presence of the press at judicial proceedings must be limited when it is apparent that the accused might otherwise be prejudiced or disadvantaged. Bearing in mind the massive pretrial publicity, the judge should have adopted stricter rules governing the use of the courtroom by newsmen, as Sheppard's counsel requested. The number of reporters in the courtroom itself could have been limited at the first sign that their presence would disrupt the trial. They certainly should not have been placed inside the bar. Furthermore, the judge should have more closely regulated the conduct of newsmen in the courtroom. For instance, the judge belatedly asked them not to handle and photograph trial exhibits lying on the counsel table during recesses.

Secondly, the court should have insulated the witnesses. All of the newspapers and radio stations apparently interviewed prospective witnesses at will, and in many instances disclosed their testimony.

Thirdly, the court should have made some effort to control the release of leads, information, and gossip to the press by police officers, witnesses, and the counsel for both sides. Much of the information thus disclosed was inaccurate, leading to groundless rumors and confusion. . . .

Defense counsel immediately brought to the court's attention the tremendous amount of publicity in the Cleveland press that "misrepresented entirely the testimony" in the case. Under such circumstances, the judge should have at least warned the newspapers to check the accuracy of their accounts. And it is obvious that the judge should have further sought to alleviate this problem by imposing control over the statements made to the news media by counsel, witnesses, and especially the Coroner and police officers. The prosecution repeatedly made evidence available to the news media which was never offered in the trial. . . .

[T]he court could also have requested the appropriate city and county officials to promulgate a regulation with respect to dissemination of information about the case by their employees. In addition, reporters who wrote or broadcast prejudicial stories, could have been warned as to the impropriety of publishing material not introduced in the proceedings. . . .

If publicity during the proceedings threatens the fairness of the trial, a new trial should be ordered. But we must remember that reversals are but palliatives; the cure lies in those remedial measures that will prevent the prejudice at its inception. The courts must take such steps by rule and regulation that will protect their processes from prejudicial outside interferences. Neither prosecutors, counsel for defense, the accused, witnesses, court staff nor enforcement officers coming under the jurisdiction of the court should be permitted to frustrate its function. Collaboration between counsel and the press as to information affecting the fairness of a criminal trial is not only subject to regulation, but is highly censurable and worthy of disciplinary measures.

Since the state trial judge did not fulfill his duty to protect Sheppard from the inherently prejudicial publicity which saturated the community and to control disruptive influences in the courtroom, we must reverse the denial of the habeas petition. The case is remanded to the District Court with instructions to issue the writ and order that Sheppard be released from custody unless the State puts him to its charges again within a reasonable time.

It is so ordered.

Source: United States Reports. Vol. 384, 333–49. Washington, D.C.: Government Printing Office, 1966.

DOCUMENT 46: *Miranda v. Arizona* (1966)

In requiring the right to counsel during the police questioning, *Escobedo v. Illinois* (see Document 42) left police unsure of what procedure would be considered constitutional. In *Miranda v. Arizona*, the Court provided very specific guidelines for police. The four-part warning required police to inform suspects that they had a right to an attorney; if they could not afford one, one would be appointed; they did not have to make any statements; and any statements made could be used against them in a trial.

That warning made this case one of the most famous in the history of the Court. Every TV and movie depicting an arrest includes the statement that police need to make before any interrogation of a suspect. The Court's reasoning was consistent with *Escobedo*, but the protection awarded to the accused include both self-incriminating statements and the right to an attorney. Thus both protections for the Fifth and Sixth Amendments were extended to pre-trial investigations and required of states. The Court added that Congress and the states could find other remedies to protect the rights of accused, but the warning was a minimum and an essential ingredient in any other remedy. The Court also ruled that any evidence gained in violation of this ruling could not be admitted at trial.

This decision caused considerable controversy. Police warned that confessions would be nonexistent and their investigations would be inhibited. Others argued that the Court was exceeding its authority and making legislation. In a strongly worded dissent, three justices stated that this decision "has no significant support in the history of the privilege or in the language of the Fifth Amendment."

Miranda v. Arizona is the lead case of four that were considered together. All had similar circumstances in that suspects were questioned by police in private and without counsel of an attorney.

* * *

Miranda v. Arizona, 384 U.S. 436

Mr. Chief Justice Warren delivered the opinion of the Court.

The cases before us raise questions which go to the roots of our concepts of American criminal jurisprudence: the restraints society must observe consistent with the Federal Constitution in prosecuting individuals for crime. More specifically, we deal with the admissibility of statements obtained from an individual who is subjected to custodial police interrogation and the necessity for procedures which assure that the individual is accorded his privilege under the Fifth Amendment to the Constitution not to be compelled to incriminate himself. . . .

Our holding will be spelled out with some specificity in the pages which follow, but, briefly stated, it is this: the prosecution may not use statements, whether exculpatory or inculpatory, stemming from custodial interrogation of the defendant unless it demonstrates the use of procedural safeguards effective to secure the privilege against self-incrimination. By custodial interrogation, we mean questioning initiated by law enforcement officers after a person has been taken into custody or otherwise deprived of his freedom of action in any significant way. As for the procedural safeguards to be employed, unless other fully effective means are devised to inform accused persons of their right of silence and to assure a continuous opportunity to exercise it, the following measures are required. Prior to any questioning, the person must be warned that he has a right to remain silent, that any statement he does make may be used as evidence against him, and that he has a right to the presence of an attorney, either retained or appointed. The defendant may waive effectuation of these rights, provided the waiver is made voluntarily, knowingly and intelligently. If, however, he indicates in any manner and at any stage of the process that he wishes to consult with an attorney before speaking, there can be no questioning. Likewise, if the individual is alone and indicates in any manner that he does not wish to be interrogated, the police may not question him. The mere fact that he may have answered some questions or volunteered some statements on his own does not deprive him of the right to refrain from answering any further inquiries until he has consulted with an attorney and thereafter consents to be questioned.

The constitutional issue we decide in each of these cases is the admissibility of statements obtained from a defendant questioned while in custody or otherwise deprived of his freedom of action in any significant way. In each, the defendant was questioned by police officers, detectives, or a prosecuting attorney in a room in which he was cut off from the outside world. In none of these cases was the defendant given a full and effective warning of his rights at the outset of the interrogation process. In all the cases, the questioning elicited oral admissions, and in three of them, signed statements as well which were admitted at their trials. They all thus share salient features—incommunicado interrogation of individuals in a police-dominated atmosphere, resulting in self-incriminating statements without full warnings of constitutional rights. . . .

Again we stress that the modern practice of in-custody interrogation is psychologically, rather than physically, oriented. As we have stated before, "Since Chambers v. Florida, this Court has recognized that coercion can be mental as well as physical, and that the blood of the accused is not the only hallmark of an unconstitutional inquisition. . . ." A valuable source of information about present police practices, however, may be found in various police manuals and texts which document procedures employed with success in the past, and which recommend various other effective tactics. These texts are used by law enforcement agencies themselves as guides. It should be noted that these texts professedly present the most enlightened and effective means presently used to obtain statements through custodial interrogation. By considering these texts and other data, it is possible to describe procedures observed and noted around the country.

The officers are told by the manuals that the "principal psychological factor contributing to a successful interrogation is privacy—being alone with the person under interrogation." . . .

To highlight the isolation and unfamiliar surroundings, the manuals instruct the police to display an air of confidence in the suspect's guilt and, from outward appearance, to maintain only an interest in confirming certain details. The guilt of the subject is to be posited as a fact. The interrogator should direct his comments toward the reasons why the subject committed the act, rather than court failure by asking the subject whether he did it. . . . These tactics are designed to put the subject in a psychological state where his story is but an elaboration of what the police purport to know already—that he is guilty. Explanations to the contrary are dismissed and discouraged.

The texts thus stress that the major qualities an interrogator should possess are patience and perseverance. . . .

When the techniques described above prove unavailing, the texts recommend they be alternated with a show of some hostility. . . .

The manuals also contain instructions for police on how to handle the individual who refuses to discuss the matter entirely, or who asks for an attorney or relatives. The examiner is to concede him the right to remain silent. "This usually has a very undermining effect. First of all, he is disappointed in his expectation of an unfavorable reaction on the part of the interrogator. Secondly, a concession of this right to remain silent impresses the subject with the apparent fairness of his interrogator." After this psychological conditioning, however, the officer is told to point out the incriminating significance of the suspect's refusal to talk:

"Joe, you have a right to remain silent. That's your privilege, and I'm the last person in the world who'll try to take it away from you. If that's the way you want to leave this, O.K. But let me ask you this. Suppose you were in my shoes, and I were in yours, and you called me in to ask me about this, and I told you, "I don't want to answer any of your questions." You'd think I had something to hide, and you'd probably be right in thinking that. That's exactly what I'll have to think about you, and so will everybody else. So let's sit here and talk this whole thing over."

Few will persist in their initial refusal to talk, it is said, if this monologue is employed correctly.

In the event that the subject wishes to speak to a relative or an attorney, the following advice is tendered:

"[T]he interrogator should respond by suggesting that the subject first tell the truth to the interrogator himself, rather than get anyone else involved in the matter. If the request is for an attorney, the interrogator may suggest that the subject save himself or his family the expense of any such professional service, particularly if he is innocent of the offense under investigation. The interrogator may also add, 'Joe, I'm only looking for the truth, and if you're telling the truth, that's it. You can handle this by yourself.' "

From these representative samples of interrogation techniques, the setting prescribed by the manuals and observed in practice becomes clear. In essence, it is this: to be alone with the subject is essential to prevent distraction and to deprive him of any outside support. The aura of confidence in his guilt undermines his will to resist. He merely confirms the preconceived story the police seek to have him describe. Patience and persistence, at times relentless questioning, are employed. To obtain a confession, the interrogator must "patiently maneuver himself or his quarry into a position from which the desired objective may be attained." When normal procedures fail to produce the needed result, the police may resort to deceptive stratagems such as giving false legal advice. It is important to keep the subject off balance, for example, by trading on his insecurity about himself or his surroundings. The police then persuade, trick, or cajole him out of exercising his constitutional rights. . . .

It is obvious that such an interrogation environment is created for no purpose other than to subjugate the individual to the will of his examiner. This atmosphere carries its own badge of intimidation. To be sure, this is not physical intimidation, but it is equally destructive of human dignity. The current practice of incommunicado interrogation is at odds with one of our Nation's most cherished principles—that the individual may not be compelled to incriminate himself. Unless adequate protective devices are employed to dispel the compulsion inherent in custodial surroundings, no statement obtained from the defendant can truly be the product of his free choice. . . .

It is impossible for us to foresee the potential alternatives for protecting the privilege which might be devised by Congress or the States in the exercise of their creative rulemaking capacities. Therefore, we cannot say that the Constitution necessarily requires adherence to any particular solution for the inherent compulsions of the interrogation process as it is presently conducted. Our decision in no way creates a constitutional straitjacket which will handicap sound efforts at reform, nor is it intended to have this effect. We encourage Congress and the States to continue their laudable search for increasingly effective ways of protecting the rights of the individual while promoting efficient enforcement of our criminal laws. However, unless we are shown other procedures which are at least as effective in apprising accused persons of their right of silence and in assuring a continuous opportunity to exercise it, the following safeguards must be observed.

At the outset, if a person in custody is to be subjected to interrogation, he must first be informed in clear and unequivocal terms that he has the right to remain silent. . . .

More important, whatever the background of the person interrogated, a warning at the time of the interrogation is indispensable to overcome its pressures and to insure that the individual knows he is free to exercise the privilege at that point in time.

The warning of the right to remain silent must be accompanied by the explanation that anything said can and will be used against the individual in court. This warning is needed in order to make him aware not only of the privilege, but also of the consequences of forgoing it. . . .

The circumstances surrounding in-custody interrogation can operate very quickly to overbear the will of one merely made aware of his privilege by his interrogators. Therefore, the right to have counsel present at the interrogation is indispensable to the protection of the Fifth Amendment privilege under the system we delineate today. . . .

The presence of counsel at the interrogation may serve several significant subsidiary functions, as well. If the accused decides to talk to his interrogators, the assistance of counsel can mitigate the dangers of untrustworthiness. With a lawyer present, the likelihood that the police will practice coercion is reduced, and, if coercion is nevertheless exercised, the lawyer can testify to it in court. The presence of a lawyer can also help to guarantee that the accused gives a fully accurate statement to the police, and that the statement is rightly reported by the prosecution at trial.

An individual need not make a pre-interrogation request for a lawyer. While such request affirmatively secures his right to have one, his failure to ask for a lawyer does not constitute a waiver. No effective waiver of the right to counsel during interrogation can be recognized unless specifically made after the warnings we here delineate have been given. . . .

Accordingly, we hold that an individual held for interrogation must be clearly informed that he has the right to consult with a lawyer and to have the lawyer with him during interrogation under the system for protecting the privilege we delineate today. As with the warnings of the right to remain silent and that anything stated can be used in evidence against him, this warning is an absolute prerequisite to interrogation. . . .

If an individual indicates that he wishes the assistance of counsel before any interrogation occurs, the authorities cannot rationally ignore or deny his request on the basis that the individual does not have or cannot afford a retained attorney. The financial ability of the individual has no relationship to the scope of the rights involved here. The privilege against self-incrimination secured by the Constitution applies to all individuals. The need for counsel in order to protect the privilege exists for the indigent as well as the affluent. . . .

In order fully to apprise a person interrogated of the extent of his rights under this system, then, it is necessary to warn him not only that he has the right to consult with an attorney, but also that, if he is indigent, a lawyer will be appointed to represent him. Without this additional warning, the admonition of the right to consult with counsel would often be understood as meaning only that he can consult with a lawyer if he has one or has the funds to obtain one. . . .

Once warnings have been given, the subsequent procedure is clear. If the individual indicates in any manner, at any time prior to or during questioning, that he wishes to remain silent, the interrogation must cease. . . . If the individual states that he wants an attorney, the interrogation must cease until an attorney is present. At that time, the individual must have an opportunity to confer with the attorney and to have him present during any subsequent questioning. If the individual cannot obtain an attorney and he indicates that he wants one before speaking to police, they must respect his decision to remain silent. . . .

If the interrogation continues without the presence of an attorney and a statement is taken, a heavy burden rests on the government to demonstrate that the defendant knowingly and intelligently waived his privilege against self-incrimination and his right to retained or appointed counsel. . . .

The warning required and the waiver necessary in accordance with our opinion today are, in the absence of a fully effective equivalent, prerequisites to the admissibility of any statement made by a defendant. . . .

The principles announced today deal with the protection which must be given to the privilege against self-incrimination when the individual is first subjected to police interrogation while in custody at the station or otherwise deprived of his freedom of action in any significant way. It is at this point that our adversary system of criminal proceedings commences, distinguishing itself at the outset from the inquisitorial system recognized in some countries. Under the system of warnings we delineate today, or under any other system which may be devised and found effective, the safeguards to be erected about the privilege must come into play at this point. . . .

In dealing with statements obtained through interrogation, we do not purport to find all confessions inadmissible. Confessions remain a proper element in law enforcement. Any statement given freely and voluntarily without any compelling influences is, of course, admissible in evidence. . . .

A recurrent argument made in these cases is that society's need for interrogation outweighs the privilege. This argument is not unfamiliar to this Court. The whole thrust of our foregoing discussion demonstrates that the Constitution has prescribed the rights of the individual when confronted with the power of government when it provided in the Fifth

Amendment that an individual cannot be compelled to be a witness against himself. That right cannot be abridged. . . .

If the individual desires to exercise his privilege, he has the right to do so. This is not for the authorities to decide. An attorney may advise his client not to talk to police until he has had an opportunity to investigate the case, or he may wish to be present with his client during any police questioning. In doing so an attorney is merely exercising the good professional judgment he has been taught. This is not cause for considering the attorney a menace to law enforcement. He is merely carrying out what he is sworn to do under his oath—to protect to the extent of his ability the rights of his client. In fulfilling this responsibility, the attorney plays a vital role in the administration of criminal justice under our Constitution.

In announcing these principles, we are not unmindful of the burdens which law enforcement officials must bear, often under trying circumstances. We also fully recognize the obligation of all citizens to aid in enforcing the criminal laws. This Court, while protecting individual rights, has always given ample latitude to law enforcement agencies in the legitimate exercise of their duties. The limits we have placed on the interrogation process should not constitute an undue interference with a proper system of law enforcement. As we have noted, our decision does not in any way preclude police from carrying out their traditional investigatory functions. . . .

Because of the nature of the problem and because of its recurrent significance in numerous cases, we have to this point discussed the relationship of the Fifth Amendment privilege to police interrogation without specific concentration on the facts of the cases before us. We turn now to these facts to consider the application to these cases of the constitutional principles discussed above. In each instance, we have concluded that statements were obtained from the defendant under circumstances that did not meet constitutional standards for protection of the privilege.

Therefore, in accordance with the foregoing, the judgments of the Supreme Court of Arizona in No. 759, of the New York Court of Appeals in No. 760, and of the Court of Appeals for the Ninth Circuit in No. 761, are reversed. The judgment of the Supreme Court of California in No. 584 is affirmed.

It is so ordered.

Source: United States Reports. Vol. 384, 436–545. Washington, D.C.: Government Printing Office, 1967.

DOCUMENT 47: *Parker v. Gladden* (1966)

Parker was convicted of second-degree murder and sentenced to life imprisonment. After his conviction, the trial court found that a bailiff assigned to shepherd the sequestered jury had made prejudicial comments to several jurors on several occassions.

The Court decided that the Sixth Amendment right to an impartial jury applied to the states and reversed his conviction. In a separate argument, Parker's lawyers argued that the comments by the bailiff constituted testimony without the accused having the opportunity to confront the witness. The Court agreed with that violation also.

* * *

Parker v. Gladden, 385 U.S. 363

Petitioner, after his conviction for second degree murder . . . filed a petition for post-conviction relief. . . . At a hearing on the petition the trial court found that a court bailiff assigned to shepherd the sequestered jury, which sat for eight days, stated to one of the jurors in the presence of others while the jury was out walking on a public sidewalk: "Oh that wicked fellow [petitioner], he is guilty"; and on another occasion said to another juror under similar circumstances, "If there is anything wrong [in finding petitioner guilty] the Supreme Court will correct it." Both statements were overheard by at least one regular juror or an alternate. The trial court found "that the unauthorized communication was prejudicial and that such conduct materially affected the rights of the [petitioner]." The Supreme Court of Oregon reversed, finding that "the bailiff's misconduct did not deprive [petitioner] of a constitutionally correct trial." . . . [W]e have concluded that the judgment must be reversed.

We believe that the statements of the bailiff to the jurors are controlled by the command of the Sixth Amendment, made applicable to the States through the Due Process Clause of the Fourteenth Amendment. It guarantees that "the accused shall enjoy the right to a . . . trial, by an impartial jury . . . [and] be confronted with the witnesses against him. . . ." As we said in Turner v. Louisiana, "the 'evidence developed' against a defendant shall come from the witness stand in a public courtroom where there is full judicial protection of the defendant's right of confrontation, of cross-examination, and of counsel." Here there is dispute neither as to what the bailiff, an officer of the State, said nor that when he said it he was not subjected to confrontation, cross-examination or other safeguards guaranteed to the petitioner. Rather, his expressions were "private talk," tending to reach the jury by "outside influence." Patterson v. Colorado. We have followed the "undeviating rule," Sheppard v. Maxwell, that the rights of confrontation and cross-examination are among the fundamental requirements of a constitutionally fair trial.

The State suggests that no prejudice was shown and that no harm could have resulted because 10 members of the jury testified that they had not heard the bailiff's statements and that Oregon law permits a verdict of guilty by 10 affirmative votes. This overlooks the fact that the official character of the bailiff—as an officer of the court as well as the State—beyond question carries great weight with a jury which he had been shepherding for eight days and nights. Moreover, the jurors deliberated for 26 hours, indicating a difference among them as to the guilt of petitioner. Finally, one of the jurors testified that she was prejudiced by the statements, which supports the trial court's finding "that the unauthorized communication was prejudicial and that such conduct materially affected the rights of the defendant." This finding was not upset by Oregon's highest court. Aside from this, we believe that the unauthorized conduct of the bailiff "involves such a probability that prejudice will result that it is deemed inherently lacking in due process," Estes v. Texas. As we said in Turner v. Louisiana, supra, "it would be blinking reality not to recognize the extreme prejudice inherent" in such statements that reached at least three members of the jury and one alternate member. The State says that 10 of the jurors testified that they had not heard the statements of the bailiff. This, however, ignores the testimony that one of the statements was made to an unidentified juror, which, including Mrs. Inwards and Mrs. Drake, makes three. In any event, petitioner was entitled to be tried by 12, not 9 or even 10, impartial and unprejudiced jurors.

Reversed.

Source: United States Reports. Vol. 385, 363–69. Washington, D.C.: Government Printing Office, 1967.

DOCUMENT 48: *Klopfer v. North Carolina* (1967)

In *Klopfer v. North Carolina*, the Supreme Court notes that the right to a speedy trial is guaranteed by the Sixth Amendment and by the Constitutions of all fifty states. Thus there is no debate about the right to a speedy trial being a fundamental right.

But what treatment is covered by the right to a speedy trial? Klopfer was charged with criminal trespass for not leaving a public restaurant when so ordered. His trial was prompt, but the jury was unable to reach a verdict and the judge declared a mistrial. The prosecutor indicated a desire to retry, but eighteen months later no trial was scheduled. Klopfer filed motions to request whether the state intended to prosecute him. Under a unique Florida law, the prosecutor moved for permission to take a *"nolle prosequi* with leave," which discharges the accused from custody but leaves him subject to presecution at any future time desired by the prosecutor. Klopfer's attorneys argued that such a delay denied him a speedy trial.

The Court agreed and used this case to add the right to a speedy trial to the list of rights incorporated into the Fourteenth Amendment and, thereby, required of all states.

* * *

Klopfer v. North Carolina, 386 U.S. 213

Mr. Chief Justice Warren delivered the opinion of the Court.

The question involved in this case is whether a State may indefinitely postpone prosecution on an indictment without stated justification over the objection of an accused who has been discharged from custody. . . .

[I]n the present case, neither the court below nor the solicitor offers any reason why the case of petitioner should have been nolle prossed except for the suggestion of the Supreme Court that the solicitor, having tried the defendant once and having obtained only a mistrial, "may have concluded that another go at it would not be worth the time and expense of another effort." . . .

The consequence of this extraordinary criminal procedure is made apparent by the case before the Court. A defendant indicted for a misdemeanor may be denied an opportunity to exonerate himself in the discretion of the solicitor and held subject to trial, over his objection, throughout the unlimited period in which the solicitor may restore the case to the calendar. During that period, there is no means by which he can obtain a dismissal or have the case restored to the calendar for trial. In spite of this result, both the Supreme Court and the Attorney General state as a fact, and rely upon it for affirmance in this case, that this procedure, as applied to the petitioner, placed no limitations upon him, and was in no way violative of his rights. With this we cannot agree. . . .

The petitioner is not relieved of the limitations placed upon his liberty by this prosecution merely because its suspension permits him to go "whithersoever he will." The pendency of the indictment may subject him to public scorn and deprive him of employment, and almost certainly will force curtailment of his speech, associations and participation in unpopular causes. By indefinitely prolonging this oppression, as well as the "anxiety and concern accompanying public accusation," the criminal procedure condoned in this case by the Supreme Court of North Carolina clearly denies the petitioner the right to a speedy trial which we hold is guaranteed to him by the Sixth Amendment of the Constitution of the United States. . . .

We hold here that the right to a speedy trial is as fundamental as any of the rights secured by the Sixth Amendment. That right has its roots at the very foundation of our English law heritage. Its first articulation in modern jurisprudence appears to have been made in Magna Carta (1215), wherein it was written, "We will sell to no man, we will not deny or defer to any man either justice or right"; but evidence of recognition of the right to speedy justice in even earlier times is found in the Assize of Clarendon (1166). By the late thirteenth century, justices, armed with commissions of gaol [jail] delivery . . . and/or were visiting the countryside three times a year. These justices, Sir Edward Coke wrote in Part II of his Institutes,

have not suffered the prisoner to be long detained, but, at their next coming, have given the prisoner full and speedy justice, . . . without detaining him long in prison. . . .

[W]hen George Mason drafted the first of the colonial bills of rights, he set forth a principle of Magna Carta. . . . "[I]n all capital or criminal prosecutions," the Virginia Declaration of Rights of 1776 provided, "a man hath a right . . . to a speedy trial. . . ." That this right was considered fundamental at this early period in our history is evidenced by its guarantee in the constitutions of several of the States of the new nation, as well as by its prominent position in the Sixth Amendment. Today, each of the 50 States guarantees the right to a speedy trial to its citizens.

The history of the right to a speedy trial and its reception in this country clearly establish that it is one of the most basic rights preserved by our Constitution.

For the reasons stated above, the judgment must be reversed and remanded for proceedings not inconsistent with the opinion of the Court.

It is so ordered.

Source: United States Reports. Vol. 386, 213–27. Washington, D.C.: Government Printing Office, 1967.

DOCUMENT 49: *In Re Gault* (1967)

Juvenile courts were started in the early part of the twentieth century to create an alternative to punishing youth with hardened adult criminals. The courts were informal; usually the judge held a casual conference with the offender and the youth's parents to determine what happened and how to treat the youth. Public jury trials were not required. Court staff specialists, including doctors, psychologists, and social workers, were available for consultation. However, by midcentury the juvenile courts were widely criticized. Charges included poorly educated judges; enormous case loads, causing "rushed justice"; insufficient funds; and nonexistent staff specialists. The "reform schools" to which offenders were sent were little more than jails for youth.

Gerald Gault was a 15-year-old charged with making obscene phone calls. He was removed from his home by police without notice to his parents, questioned, and held. Shortly thereafter, he was charged with being a "delinquent minor." At his hearing, the complaining witness did not appear. He was judged to be delinquent and sentenced to the State Industrial School for the rest of minority, six years. Had he been an adult, the maximum penalty permitted would have been $5 to $50 and imprisonment for not more than two months.

Gault's parents filed petitions and appeals that led to the Supreme Court. It ruled that Gault was denied due process guaranteed under the Fourteenth Amendment. This decision revolutionized the treatment of minors in juvenile courts throughout the nation. It listed specific due process rights that must be incorporated into juvenile procedures.

* * *

In Re Gault, 387 U.S. 1

Mr. Justice Fortas delivered the opinion of the Court. . . .

We consider only the problems presented to us by this case. These relate to the proceedings by which a determination is made as to whether a juvenile is a "delinquent" as a result of alleged misconduct on his part, with the consequence that he may be committed to a state institution. As to these proceedings, there appears to be little current dissent from the proposition that the Due Process Clause has a role to play. The problem is to ascertain the precise impact of the due process requirement upon such proceedings.

From the inception of the juvenile court system, wide differences have been tolerated—indeed insisted upon—between the procedural rights accorded to adults and those of juveniles. In practically all jurisdictions, there are rights granted to adults which are withheld from juveniles. In addition to the specific problems involved in the present case, for example, it has been held that the juvenile is not entitled to bail, to indictment by grand jury, to a public trial or to trial by jury. It is frequent practice that rules governing the arrest and interrogation of adults by the police are not observed in the case of juveniles.

The history and theory underlying this development are well-known, but a recapitulation is necessary for purposes of this opinion. The Juvenile Court movement began in this country at the end of the last century. From the juvenile court statute adopted in Illinois in 1899, the system has spread to every State in the Union, the District of Columbia, and Puerto Rico. The constitutionality of Juvenile Court laws has been sustained in over 40 jurisdictions against a variety of attacks.

The early reformers were appalled by adult procedures and penalties, and by the fact that children could be given long prison sentences and mixed in jails with hardened criminals. They were profoundly convinced that society's duty to the child could not be confined by the concept of justice alone. They believed that society's role was not to ascertain whether the child was "guilty" or "innocent," but "What is he, how has he become what he is, and what had best be done in his interest and in the interest of the state to save him from a downward career." The child essentially good, as they saw it was to be made "to feel that he is the object of [the state's] care and solicitude," not that he was under arrest or on trial. The rules of criminal procedure were therefore altogether inapplicable. The apparent rigidities, technicalities, and harshness which they observed in both substantive and procedural criminal law were therefore to be discarded. The idea of crime and punishment was to be abandoned. The child was to be "treated" and "rehabilitated" and the procedures, from apprehension through institutionalization, were to be "clinical" rather than punitive. . . .

Failure to observe the fundamental requirements of due process has resulted in instances, which might have been avoided, of unfairness to individuals and inadequate or inaccurate findings of fact and unfortunate prescriptions of remedy. Due process of law is the primary and indispensable foundation of individual freedom. It is the basic and essential term in the social compact which defines the rights of the individual and delimits the powers which the state may exercise. . . .

It is claimed that juveniles obtain benefits from the special procedures applicable to them which more than offset the disadvantages of denial of the substance of normal due process. As we shall discuss, the observance of due process standards, intelligently and not ruthlessly administered, will not compel the States to abandon or displace any of the substantive benefits of the juvenile process. But it is important, we think, that the claimed benefits of the juvenile process should be candidly appraised. . . .

In view of this, it would be extraordinary if our Constitution did not require the procedural regularity and the exercise of care implied in the phrase "due process." Under our Constitution, the condition of being a boy does not justify a kangaroo court. . . . The essential difference between Gerald's case and a normal criminal case is that safeguards available to adults were discarded in Gerald's case. The summary procedure as well as the long commitment was possible because Gerald was 15 years of age instead of over 18. . . .

Due process of law requires notice of the sort we have described—that is, notice which would be deemed constitutionally adequate in a civil or criminal proceeding. It does not allow a hearing to be held in which a youth's freedom and his parents' right to his custody are at stake without giving them timely notice, in advance of the hearing, of the specific issues that they must meet. Nor, in the circumstances of this case, can it reasonably be said that the requirement of notice was waived. . . .

We conclude that the Due Process Clause of the Fourteenth Amendment requires that in respect of proceedings to determine delinquency which may result in commitment to an institution in which the juvenile's freedom is curtailed, the child and his parents must be notified of the child's right to be represented by counsel retained by them, or if they are unable to afford counsel, that counsel will be appointed to represent the child.

We conclude that the constitutional privilege against self-incrimination is applicable in the case of juveniles as it is with respect to adults. We appreciate that special problems may arise with respect to waiver of the privilege by or on behalf of children, and that there may well be some differences in technique—but not in principle—depending upon the age of the child and the presence and competence of parents. The participation of counsel will, of course, assist the police, Juvenile Courts and appellate tribunals in administering the privilege. If counsel was not present for some permissible reason when an admission was obtained, the greatest care must be taken to assure that the admission was voluntary, in the sense not only that it was not coerced or suggested, but also that it was not the product of ignorance of rights or of adolescent fantasy, fright or despair.

For the reasons stated, the judgment of the Supreme Court of Arizona is reversed and the cause remanded for further proceedings not inconsistent with this opinion.

It is so ordered.

Source: United States Reports. Vol. 387, 1–81. Washington, D.C.: Government Printing Office, 1967.

DOCUMENT 50: *Washington v. Texas* (1967)

Jackie Washington and another man were tried separately for a fatal shooting. His co-participant was tried and convicted of murder. During Washington's trial, his co-participant was not allowed to testify under Texas laws that barred a participant accused of a crime from testifying for his co-participant.

The Court found that the barred testimony would have been relevant in Washington's trial and could find no justification for the Texas laws that barred his testimony. In this decision, the Court ruled that Washington had been denied the right to obtain witnesses in his favor and also ruled that that right was required of states under the due process clause of the Fourteenth Amendment.

* * *

Washington v. Texas, 388 U.S. 14

Mr. Chief Justice Warren delivered the opinion of the Court.

We granted certiorari in this case to determine whether the right of a defendant in a criminal case under the Sixth Amendment to have compulsory process for obtaining witnesses in his favor is applicable to the States through the Fourteenth Amendment, and whether that right was violated by a state procedural statute providing that persons charged as principals, accomplices, or accessories in the same crime cannot be introduced as witnesses for each other. . . .

We have not previously been called upon to decide whether the right of an accused to have compulsory process for obtaining witnesses in his favor, guaranteed in federal trials by the Sixth Amendment, is so fundamental and essential to a fair trial that it is incorporated in the Due Process Clause of the Fourteenth Amendment. At one time, it was thought that the Sixth Amendment had no application to state criminal trials. That view no longer prevails, and, in recent years, we have increasingly looked to the specific guarantees of the Sixth Amendment to determine whether a state criminal trial was conducted with due process of law. We have held that due process requires that the accused have the assistance of counsel for his defense, that he be confronted with the witnesses against him, and that he have the right to a speedy and public trial.

The right of an accused to have compulsory process for obtaining witnesses in his favor stands on no lesser footing than the other Sixth Amendment rights that we have previously held applicable to the States. This Court had occasion in In re Oliver to describe what it regarded as the most basic ingredients of due process of law. It observed that:

"A person's right to reasonable notice of a charge against him, and an opportunity to be heard in his defense—a right to his day in court—are basic in our system of jurisprudence, and these rights include, as a minimum, a right to examine the witnesses against him, to offer testimony, and to be represented by counsel."

The right to offer the testimony of witnesses, and to compel their attendance, if necessary, is in plain terms the right to present a defense, the right to present the defendant's version of the facts as well as the prosecution's to the jury, so it may decide where the truth lies. Just as an accused has the right to confront the prosecution's witnesses for the purpose of challenging their testimony, he has the right to present his own witnesses to establish a defense. This right is a fundamental element of due process of law.

Since the right to compulsory process is applicable in this state proceeding, the question remains whether it was violated in the circumstances of this case. The testimony of Charles Fuller was denied to the defense not because the State refused to compel his attendance, but because a state statute made his testimony inadmissible whether he was present in the courtroom or not. We are thus called upon to decide whether the Sixth Amendment guarantees a defendant the right under any circumstances to put his witnesses on the stand, as well as the right to compel their attendance in court.

We hold that the petitioner in this case was denied his right to have compulsory process for obtaining witnesses in his favor because the State arbitrarily denied him the right to put on the stand a witness who was physically and mentally capable of testifying to events that he had personally observed, and whose testimony would have been relevant and material to the defense. The Framers of the Constitution did not intend to commit the futile act of giving to a defendant the right to secure the attendance of witnesses whose testimony he had no right to use. The judgment of conviction must be reversed.

It is so ordered.

Source: United States Reports. Vol. 388, 14–25. Washington, D.C.: Government Printing Office, 1968.

DOCUMENT 51: *Bruton v. United States* (1968)

Bruton and co-defendant Evans were both convicted of armed postal robbery. This is a federal offense. Both were prosecuted in a joint trial. Trial of two accomplices together had become common, since it saved money and time. During their trial, a confession given by Evans was presented. In that confession, he admitted the crime and stated he had an accomplice whom he refused to identify. The trial judge instructed the jury that they were to consider the confession as evidence only against Evans and to disregard it in terms of Bruton. Evans never testified during the trial to avoid giving self-incriminating evidence.

In a previous case, *Delli Paoli v. United States* (1957), the Court had ruled that instructions from the judge to the jury to ignore certain evidence protected the accused. In Bruton, the Court reversed itself. It reasoned that Bruton had no opportunity to cross-examine Evans because he never testified. This violated his Sixth Amendment right to confront and question witnesses. Further, it was not possible to be sure that the jury was able to follow the court's instruction. The confession may have influenced the jury.

* * *

Bruton v. United States, 391 U.S. 123

Mr. Justice Brennan delivered the opinion of the Court.

A joint trial of petitioner and one Evans in the District Court for the Eastern District of Missouri resulted in the conviction of both by a jury on a federal charge of armed postal robbery. A postal inspector testified that Evans orally confessed to him that Evans and petitioner committed the armed robbery. The postal inspector obtained the oral confession, and another in which Evans admitted he had an accomplice whom he would not name, in the course of two interrogations of Evans at the city jail in St. Louis, Missouri, where Evans was held in custody on state criminal charges. Both petitioner and Evans appealed their convictions to the Court of Appeals for the Eighth Circuit. . . . The Court . . . affirmed petitioner's conviction because the trial judge instructed the jury that although Evans' confession was competent evidence against Evans it was inadmissible hearsay against petitioner and therefore had to be disregarded in determining petitioner's guilt or innocence. We hold that, because of the substantial risk that the jury, despite instructions to the contrary, looked to the incriminating extrajudicial statements in determining petitioner's guilt, admission of Evans' confession in this joint trial violated petitioner's right of cross-examination secured by the Confrontation Clause of the Sixth Amendment.

Evans' oral confessions were in fact testified to, and were therefore actually in evidence. That testimony was legitimate evidence against Evans and to that extent was properly before the jury during its deliberations. Even greater, then, was the likelihood that the jury would believe Evans made the statements and that they were true—not just the self-incriminating portions but those implicating petitioner as well. Plainly, the introduction of Evans' confession added substantial, perhaps even critical, weight to the Government's case in a form not subject to cross-examination, since Evans did not take the stand. Petitioner thus was denied his constitutional right of confrontation. . . .

Those who have defended reliance on the limiting instruction in this area have cited several reasons in support. . . . In Judge Hand's view the limiting instruction, although not really capable of preventing the jury from considering the prejudicial evidence, does as a matter of form provide a way around the exclusionary rules of evidence that is defensible because it "probably furthers, rather than impedes, the search for truth. . . ." Nash v. United States. Insofar as this implies the prosecution ought not to be denied the benefit of the confession to prove the confessor's guilt, however, it overlooks alternative ways of achieving that benefit without at the same time infringing the nonconfessor's right of confrontation. Where viable alternatives do exist, it is deceptive to rely on the pursuit of truth to defend a clearly harmful practice.

Another reason . . . is the justification for joint trials in general, the argument being that the benefits of joint proceedings should not have to be sacrificed by requiring separate trials in order to use the confession against the declarant. Joint trials do conserve state funds, diminish inconvenience to witnesses and public authorities, and avoid delays in bringing those accused of crime to trial. But the answer to this argument was cogently stated by Judge Lehman of the New York Court of Appeals, dissenting in People v. Fisher:

"We still adhere to the rule that an accused is entitled to confrontation of the witnesses against him and the right to cross-examine them. . . . We destroy the age-old rule which in the past has been regarded as a fundamental principle of our jurisprudence by a legalistic formula, required of the judge, that the jury may not consider any admissions against any party who did not join in them. We secure greater speed, economy and convenience in the administration of the law at the price of fundamental principles of constitutional liberty. That price is too high."

Finally, the reason . . . was to tie the result to maintenance of the jury system. "Unless we proceed on the basis that the jury will follow the court's instructions where those instructions are clear and the circumstances are such that the jury can reasonably be expected to follow them, the jury system makes little sense." We agree that there are many circumstances in which this reliance is justified. Not every admission of inadmissible hearsay or other evidence can be considered to be reversible error unavoidable through limiting instructions; instances occur in almost every trial where inadmissible evidence creeps in, usually inadvertently. "A defendant is entitled to a fair trial but not a perfect one." Lutwak v. United States. It is not unreasonable to conclude that in many such cases the jury can and will follow the trial judge's instructions to disregard such information. Nevertheless, as was recognized in Jackson v. Denno, there are some contexts in which the risk that the jury will not, or cannot, follow instructions is so great, and the consequences of failure so vital to the defendant, that the practical and human limitations of the jury system cannot be ignored. Such a context is presented here, where the powerfully incriminating extrajudicial statements of a codefendant, who stands accused side-by-side with the defendant, are deliberately spread before the jury in a joint trial. Not only are the incriminations devastating to the defendant but their credibility is inevitably suspect, a fact recognized when accomplices do take the stand and the jury is instructed to weigh their testimony carefully given the recognized motivation to shift blame onto others. The unreliability of such evidence is intolerably compounded when the alleged accomplice, as here, does not testify and cannot be tested by cross-examination. It was against such threats to a fair trial that the Confrontation Clause was directed.

We, of course, acknowledge the impossibility of determining whether in fact the jury did or did not ignore Evans' statement inculpating petitioner in determining petitioner's guilt. . . . It was enough that that procedure posed "substantial threats to a defendant's constitutional rights to have an involuntary confession entirely disregarded and to have the coercion issue fairly and reliably determined. These hazards we cannot ignore." Here the introduction of Evans' confession posed a substantial threat to petitioner's right to confront the witnesses against him, and this is a hazard we cannot ignore. Despite the concededly clear instructions to the jury to disregard Evans' inadmissible hearsay evidence inculpating petitioner, in the context of a joint trial we cannot accept limiting instructions as an adequate substitute for petitioner's constitutional right of cross-examination. The effect is the same as if there had been no instruction at all.

Reversed.

Source: *United States Reports*, Vol. 391, 123–25. Washington, D.C: Government
Printing Office, 1968.

DOCUMENT 52: *Duncan v. Louisiana* (1968)

The right to a jury trial is a most fundamental right, but must it be
available in all cases? Which cases are too minor to require the expense and time of a jury trial? Duncan was denied his request for a
jury trial on his battery charge. Simple battery is a misdemeanor in
Louisiana punishable by up to two years' imprisonment and a fine of
$300. Under the Louisiana Constitution, jury trials are required only
in cases in which capital punishment or imprisonment at hard labor
may be imposed. Duncan was found guilty and sentenced to sixty
days in prison and a fine of $150.

On appeal, the Supreme Court ruled that he was entitled to a jury
trial even though the crime was a misdemeanor. He could have been
punished with up to two years in jail. The possible amount of punishment determines when a jury trial is needed. The Court ruled that
the right to a jury trial is required of states under the Fourteenth
Amendment due process clause. The new standard established by this
case is that states must provide a jury trial in those cases where one
is required in the federal courts. In federal cases, any crime that could
result in a jail sentence of more than six months requires a jury trial.

* * *

Duncan v. Louisiana, 391 U.S. 145

Mr. Justice White delivered the opinion of the Court. . . .

The test for determining whether a right extended by the Fifth and
Sixth Amendments with respect to federal criminal proceedings is also
protected against state action by the Fourteenth Amendment has been
phrased in a variety of ways in the opinions of this Court. The question
has been asked whether a right is among those "fundamental principles
of liberty and justice which lie at the base of all our civil and political
institutions," whether it is "basic in our system of jurisprudence." The
claim before us is that the right to trial by jury guaranteed by the Sixth
Amendment meets these tests. The position of Louisiana, on the other
hand, is that the Constitution imposes upon the States no duty to give
a jury trial in any criminal case, regardless of the seriousness of the crime
or the size of the punishment which may be imposed. Because we believe
that trial by jury in criminal cases is fundamental to the American

scheme of justice, we hold that the Fourteenth Amendment guarantees a right of jury trial in all criminal cases which—were they to be tried in a federal court—would come within the Sixth Amendment's guarantee. Since we consider the appeal before us to be such a case, we hold that the Constitution was violated when appellant's demand for jury trial was refused. . . .

The history of trial by jury . . . is impressive support for considering the right to jury trial in criminal cases to be fundamental to our system of justice, an importance frequently recognized in the opinions of this Court. . . .

Jury trial continues to receive strong support. The laws of every State guarantee a right to jury trial in serious criminal cases; no State has dispensed with it; nor are there significant movements underway to do so. Indeed, the three most recent state constitutional revisions, in Maryland, Michigan, and New York, carefully preserved the right of the accused to have the judgment of a jury when tried for a serious crime. . . .

The guarantees of jury trial in the Federal and State Constitutions reflect a profound judgment about the way in which law should be enforced and justice administered. A right to jury trial is granted to criminal defendants in order to prevent oppression by the Government. Those who wrote our constitutions knew from history and experience that it was necessary to protect against unfounded criminal charges brought to eliminate enemies and against judges too responsive to the voice of higher authority. The framers of the constitutions strove to create an independent judiciary, but insisted upon further protection against arbitrary action. Providing an accused with the right to be tried by a jury of his peers gave him an inestimable safeguard against the corrupt or overzealous prosecutor and against the compliant, biased, or eccentric judge. If the defendant preferred the common sense judgment of a jury to the more tutored but perhaps less sympathetic reaction of the single judge, he was to have it. Beyond this, the jury trial provisions in the Federal and State Constitutions reflect a fundamental decision about the exercise of official power—a reluctance to entrust plenary powers over the life and liberty of the citizen to one judge or to a group of judges. Fear of unchecked power, so typical of our State and Federal Governments in other respects, found expression in the criminal law in this insistence upon community participation in the determination of guilt or innocence. The deep commitment of the Nation to the right of jury trial in serious criminal cases as a defense against arbitrary law enforcement qualifies for protection under the Due Process Clause of the Fourteenth Amendment, and must therefore be respected by the States. . . .

Louisiana's final contention is that even if it must grant jury trials in serious criminal cases, the conviction before us is valid and constitutional because here the petitioner was tried for simple battery and was sentenced to only 60 days in the parish prison. We are not persuaded. It is doubtless true that there is a category of petty crimes or offenses which is not subject to the Sixth Amendment jury trial provision and should not be subject to the Fourteenth Amendment jury trial requirement here applied to the States. Crimes carrying possible penalties up to six months do not require a jury trial if they otherwise qualify as petty offenses. But the penalty authorized for a particular crime is of major relevance in determining whether it is serious or not and may in itself, if severe enough, subject the trial to the mandates of the Sixth Amendment. The penalty authorized by the law of the locality may be taken "as a gauge of its social and ethical judgments," of the crime in question. . . . In the case before us, the Legislature of Louisiana has made simple battery a criminal offense punishable by imprisonment for up to two years and a fine. The question, then, is whether a crime carrying such a penalty is an offense which Louisiana may insist on trying without a jury.

We think not. . . . Of course, the boundaries of the petty offense category have always been ill-defined, if not ambulatory. In the absence of an explicit constitutional provision, the definitional task necessarily falls on the courts, which must either pass upon the validity of legislative attempts to identify those petty offenses which are exempt from jury trial or, where the legislature has not addressed itself to the problem, themselves face the question in the first instance. In either case, it is necessary to draw a line in the spectrum of crime, separating petty from serious infractions. This process, although essential, cannot be wholly satisfactory, for it requires attaching different consequences to events which, when they lie near the line, actually differ very little.

In the federal system, petty offenses are defined as those punishable by no more than six months in prison and a $500 fine. In 49 of the 50 States, crimes subject to trial without a jury, which occasionally include simple battery, are punishable by no more than one year in jail. Moreover, in the late 18th century in America, crimes triable without a jury were, for the most part, punishable by no more than a six-month prison term, although there appear to have been exceptions to this rule. We need not, however, settle in this case the exact location of the line between petty offenses and serious crimes. It is sufficient for our purposes to hold that a crime punishable by two years in prison is, based on past and contemporary standards in this country, a serious crime, and not a petty offense. Consequently, appellant was entitled to a jury trial, and it was error to deny it.

The judgment below is reversed and the case is remanded for proceedings not inconsistent with this opinion.

Source: United States Reports. Vol. 391, 145–93. Washington, D.C.: Government Printing Office, 1968.

DOCUMENT 53: *Benton v. Maryland* (1969)

Benton was charged with burglary and larceny, tried, convicted only of the burglary charge, and sentenced to ten years in prison. The grand jury and petit jury in his case were later determined to have been selected under an invalid constitutional provision of the Maryland Constitution. Benton was given the choice of being retried, which he elected. He was charged again for both burglary and larceny. His lawyers argued that he had already been acquitted of the larceny charge and retrial on that charge was a violation of the double jeopardy protection. The state, however, retried him on both counts and found him guilty on both. His sentence was fifteen years for burglary and five years for larceny to be served concurrently.

On appeal, the state reasoned that he requested the retrial and, even if the larceny charge was double jeopardy, the sentences were served concurrently, so the conviction for larceny made no material difference in his prison sentence.

The Supreme Court did not agree. It ruled that the double jeopardy clause of the Fifth Amendment is enforceable against the states through the Fourteenth Amendment. That the sentences were concurrent did not change the reality that the state's action placed Benton in double jeopardy.

* * *

Benton v. Maryland, 395 U.S. 784

Mr. Justice Marshall delivered the opinion of the Court. . . .

On the merits, we hold that the Double Jeopardy Clause of the Fifth Amendment is applicable to the States through the Fourteenth Amendment, and we reverse petitioner's conviction for larceny.

At the outset of this case, we are confronted with a jurisdictional problem. If the error specified in the original writ of certiorari were found to affect only petitioner's larceny conviction, reversal of that conviction would not require the State to change the terms of petitioner's confinement. Whatever the status of his sentence on the larceny conviction, petitioner would probably stay in prison until he had served out his sentence for burglary. Is there, in these circumstances, a live "case" or "controversy" suitable for resolution by this Court, or is the issue moot? Is petitioner asking for an advisory opinion on an abstract or hypothetical question? The answer to these questions is crucial, for it is well settled that federal courts may act only in the context of a justifiable case or controversy. . . .

It is sufficient for present purposes to hold that there is no jurisdictional bar to consideration of challenges to multiple convictions, even though concurrent sentences were imposed.

In 1937, this Court decided the landmark case of Palko v. Connecticut. . . . Federal double jeopardy standards were not applicable against the States. . . .

Recently, however, this Court has increasingly looked to the specific guarantees of the [Bill of Rights] to determine whether a state criminal trial was conducted with due process of law. In an increasing number of cases, the Court has rejected the notion that the Fourteenth Amendment applies to the States only a "watered-down, subjective version of the individual guarantees of the Bill of Rights. . . ." Only last Term, we found that the right to trial by jury in criminal cases was "fundamental to the American scheme of justice" Duncan v. Louisiana (1968) and held that the Sixth Amendment right to a jury trial was applicable to the States through the Fourteenth Amendment. For the same reasons, we today find that the double jeopardy prohibition of the Fifth Amendment represents a fundamental ideal in our constitutional heritage, and that it should apply to the States through the Fourteenth Amendment. Insofar as it is inconsistent with this holding, Palko v. Connecticut is overruled.

Palko represented an approach to basic constitutional rights which this Court's recent decisions have rejected. It was cut of the same cloth as Betts v. Brady, the case which held that a criminal defendant's right to counsel was to be determined by deciding in each case whether the denial of that right was "shocking to the universal sense of justice." It relied upon Twining v. New Jersey, which held that the right against compulsory self-incrimination was not an element of Fourteenth Amendment due process. Betts was overruled by Gideon v. Wainwright, Twining by Malloy v. Hogan. Our recent cases have thoroughly rejected the Palko notion that basic constitutional rights can be denied by the States as long as the totality of the circumstances does not disclose a denial of "fundamental fairness." Once it is decided that a particular Bill of Rights guarantee is "fundamental to the American scheme of justice," Duncan v. Louisiana, supra . . . the same constitutional standards apply against both the State and Federal Governments. Palko's roots had thus been cut away years ago. We today only recognize the inevitable. . . .

It is clear that petitioner's larceny conviction cannot stand once federal double jeopardy standards are applied. Petitioner was acquitted of larceny in his first trial. Because he decided to appeal his burglary conviction, he is forced to suffer retrial on the larceny count as well. . . .

The judgment is vacated, and the case is remanded for further proceedings not inconsistent with this opinion.

It is so ordered.

Source: United States Reports. Vol. 395, 784–813. Washington, D.C.: Government Printing Office, 1969.

Part V

Sustaining the Due Process Revolution

DOCUMENT 54: *Williams v. Florida* (1970)

Traditionally, juries have consisted of twelve members, peers of the accused. The Supreme Court in decisions dating from *Thompson v. Utah* (1898) had upheld the twelve-person jury as a constitutional requirement in federal cases; when the right to a jury trial was required of states in *Duncan v. Louisiana* (see Document 52), the twelve-person jury was also required in state trials. Florida's laws permitted a six-member jury for noncapital cases. Williams had been charged and convicted of robbery. In a series of cases starting with *Thompson v. Utah* (1898), the Court had held that a jury consisted of twelve members. In a surprise change, the Court ruled that the twelve-member jury was a historical accident and was not a requirement of the Sixth Amendment. Juries can consist of various sizes.

Williams's lawyers also argued that a discovery procedure required by Florida state law violated the Fifth Amendment protection against self-incrimination. The law required defendants to disclose before the start of a trial whether or not they intended to present an alibi and provide a list of alibi witnesses. The state was required to submit to defense a list of rebuttal witnesses. The Court found that this procedure was not a violation of the Fifth Amendment.

* * *

Williams v. Florida, 399 U.S. 78

Mr. Justice White delivered the opinion of the Court.

Prior to his trial for robbery in the State of Florida, petitioner filed a "Motion for a Protective Order," seeking to be excused from the requirements of Rule 1.200 of the Florida Rules of Criminal Procedure. That rule requires a defendant, on written demand of the prosecuting attorney, to give notice in advance of trial if the defendant intends to claim an alibi, and to furnish the prosecuting attorney with information as to the place where he claims to have been and with the names and addresses of the alibi witnesses he intends to use. In his motion, petitioner openly declared his intent to claim an alibi, but objected to the further disclosure requirements on the ground that the rule "compels the Defendant in a criminal case to be a witness against himself" in violation of his Fifth and Fourteenth Amendment rights. The motion was denied. Petitioner also filed a pretrial motion to impanel a 12-man jury instead of the six-man jury provided by Florida law in all but capital cases. That motion too was denied. Petitioner was convicted as charged and was sentenced to life imprisonment. The District Court of Appeal affirmed, rejecting petitioner's claims that his Fifth and Sixth Amendment rights had been violated. . . .

Florida's "notice of alibi" rule is, in essence, a requirement that a defendant submit to a limited form of pretrial discovery by the State whenever he intends to rely at trial on the defense of alibi. In exchange for the defendant's disclosure of the witnesses he proposes to use to establish that defense, the State, in turn, is required to notify the defendant of any witnesses it proposes to offer in rebuttal to that defense.

We need not linger over the suggestion that the discovery permitted the State against petitioner in this case deprived him of "due process" or a "fair trial." Florida law provides for liberal discovery by the defendant against the State, and the "notice of alibi" rule is itself carefully hedged with reciprocal duties requiring state disclosure to the defendant. Given the ease with which an alibi can be fabricated, the State's interest in protecting itself against an eleventh-hour defense is both obvious and legitimate. Reflecting this interest, "notice of alibi" provisions, dating at least from 1927, are now in existence in a substantial number of States. The adversary system of trial is hardly an end in itself; it is not yet a poker game in which players enjoy an absolute right always to conceal their cards until played. We find ample room in that system, at least as far as "due process" is concerned, for the instant Florida rule, which is designed to enhance the search for truth in the criminal trial by insuring both the defendant and the State ample opportunity to investigate certain facts crucial to the determination of guilt or innocence.

Petitioner's major contention is that he was "compelled . . . to be a witness against himself," contrary to the command of the Fifth and Fourteenth Amendments. . . . We conclude, however, as has apparently every other court that has considered the issue, that the privilege against self-incrimination is not violated by a requirement that the defendant give notice of an alibi defense and disclose his alibi witnesses. . . .

. . . The question in this case, then, is whether the constitutional guarantee of a trial by "jury" necessarily requires trial by exactly 12 persons, rather than some lesser number—in this case, six. We hold that the 12-man panel is not a necessary ingredient of "trial by jury," and that respondent's refusal to impanel more than the six members provided for by Florida law did not violate petitioner's Sixth Amendment rights as applied to the States through the Fourteenth.

We had occasion in Duncan v. Louisiana . . . to review briefly the oft-told history of the development of trial by jury in criminal cases. That history revealed . . . sometime in the 14th century, the size of the jury at common law came to be fixed generally at 12, that particular feature of the jury system appears to have been a historical accident, unrelated to the great purposes which gave rise to the jury in the first place. The question before us is whether this accidental feature of the jury has been immutably codified into our Constitution.

This Court's earlier decisions have assumed an affirmative answer to this question. The leading case so construing the Sixth Amendment is Thompson v. Utah. . . . In reaching its conclusion, the Court announced that . . . the jury referred to in the Amendment was a jury "constituted, as it was at common law, of twelve persons, neither more nor less." . . .

. . . [T]he relevant constitutional history casts considerable doubt on the easy assumption in our past decisions that, if a given feature existed in a jury at common law in 1789, then it was necessarily preserved in the Constitution.

Three significant features may be observed in . . . the background of the Constitution's jury trial provisions. First, even though the vicinage requirement was as much a feature of the common law jury as was the 12-man requirement, the mere reference to "trial by jury" in Article III was not interpreted to include that feature. . . . Second, provisions that would have explicitly tied the "jury" concept to the "accustomed requisites" of the time were eliminated. . . . Finally, contemporary legislative and constitutional provisions indicate that, where Congress wanted to leave no doubt that it was incorporating existing common law features of the jury system, it knew how to use express language to that effect. . . . It may well be that the usual expectation was that the jury would consist of 12, and that hence, the most likely conclusion to be drawn is simply that little thought was actually given to the specific question we face today. But there is absolutely no indication in "the intent of the Framers" of an explicit decision to equate the constitutional and common-law characteristics of the jury. Nothing in this history suggests, then, that we do violence to the letter of the Constitution by turning to other than purely historical considerations to determine which features of the jury system, as it existed in common law, were preserved in the Constitution. . . .

The purpose of the jury trial, as we noted in Duncan, is to prevent oppression by the Government. . . . Given this purpose, the essential feature of a jury obviously lies in the interposition between the accused and his accuser of the common sense judgment of a group of laymen, and in the community participation and shared responsibility that results from that group's determination of guilt or innocence. The performance of this role is not a function of the particular number of the body that makes up the jury. . . .

. . . [N]either currently available evidence nor theory suggests that the 12-man jury is necessarily more advantageous to the defendant than a jury composed of fewer members.

We conclude, in short, as we began: the fact that the jury at common law was composed of precisely 12 is a historical accident, unnecessary to effect the purposes of the jury system and wholly without significance. . . . To read the Sixth Amendment as forever codifying a feature so incidental to the real purpose of the Amendment is to ascribe a blind formalism to the Framers which would require considerably more evidence than we have been able to discover in the history and language of the Constitution or in the reasoning of our past decisions. We do not mean to intimate that legislatures can never have good reasons for concluding that the 12-man jury is preferable to the smaller jury, or that such conclusions—reflected in the provisions of most States and in our federal system—are in any sense unwise. . . . Our holding does no more than leave these considerations to Congress and the States, unrestrained by an interpretation of the Sixth Amendment that would forever dictate the precise number that can constitute a jury. Consistent with this holding, we conclude that petitioner's Sixth Amendment rights, as applied to the States through the Fourteenth Amendment, were not violated by Florida's decision to provide a six-man, rather than a 12-man, jury.

The judgment of the Florida District Court of Appeal is affirmed.

Source: United States Reports. Vol. 399, 78–145. Washington, D.C.: Government Printing Office, 1971.

DOCUMENT 55: *Johnson v. Louisiana* (1972)

In *William v. Florida* (see Document 54), 1970, the Supreme Court held that juries did not have to consist of twelve members always.

Thus, that traditional requirement was set aside. In *Johnson v. Louisiana*, the Court upheld a Louisiana law that allowed conviction without unanimity of the jury.

Johnson was arrested and tried for robbery. He was convicted when nine of the twelve jurors decided he was guilty. Johnson's lawyers argued that the jury decision could not have been beyond a reasonable doubt if three jurors were not voting for conviction. If he had been charged with a capital offense, unanimity of the jury would have been required.

The Court found no conflict between the Louisiana law and the Sixth Amendment. In no previous ruling had the Court ever required jury unanimity, and jury unanimity is not a requirement of due process either. The Louisiana laws that permitted different levels of jury unanimity were found reasonable as a way to expedite the administration of the courts.

Four justices voiced dissent. They found the lack of jury unanimity to be a lowered standard of justice. The dissent of Justice Stewart voices their concerns clearly.

* * *

Johnson v. Louisiana, 406 U.S. 356

Mr. Justice White delivered the opinion of the Court.

Under both the Louisiana Constitution and Code of Criminal Procedure, criminal cases in which the punishment is necessarily at hard labor are tried to a jury of 12, and the vote of nine jurors is sufficient to return either a guilty or not guilty verdict. The principal question in this case is whether these provisions allowing less than unanimous verdicts in certain cases are valid under the Due Process and Equal Protection Clauses of the Fourteenth Amendment.

. . . Johnson pleaded not guilty, was tried on May 14, 1968, by a 12-man jury, and was convicted by a nine-to-three verdict. . . .

Appellant argues that, in order to give substance to the reasonable doubt standard, which the State, by virtue of the Due Process Clause of the Fourteenth Amendment, must satisfy in criminal cases, that clause must be construed to require a unanimous jury verdict in all criminal cases. . . . Appellant focuses instead on the fact that less than all jurors voted to convict, and argues that, because three voted to acquit, the reasonable doubt standard has not been satisfied, and his conviction is therefore infirm.

We note at the outset that this Court has never held jury unanimity to be a requisite of due process of law. . . .

. . . [I]t is our view that the fact of three dissenting votes to acquit raises no question of constitutional substance about either the integrity or the accuracy of the majority verdict of guilt. Appellant's contrary argument breaks down into two parts, each of which we shall consider separately: first, that nine individual jurors will be unable to vote conscientiously in favor of guilt beyond a reasonable doubt when three of their colleagues are arguing for acquittal, and, second, that guilt cannot be said to have been proved beyond a reasonable doubt when one or more of a jury's members at the conclusion of deliberation still possess such a doubt. Neither argument is persuasive. . . .

We conclude, therefore, that, as to the nine jurors who voted to convict, the State satisfied its burden of proving guilt beyond any reasonable doubt. The remaining question under the Due Process Clause is whether the vote of three jurors for acquittal can be said to impeach the verdict of the other nine and to demonstrate that guilt was not in fact, proved beyond such doubt. We hold that it cannot. . . .

Appellant also attacks as violative of the Equal Protection Clause the provisions of Louisiana law requiring unanimous verdicts in capital and five-man jury cases, but permitting less than unanimous verdicts in cases such as his. We conclude, however, that the Louisiana statutory scheme serves a rational purpose, and is not subject to constitutional challenge.

In order to "facilitate, expedite, and reduce expense in the administration of criminal justice," State v. Lewis, Louisiana has permitted less serious crimes to be tried by five jurors with unanimous verdicts, more serious crimes have required the assent of nine of 12 jurors, and, for the most serious crimes, a unanimous verdict of 12 jurors is stipulated. In appellant's case, nine jurors, rather than five or 12, were required for a verdict. We discern nothing invidious in this classification. . . .

The judgment of the Supreme Court of Louisiana is therefore affirmed.

Mr. Justice Stewart, with whom Mr. Justice Brennan and Mr. Justice Marshall join, dissenting.

. . . I think the Fourteenth Amendment alone clearly requires that, if a State purports to accord the right of trial by jury in a criminal case, then only a unanimous jury can return a constitutionally valid verdict.

The guarantee against systematic discrimination in the selection of criminal court juries is a fundamental of the Fourteenth Amendment. That has been the insistent message of this Court in a line of decisions extending over nearly a century. . . . The clear purpose of these decisions has been to ensure universal participation of the citizenry in the administration of criminal justice. Yet today's judgment approves the elimination of the one rule that can ensure that such participation will be meaningful—the rule requiring the assent of all jurors before a verdict of conviction or acquittal can be returned. Under today's judgment, nine jurors can simply ignore the views of their fellow panel members of a different race or class.

The constitutional guarantee of an impartial system of jury selection in a state criminal trial rests on the Due Process and Equal Protection Clauses of the Fourteenth Amendment. See, e.g., Whitus v. Georgia; Carter v. Texas; Strauder v. West Virginia. Only a jury so selected can assure both a fair criminal trial and public confidence in its result. Today's decision grossly undermines those basic assurances. For only a unanimous jury so selected can serve to minimize the potential bigotry of those who might convict on inadequate evidence, or acquit when evidence of guilt was clear. . . .

. . . The requirement that the verdict of the jury be unanimous . . . preserves the jury's function in linking law with contemporary society. It provides the simple and effective method endorsed by centuries of experience and history to combat the injuries to the fair administration of justice that can be inflicted by community passion and prejudice.

I dissent.

Source: United States Reports. Vol. 406, 356–403. Washington, D.C.: Government Printing Office, 1973.

DOCUMENT 56: *Kastigar v. United States* (1972)

It has long been the practice of prosecutors to offer immunity to individuals to compel their testimony against their claim of Fifth Amendment rights against self-incrimination. From the 1890s, the immunity granted in federal cases prevented any future prosecution for that incident of the crime of the person compelled to testify. Even if the testimony showed the person to be guilty of a crime, no prosecution could follow.

In 1970, Congress enacted a new law that provided a different form of immunity known as use and derivative use. Under this immunity, the individual compelled to testify could still be prosecuted for the crime, but that prosecution needed to be based on evidence other than the testimony and information derived from it.

Kastigar refused to testify claiming that the immunity he was granted was not as broad as the self-incrimination right of the Fifth Amendment. The Court decided that use and derivative use immunity is consistent with the individual's self-incrimination right. The requirement that prosecution must be based on other evidence, and that the prosecution must prove that is so, provides adequate protection.

* * *

Kastigar v. United States, 406 U.S. 441

Mr. Justice Powell delivered the opinion of the Court.

This case presents the question whether the United States Government may compel testimony from an unwilling witness, who invokes the Fifth Amendment privilege against compulsory self-incrimination, by conferring on the witness immunity from use of the compelled testimony in subsequent criminal proceedings, as well as immunity from use of evidence derived from the testimony. . . .

This Court granted certiorari to resolve the important question whether testimony may be compelled by granting immunity from the use of compelled testimony and evidence derived therefrom ("use and derivative use" immunity), or whether it is necessary to grant immunity from prosecution for offenses to which compelled testimony relates ("transactional" immunity). (1971). . . .

Petitioners' . . . contention is that the scope of immunity provided by the federal witness immunity statute, 18 U.S.C. 6002, is not coextensive with the scope of the Fifth Amendment privilege against compulsory self-incrimination, and therefore is not sufficient to supplant the privilege and compel testimony over a claim of the privilege. The statute provides that when a witness is compelled by district court order to testify over a claim of the privilege:

"the witness may not refuse to comply with the order on the basis of his privilege against self-incrimination; but no testimony or other information compelled under the order (or any information directly or indirectly derived from such testimony or other information) may be used against the witness in any criminal case, except a prosecution for perjury, giving a false statement, or otherwise failing to comply with the order." 18 U.S.C. 6002.

The constitutional inquiry, rooted in logic and history, as well as in the decisions of this Court, is whether the immunity granted under this statute is coextensive with the scope of the privilege. If so, petitioners' refusals to answer based on the privilege were unjustified, and the judgments of contempt were proper, for the grant of immunity has removed the dangers against which the privilege protects. If, on the other hand, the immunity granted is not as comprehensive as the protection afforded by the privilege, petitioners were justified in refusing to answer, and the judgments of contempt must be vacated. McCarthy v. Arndstein (1924). . . .

Petitioners draw a distinction between statutes that provide transactional immunity and those that provide, as does the statute before us, immunity from use and derivative use. They contend that a statute must at a minimum grant full transactional immunity. . . .

[In 1970] Congress enacted the statute here under consideration. The new statute, which does not "afford [the] absolute immunity against future prosecution" . . . was drafted to meet what Congress judged to be the conceptual basis of . . . decisions of the Court, namely, that immunity from the use of compelled testimony and evidence derived therefrom is coextensive with the scope of the privilege.

The statute's explicit proscription of the use in any criminal case of "testimony or other information compelled under the order (or any information directly or indirectly derived from such testimony or other information)" is consonant with Fifth Amendment standards. We hold that such immunity from use and derivative use is coextensive with the scope of the privilege against self-incrimination, and therefore is sufficient to compel testimony over a claim of the privilege. While a grant of immunity must afford protection commensurate with that afforded by the privilege, it need not be broader. Transactional immunity, which accords full immunity from prosecution for the offense to which the compelled testimony relates, affords the witness considerably broader protection than does the Fifth Amendment privilege. The privilege has never been construed to mean that one who invokes it cannot subsequently be prosecuted. Its sole concern is to afford protection against being "forced to give testimony leading to the infliction of 'penalties affixed to . . . criminal acts." Immunity from the use of compelled testimony, as well as evidence derived directly and indirectly therefrom, affords this protection. It prohibits the prosecutorial authorities from using the compelled testimony in any respect, and it therefore insures that the testimony cannot lead to the infliction of criminal penalties on the witness. . . .

Petitioners argue that use and derivative-use immunity will not adequately protect a witness from various possible incriminating uses of the compelled testimony: for example, the prosecutor or other law enforcement officials may obtain leads, names of witnesses, or other information not otherwise available that might result in a prosecution. It will be difficult and perhaps impossible, the argument goes, to identify, by testimony or cross-examination, the subtle ways in which the compelled testimony may disadvantage a witness, especially in the jurisdiction granting the immunity.

This argument presupposes that the statute's prohibition will prove impossible to enforce. The statute provides a sweeping proscription of any use, direct or indirect, of the compelled testimony and any information derived therefrom:

"[N]o testimony or other information compelled under the order (or any information directly or indirectly derived from such testimony or other information) may be used against the witness in any criminal case. . . ." 18 U.S.C. 6002.

This total prohibition on use provides a comprehensive safeguard, barring the use of compelled testimony as an "investigatory lead," and also barring the use of any evidence obtained by focusing investigation on a witness as a result of his compelled disclosures. . . .

This burden of proof, which we reaffirm as appropriate, is not limited to a negation of taint; rather, it imposes on the prosecution the affirmative duty to prove that the evidence it proposes to use is derived from a legitimate source wholly independent of the compelled testimony.

This is very substantial protection commensurate with that resulting from invoking the privilege itself. The privilege assures that a citizen is not compelled to incriminate himself by his own testimony. It usually operates to allow a citizen to remain silent when asked a question requiring an incriminatory answer. This statute, which operates after a witness has given incriminatory testimony, affords the same protection by assuring that the compelled testimony can in no way lead to the infliction of criminal penalties. The statute, like the Fifth Amendment, grants neither pardon nor amnesty. Both the statute and the Fifth Amendment allow the government to prosecute using evidence from legitimate independent sources. . . .

There can be no justification in reason or policy for holding that the Constitution requires an amnesty grant where, acting pursuant to statute and accompanying safeguards, testimony is compelled in exchange for immunity from use and derivative use when no such amnesty is required where the government, acting without colorable right, coerces a defendant into incriminating himself.

We conclude that the immunity provided by 18 U.S.C. 6002 leaves the witness and the prosecutorial authorities in substantially the same position as if the witness had claimed the Fifth Amendment privilege. The immunity therefore is coextensive with the privilege and suffices to supplant it. The judgment of the Court of Appeals for the Ninth Circuit accordingly is

Affirmed.

Source: United States Reports. Vol. 406, 441–53. Washington, D.C.: Government Printing Office, 1972.

DOCUMENT 57: *Argersinger v. Hamlin* (1972)

Argersinger was indigent and charged with carrying a concealed weapon. His request for an attorney was denied because his potential penalty was six months or less. In *Gideon v. Wainwright* (see Document 37), the Court had ruled that in every trial involving imprisonment of six months or more, the accused was entitled to be represented by counsel.

In this decision, the Court expanded the *Gideon v. Wainwright* requirement of an attorney to include any trial where the accused could be sentenced to any prison confinement, no matter how short. The Court reasoned that trials involving short prison terms can be as complex as trials resulting in long prison terms. The very essence of a fair trial is to be represented by an attorney in our adversarial system.

* * *

Argersinger v. Hamlin, 407 U.S. 25

Mr. Justice Douglas delivered the opinion of the Court.

Petitioner, an indigent, was charged in Florida with carrying a concealed weapon, an offense punishable by imprisonment up to six months, a $1,000 fine, or both. The trial was to a judge, and petitioner was unrepresented by counsel. He was sentenced to serve 90 days in jail, and brought this habeas corpus action in the Florida Supreme Court, alleging that, being deprived of his right to counsel, he was unable as an indigent layman properly to raise and present to the trial court good and sufficient defenses to the charge for which he stands convicted. The Florida Supreme Court, by a four-to-three decision, in ruling on the right to counsel, followed the line we marked out in Duncan v. Louisiana, as respects the right to trial by jury, and held that the right to court-appointed counsel extends only to trials "for non-petty offenses punishable by more than six months imprisonment." ...

The Sixth Amendment, which, in enumerated situations, has been made applicable to the States by reason of the Fourteenth Amendment provides specified standards for "all criminal prosecutions."

One is the requirement of a "public trial." In re Oliver, supra, held that the right to a "public trial" was applicable to a state proceeding even though only a 60-day sentence was involved.

Another guarantee is the right to be informed of the nature and cause of the accusation. Still another, the right of confrontation.... And another, compulsory process for obtaining witnesses in one's favor.... We have never limited these rights to felonies or to lesser but serious offenses....

... [T]here is nothing in the language of the Amendment, its history, or in the decisions of this Court to indicate that it was intended to embody a retraction of the right in petty offenses wherein the common law previously did require that counsel be provided....

We reject, therefore, the premise that, since prosecutions for crimes punishable by imprisonment for less than six months may be tried without a jury, they may also be tried without a lawyer.

The assistance of counsel is often a requisite to the very existence of a fair trial. . . .

The requirement of counsel may well be necessary for a fair trial even in a petty offense prosecution. We are by no means convinced that legal and constitutional questions involved in a case that actually leads to imprisonment even for a brief period are any less complex than when a person can be sent off for six months or more. . . .

In addition, the volume of misdemeanor cases, far greater in number than felony prosecutions, may create an obsession for speedy dispositions, regardless of the fairness of the result.

There is evidence of the prejudice which results to misdemeanor defendants from this "assembly line justice." One study concluded that

[m]isdemeanants represented by attorneys are five times as likely to emerge from police court with all charges dismissed as are defendants who face similar charges without counsel.

American Civil Liberties Union, Legal Counsel for Misdemeanants, Preliminary Report 1 (1970).

We must conclude, therefore, that the problems associated with misdemeanor and petty offenses often require the presence of counsel to insure the accused a fair trial. . . .

We hold, therefore, that, absent a knowing and intelligent waiver, no person may be imprisoned for any offense, whether classified as petty, misdemeanor, or felony, unless he was represented by counsel at his trial.

We hold that no person may be deprived of his liberty who has been denied the assistance of counsel as guaranteed by the Sixth Amendment. This holding is applicable to all criminal prosecutions, including prosecutions for violations of municipal ordinances. The denial of the assistance of counsel will preclude the imposition of a jail sentence.

Under the rule we announce today, every judge will know when the trial of a misdemeanor starts that no imprisonment may be imposed, even though local law permits it, unless the accused is represented by counsel. He will have a measure of the seriousness and gravity of the offense, and therefore know when to name a lawyer to represent the accused before the trial starts.

The run of misdemeanors will not be affected by today's ruling. But, in those that end up in the actual deprivation of a person's liberty, the accused will receive the benefit of "the guiding hand of counsel" so necessary when one's liberty is in jeopardy.

Reversed.

Source: United States Reports. Vol. 407, 25–66. Washington, D.C.: Government Printing Office, 1972.

DOCUMENT 58: *Barker v. Wingo* (1972)

The Sixth Amendment to the Constitution guarantees defendants the right to a speedy trial. The Supreme Court decided in *Klopfer v. North Carolina* (see Document 48) that a speedy trial is imposed on the states through the due process clause of the Fourteenth Amendment. A question which the court had not addressed is how much delay could be permitted before the constitutional right to a speedy trial was violated.

Barker was charged for murder. A co-defendant, Manning, was also arrested. Since the prosecutors believed the case against Manning was stronger, they tried him first. Because of an unusual set of circumstances, Manning had to be tried six times before he was convicted. His first five trials were not completed. Barker was then scheduled for trial, but his trial was further delayed several times by the illness of a key witness. Barker made no protest about the delays until three and half years had passed, and then he did not consistently protest. His trial finally began more than five years after he had been arrested. He was convicted. He appealed his case claiming his right to a speedy trial had been violated.

The Court used this case to comment on the meaning of a speedy trial. The Court reasoned that no firm timetable could be proposed that would apply in all cases. Each case would have to be judged by its own circumstances. One of the key factors in determining if the delay violates the speedy trial requirement is if the defendant's case is prejudiced by the delay. The Court did not feel that Barker's case suffered from the delays, and there was even evidence that he welcomed them. The Court ruled that the delays in this case were not a violation of the right to a speedy trial.

The Court's unwillingness to set a firm timetable for a speedy trial will prompt Congress to pass legislation to create one. See the next document.

* * *

Barker v. Wingo, 407 U.S. 514

Mr. Justice Powell delivered the opinion of the Court.
Although a speedy trial is guaranteed the accused by the Sixth Amend-

ment to the Constitution, this Court has dealt with that right on infrequent occasions. . . . The Court's opinion in Klopfer v. North Carolina established that the right to a speedy trial is "fundamental" and is imposed by the Due Process Clause of the Fourteenth Amendment on the States. . . . [I]n none of these cases have we attempted to set out the criteria by which the speedy trial right is to be judged. This case compels us to make such an attempt.

The right to a speedy trial is generically different from any of the other rights enshrined in the Constitution for the protection of the accused. In addition to the general concern that all accused persons be treated according to decent and fair procedures, there is a societal interest in providing a speedy trial which exists separate from, and at times in opposition to, the interests of the accused. The inability of courts to provide a prompt trial has contributed to a large backlog of cases in urban courts which, among other things, enables defendants to negotiate more effectively for pleas of guilty to lesser offenses and otherwise manipulate the system. In addition, persons released on bond for lengthy periods awaiting trial have an opportunity to commit other crimes. It must be of little comfort to the residents of Christian County, Kentucky, to know that Barker was at large on bail for over four years while accused of a vicious and brutal murder of which he was ultimately convicted. Moreover, the longer an accused is free awaiting trial, the more tempting becomes his opportunity to jump bail and escape. Finally, delay between arrest and punishment may have a detrimental effect on rehabilitation.

A second difference between the right to speedy trial and the accused's other constitutional rights is that deprivation of the right may work to the accused's advantage. Delay is not an uncommon defense tactic. As the time between the commission of the crime and trial lengthens, witnesses may become unavailable or their memories may fade. . . . Thus, unlike the right to counsel or the right to be free from compelled self-incrimination, deprivation of the right to speedy trial does not per se prejudice the accused's ability to defend himself.

Finally, and perhaps most importantly, the right to speedy trial is a more vague concept than other procedural rights. It is, for example, impossible to determine with precision when the right has been denied. We cannot definitely say how long is too long in a system where justice is supposed to be swift but deliberate. As a consequence, there is no fixed point in the criminal process when the State can put the defendant to the choice of either exercising or waiving the right to a speedy trial. . . .

The amorphous quality of the right also leads to the unsatisfactorily severe remedy of dismissal of the indictment when the right has been deprived. This is indeed a serious consequence because it means that a defendant who may be guilty of a serious crime will go free, without having been tried. Such a remedy is more serious than an exclusionary rule or a reversal for a new trial, but it is the only possible remedy.

Perhaps because the speedy trial right is so slippery, two rigid approaches are urged upon us as ways of eliminating some of the uncertainty which courts experience in protecting the right. The first suggestion is that we hold that the Constitution requires a criminal defendant to be offered a trial within a specified time period.

The second suggested alternative would restrict consideration of the right to those cases in which the accused has demanded a speedy trial. Most States have recognized what is loosely referred to as the "demand rule," although eight States reject it. . . .

We, therefore, reject both of the inflexible approaches—the fixed-time period because it goes further than the Constitution requires; the demand-waiver rule because it is insensitive to a right which we have deemed fundamental. The approach we accept is a balancing test, in which the conduct of both the prosecution and the defendant are weighed.

A balancing test necessarily compels courts to approach speedy trial cases on an ad hoc basis. We can do little more than identify some of the factors which courts should assess in determining whether a particular defendant has been deprived of his right. Though some might express them in different ways, we identify four such factors: Length of delay, the reason for the delay, the defendant's assertion of his right, and prejudice to the defendant.

The length of the delay is to some extent a triggering mechanism. Until there is some delay which is presumptively prejudicial, there is no necessity for inquiry into the other factors that go into the balance. Nevertheless, because of the imprecision of the right to speedy trial, the length of delay that will provoke such an inquiry is necessarily dependent upon the peculiar circumstances of the case. . . . [D]ifferent weights should be assigned to different reasons. A deliberate attempt to delay the trial in order to hamper the defense should be weighted heavily against the government. A more neutral reason such as negligence or overcrowded courts should be weighted less heavily but nevertheless should be considered since the ultimate responsibility for such circumstances must rest with the government rather than with the defendant. Finally, a valid reason, such as a missing witness, should serve to justify appropriate delay.

. . . Whether and how a defendant asserts his right is closely related to the other factors we have mentioned. . . . The more serious the deprivation, the more likely a defendant is to complain. The defendant's assertion of his speedy trial right, then, is entitled to strong evidentiary weight in determining whether the defendant is being deprived of the right. We emphasize that failure to assert the right will make it difficult for a defendant to prove that he was denied a speedy trial.

A fourth factor is prejudice to the defendant. Prejudice, of course, should be assessed in the light of the interests of defendants which the speedy trial right was designed to protect. This Court has identified three such interests: (i) to prevent oppressive pretrial incarceration; (ii) to minimize anxiety and concern of the accused; and (iii) to limit the possibility that the defense will be impaired. Of these, the most serious is the last. . . .

We regard none of the four factors identified above as either a necessary or sufficient condition to the finding of a deprivation of the right of speedy trial. Rather, they are related factors and must be considered together with such other circumstances as may be relevant. . . .

The difficulty of the task of balancing these factors is illustrated by this case, which we consider to be close. It is clear that the length of delay between arrest and trial—well over five years—was extraordinary. Only seven months of that period can be attributed to a strong excuse, the illness of the ex-sheriff who was in charge of the investigation. Perhaps some delay would have been permissible under ordinary circumstances, so that Manning could be utilized as a witness in Barker's trial, but more than four years was too long a period, particularly since a good part of that period was attributable to the Commonwealth's failure or inability to try Manning under circumstances that comported with due process.

Two counterbalancing factors, however, outweigh these deficiencies. The first is that prejudice was minimal. . . .

More important than the absence of serious prejudice, is the fact that Barker did not want a speedy trial. Counsel was appointed for Barker immediately after his indictment and represented him throughout the period. . . . Despite the fact that counsel had notice of the motions for continuances, the record shows no action whatever taken between October 21, 1958, and February 12, 1962, that could be construed as the assertion of the speedy trial right. On the latter date, in response to another motion for continuance, Barker moved to dismiss the indictment. The record does not show on what ground this motion was based, although it is clear that no alternative motion was made for an immediate trial. Instead the record strongly suggests that while he hoped to take advantage of the delay in which he had acquiesced, and thereby obtain a dismissal of the charges, he definitely did not want to be tried . . . :

The probable reason for Barker's attitude was that he was gambling on Manning's acquittal. . . . Barker undoubtedly thought that if Manning were acquitted, he would never be tried. . . .

That Barker was gambling on Manning's acquittal is also suggested by his failure, following the pro forma motion to dismiss filed in February 1962, to object to the Commonwealth's next two motions for continuances. Indeed, it was not until March 1963, after Manning's convictions were final, that Barker, having lost his gamble, began to object to further continuances. . . .

We do not hold that there may never be a situation in which an indictment may be dismissed on speedy trial grounds where the defendant has failed to object to continuances. . . . But barring extraordinary circumstances, we would be reluctant indeed to rule that a defendant was denied this constitutional right on a record that strongly indicates, as does this one, that the defendant did not want a speedy trial. We hold, therefore, that Barker was not deprived of his due process right to a speedy trial.

The judgment of the Court of Appeals is affirmed.

Source: United States Reports. Vol. 407, 514–38, Washington, D.C.: Government Printing Office, 1973.

DOCUMENT 59: Speedy Trial Act of 1974

Congress responded to the Supreme Court's reluctance in *Barker v. Wingo* (see Document 58), 1972, to establish specified periods of time in which a defendant must be brought to trial. Congress passed the Speedy Trial Act to provide specific time limits for judicial proceeding. The many details in the law show how difficult it is to anticipate all the various factors that could influence the speediness of a trial. Note also that specific penalties were included if the time limits were exceeded.

* * *

Speedy Trial Act of 1974, P.L. 93–619

Sec. 3161. Time limits and exclusions

(a) In any case involving a defendant charged with an offense, the appropriate judicial officer, at the earliest practicable time, shall, after consultation with the counsel for the defendant and the attorney for the Government, set the case for trial on a day certain, or list it for trial on a weekly or other short-term trial calendar at a place within the judicial district, so as to assure a speedy trial.

(b) Any information or indictment charging an individual with the commission of an offense shall be filed within thirty days from the date on which such individual was arrested or served with a summons in connection with such charges. If an individual has been charged with a felony in a district in which no grand jury has been in session during such thirty-day period, the period of time for filing of the indictment shall be extended an additional thirty days.

(c) The arrangement of a defendant charged in an information or indictment with the commission of an offense shall be held within ten days from the filing date (and making public) of the information or indictment, or from the date a defendant has been ordered held to answer and has appeared before a judicial officer of the court in which such charge is pending whichever date last occurs. Thereafter, where a plea of not guilty is entered, the trial of the defendant shall commence within sixty days from arraignment on the information or indictment at such place, within the district, as fixed by the appropriate judicial officer.

(d) If any indictment or information is dismissed upon motion of the defendant, or any charge contained in a complaint filed against an individual is dismissed or otherwise dropped, and thereafter a complaint is filed against such defendant or individual charging him with the same offense or an offense based on the same conduct or arising from the same criminal episode, or an information or indictment is filed charging such defendant with the same offense or an offense based on the same conduct or arising from the same criminal episode, the provisions of subsections (b) and (c) of this section shall be applicable with respect to such subsequent complaint, indictment, or information, as the case may be.

(e) If the defendant is to be tried again following a declaration by the trial judge of a mistrial or following an order of such judge for a new trial, the trial shall commence within sixty days from the date the action occasioning the retrial becomes final. If the defendant is to be tried again following an appeal or a collateral attack, the trial shall commence within sixty days from the date the action occasioning the retrial becomes final, except that the court retrying the case may extend the period for retrial not to exceed one hundred and eighty days from the date the action occasioning the retrial becomes final if unavailability of witnesses or other factors resulting from passage of time shall make trial within sixty days impractical. . . .

(h) The following periods of delay shall be excluded in computing the time within which an information or an indictment must be filed, or in computing the time within which the trial of any such offense must commence:

(1) Any period of delay resulting from other proceedings concerning the defendant, including but not limited to—

(A) delay resulting from an examination of the defendant and hearing on, his mental competency, or physical incapacity;

(B) delay resulting from an examination of the defendant pursuant to section 2902 of title 28, United States Code;

(C) delay resulting from trials with respect to other charges against the defendant;

(D) delay resulting from interlocutory appeals;

(E) delay resulting from hearings on pretrial motions;

(F) delay resulting from proceedings relating to transfer from other districts under the Federal Rules of Criminal Procedure; and

(G) delay reasonably attributable to any period, not to exceed thirty days, during which any proceeding concerning the defendant is actually under advisement.

(2) Any period of delay during which prosecution is deferred by the attorney for the Government pursuant to written agreement with the defendant, with the approval of the court, for the purpose of allowing the defendant to demonstrate his good conduct.

(3) (A) Any period of delay resulting from the absence or unavailability of the defendant or an essential witness.

(B) For purposes of subparagraph (A) of this paragraph, a defendant or an essential witness shall be considered absent when his whereabouts are unknown and, in addition, he is attempting to avoid apprehension or prosecution or his whereabouts cannot be determined by due diligence. For purposes of such subparagraph, a defendant or an essential witness shall be considered unavailable whenever his whereabouts are known but his presence for trial cannot be obtained by due diligence or he resists appearing at or being returned for trial.

(4) Any period of delay resulting from the fact that the defendant is mentally incompetent or physically unable to stand trial.

(5) Any period of delay resulting from the treatment of the defendant pursuant to section 2902 of title 28, United States Code.

(6) If the information or indictment is dismissed upon motion of the attorney for the Government and thereafter a charge is filed against the defendant for the same offense, or any offense required to be joined with that offense, any period of delay from the date the charge was dismissed to the date the time limitation would commence to run as to the subsequent charge had there been no previous charge.

(7) A reasonable period of delay when the defendant is joined for trial with a codefendant as to whom the time for trial has not run and no motion for severance has been granted.

(8) (A) Any period of delay resulting from a continuance granted by any judge on his own motion or at the request of the defendant or his counsel or at the request of the attorney for the Government, if the judge granted such continuance on the basis of his findings that the ends of justice served by taking such action outweigh the best interest of the public and the defendant in a speedy trial. No such period of delay resulting from a continuance granted by the court in

accordance with this paragraph shall be excludable under this subsection unless the court sets forth, in the record of the case, either orally or in writing, its reasons for finding that the ends of justice served by the granting of such continuance outweigh the best interests of the public and the defendant in a speedy trial.

(B) The factors, among others, which a judge shall consider in determining whether to grant a continuance under subparagraph (A) of this paragraph in any case are as follows:

(i)   Whether the failure to grant such a continuance in the proceeding would be likely to make a continuation of such proceeding impossible, or result in a miscarriage of justice.

(ii) Whether the case taken as a whole is so unusual and so complex, due to the number of defendants or the nature of the prosecution or otherwise, that it is unreasonable to expect adequate preparation within the periods of time established by this section.

(iii) Whether delay after the grand jury proceedings have commenced, in a case where arrest precedes indictment, is caused by the unusual complexity of the factual determination to be made by the grand jury or by events beyond the control of the court or the Government. . . .

(C) No continuance under paragraph (8) (A) of this subsection shall be granted because of general congestion of the court's calendar, or lack of diligent preparation or failure to obtain available witnesses on the part of the attorney for the Government.

(i) If trial did not commence within the time limitation specified in section 3161 because the defendant had entered a plea of guilty or nolo contendere subsequently withdrawn to any or all charges in an indictment or information, the defendant shall be deemed indicted with respect to all charges therein contained within the meaning of section 3161, on the day the order permitting withdrawal of the plea becomes final. . . .

Section 3162 Sanctions.

(a) (1) If, in the case of any individual against whom a complaint is filed charging such individual with an offense, no indictment or information is filed within the time limit required by section 3161(b) as extended by sections 3161(h) of this chapter, such charge against that individual contained in such complaint shall be dismissed or otherwise dropped. In determining whether to dismiss the case with or without prejudice, the court shall consider, among others, each of the following factors: the seriousness of the offense; the facts and circumstances of the case which led to the dismissal; and the impact of a reprosecution on the administration of this chapter and on the administration of justice.

(2) If a defendant is not brought to trial within the time limit required by section 3161 (c) as extended by section 3161(h), the information or indictment shall be dismissed on motion of the defendant. The defendant shall have the burden of proof of supporting such motion but the Government shall have the burden of going forward with the evidence in connection with any exclusion of time under subparagraph 3161(h) (3). In determining whether to dismiss the case with or without prejudice, the court shall consider, among others, each of the following factors: the seriousness of the offense; the facts and circumstances of the case which led to the dismissal; and the impact of a reprosecution on the administration of this chapter and on the administration of justice. Failure of the defendant to move for dismissal prior to trial or entry of a plea of guilty or nolo contendere shall constitute a waiver of the right to dismissal under this section.

(h) In any case in which counsel for the defendant or the attorney for the Government (1) knowingly allows the case to be set for trial without disclosing the fact that a necessary witness would be unavailable for trial; (2) files a motion solely for the purpose of delay which he knows is totally frivolous and without merit; (3) makes a statement for the purpose of obtaining a continuance which he knows to be false and which is material to the granting of a continuance; or (4) otherwise willfully fails to proceed to trial without justification consistent with section 3161 of this chapter, the court may punish any such counsel or attorney, as follows:

(A) in the case of an appointed defense counsel, by reducing the amount of compensation that otherwise would have been paid to such counsel pursuant to section 3006A of this title in an amount not to exceed 25 per centum thereof;

(B) in the case of a counsel retained in connection with the defense of a defendant, by imposing on such counsel a fine of not to exceed 25 per centum of the compensation to which he is entitled in connection with his defense of such defendant;

(C) by imposing on any attorney for the Government a fine of not to exceed $250;

(D) by denying any such counsel or attorney for the Government the right to practice before the court considering such case for a period of not to exceed ninety days; or

(E) by filing a report with an appropriate disciplinary committee.

The authority to punish provided for by this subsection shall be in addition to any other authority or power available to such court.

(c) The court shall follow procedures established in the Federal rules of Criminal Procedure in punishing any counsel or attorney for the Government pursuant to this section. . . .

Source: United States Statutes at Large. Vol. 88, Part 2. Washington, D.C.: Government Printing Office, 1976.

DOCUMENT 60: *Edwards v. Arizona* (1981)

Miranda (see Document 46) directed police to inform suspects of their right to an attorney. This right is available even before being charged with a crime. Police, however, are charged with gathering evidence to be used to convict and police were very unhappy with the *Miranda* decision, believing it would make their job more difficult.

Edwards had been arrested and informed of his Miranda rights. He was questioned by police until he asked for an attorney. Police questioning stopped, but the next day officers again questioned him after warning him of his Miranda rights. Edwards agreed to talk and made a confession. At his trial, his lawyer attempted to have the confession suppressed, claiming it was taken in violation of *Miranda.* The police said the confession was freely given.

Those accused can waive their Miranda rights. This case turned on whether Edwards had knowingly given up his right to an attorney when he answered police questions on the second day. Of course, police would like a suspect's waiver of Miranda rights to be liberally defined so a waiver could easily be given. The Court, instead, used a stringent rule. Once Edwards had requested an attorney, no further questioning should have occurred until an attorney was present, the Court ruled. Further, simply answering questions of police on the second day did not constitute a valid waiver of Miranda rights. The police violated Edwards's Fifth and Fourteenth Amendment rights, and the confession should not have been admitted.

* * *

Edwards v. Arizona, 451 U.S. 477

Justice White delivered the opinion of the Court.

We granted certiorari in this case limited to Question 1 presented in the petition, which in relevant part was "whether the Fifth, Sixth, and Fourteenth Amendments require suppression of a post-arrest confession, which was obtained after Edwards had invoked his right to consult counsel before further interrogation. . . ."

On January 19, 1976, a sworn complaint was filed against Edwards in Arizona state court charging him with robbery, burglary, and first-degree murder. An arrest warrant was issued pursuant to the complaint, and Edwards was arrested at his home later that same day. At the police station, he was informed of his rights as required by Miranda v. Arizona, (1966). Petitioner stated that he understood his rights, and was willing to submit to questioning. After being told that another suspect already in custody had implicated him in the crime, Edwards denied involvement and gave a taped statement presenting an alibi defense. He then sought to "make a deal." . . . Edwards then said: "I want an attorney before making a deal." At that point, questioning ceased and Edwards was taken to county jail.

At 9:15 the next morning, two detectives, colleagues of the officer who had interrogated Edwards the previous night, came to the jail and asked to see Edwards. When the detention officer informed Edwards that the detectives wished to speak with him, he replied that he did not want to talk to anyone. The guard told him that "he had" to talk and then took him to meet with the detectives. The officers identified themselves, stated they wanted to talk to him, and informed him of his Miranda rights. Edwards was willing to talk, but he first wanted to hear the taped statement of the alleged accomplice who had implicated him. After listening to the tape for several minutes, petitioner said that he would make a statement so long as it was not tape-recorded. The detectives informed him that the recording was irrelevant since they could testify in court concerning whatever he said. Edwards replied: "I'll tell you anything you want to know, but I don't want it on tape." He thereupon implicated himself in the crime.

Prior to trial, Edwards moved to suppress his confession on the ground that his Miranda rights had been violated. . . . The trial court . . . stated without explanation that it found Edwards' statement to be voluntary. Edwards was tried twice and convicted. Evidence concerning his confession was admitted at both trials. On appeal, the Arizona Supreme Court held. . . . "The trial court's finding that the waiver and confession were voluntarily and knowingly made is upheld."

Because the use of Edwards' confession against him at his trial violated his rights under the Fifth and Fourteenth Amendments as construed in Miranda v. Arizona, we reverse the judgment of the Arizona Supreme Court. . . .

Contrary to the holdings of the state courts, Edwards insists that having exercised his right on the 19th to have counsel present during interrogation, he did not validly waive that right on the 20th. For the following reasons, we agree.

First, the Arizona Supreme Court applied an erroneous standard for determining waiver where the accused has specifically invoked his right to counsel. It is reasonably clear under our cases that waivers of counsel must not only be voluntary, but must also constitute a knowing and intelligent relinquishment or abandonment of a known right or privilege, a matter which depends in each case "upon the particular facts and circumstances surrounding that case, including the background, experience, and conduct of the accused."

Considering the proceedings in the state courts in the light of this standard, we note that in denying petitioner's motion to suppress, the trial court found the admission to have been "voluntary," App. 3, 95, without separately focusing on whether Edwards had knowingly and intelligently relinquished his right to counsel. . . .

Here, however sound the conclusion of the state courts as to the voluntariness of Edwards' admission may be, neither the trial court nor the Arizona Supreme Court undertook to focus on whether Edwards understood his right to counsel and intelligently and knowingly relinquished it. It is thus apparent that the decision below misunderstood the requirement for finding a valid waiver of the right to counsel, once invoked. . . .

[W]e now hold that when an accused has invoked his right to have counsel present during custodial interrogation, a valid waiver of that right cannot be established by showing only that he responded to further police-initiated custodial interrogation even if he has been advised of his rights. We further hold that an accused, such as Edwards, having expressed his desire to deal with the police only through counsel, is not subject to further interrogation by the authorities until counsel has been made available to him, unless the accused himself initiates further communication, exchanges, or conversations with the police.

Miranda itself indicated that the assertion of the right to counsel was a significant event and that once exercised by the accused, "the interrogation must cease until an attorney is present." Our later cases have not abandoned that view.

In concluding that the fruits of the interrogation initiated by the police on January 20 could not be used against Edwards, we do not hold or imply that Edwards was powerless to countermand his election or that the authorities could in no event use any incriminating statements made by Edwards prior to his having access to counsel. Had Edwards initiated the meeting on January 20, nothing in the Fifth and Fourteenth Amendments would prohibit the police from merely listening to his voluntary, volunteered statements and using them against him at the trial.

But this is not what the facts of this case show. Here, the officers conducting the interrogation on the evening of January 19 ceased interrogation when Edwards requested counsel as he had been advised he had the right to do. The Arizona Supreme Court was of the opinion that this was a sufficient invocation of his Miranda rights, and we are in accord. It is also clear that without making counsel available to Edwards, the police returned to him the next day. This was not at his suggestion or request. . . . We think it is clear that Edwards was subjected to custodial interrogation on January 20 . . . and that this occurred at the instance of the authorities. His statement, made without having had access to counsel, did not amount to a valid waiver and hence was inadmissible.

Accordingly, the holding of the Arizona Supreme Court that Edwards had waived his right to counsel was infirm, and the judgment of that court is reversed.

So ordered.

Source: United States Reports. Vol. 451, 477–86. Washington, D.C.: Government Printing Office, 1981.

DOCUMENT 61: *Strickland v. Washington* (1984)

The Fifth Amendment guarantees counsel for the accused. But what if the counsel is inadequate or makes errors? Then the accused can appeal a conviction based on violation of right to counsel. Strickland did just that. He appealed his convictions for three capital murders and other crimes claiming his counsel was incompetent. He listed specific ways his counsel had been inadequate. Strickland had pleaded guilty and waived the right to an advisory jury at his sentencing hearing. These decisions and others he made were against the advice of his counsel. He was sentenced to death on each of the three murder counts and prison for various other crimes.

In state courts, his counsel was found to be adequate, but an appellate court having just derived revised rules for judging competence of counsel ordered that lower courts review his case again using the new standard. That decision was appealed to the Supreme Court. The Supreme Court accepted this case to have the opportunity to provide guidance regarding when a criminal judgment should be overturned because of actual ineffective assistance of counsel.

The Court reasoned that for a case to be overturned, the defendant must show the counsel's performance was deficient and that the deficiency was so serious as to deprive the defendant of a fair trial. The burden of proof rests with the defendant.

In Strickland's case, the Court found that he had adequate counsel and his conviction was sustained.

* * *

Strickland v. Washington, 466 U.S. 668

Justice O'Connor delivered the opinion of the Court.

This case requires us to consider the proper standards for judging a criminal defendant's contention that the Constitution requires a conviction or death sentence to be set aside because counsel's assistance at the trial or sentencing was ineffective.

During a 10-day period in September 1976, respondent planned and committed three groups of crimes, which included three brutal stabbing murders, torture, kidnaping, severe assaults, attempted murders, attempted extortion, and theft. After his two accomplices were arrested, respondent surrendered to police and voluntarily gave a lengthy statement confessing to the third of the criminal episodes. The State of Florida indicted respondent for kidnaping and murder and appointed an experienced criminal lawyer to represent him.

Counsel actively pursued pretrial motions and discovery. He cut his efforts short, however, and he experienced a sense of hopelessness about the case, when he learned that, against his specific advice, respondent had also confessed to the first two murders. By the date set for trial, respondent was subject to indictment for three counts of first-degree murder and multiple counts of robbery, kidnaping for ransom, breaking and entering and assault, attempted murder, and conspiracy to commit robbery. Respondent waived his right to a jury trial, again acting against counsel's advice, and pleaded guilty to all charges, including the three capital murder charges. . . .

Counsel advised respondent to invoke his right under Florida law to an advisory jury at his capital sentencing hearing. Respondent rejected the advice and waived the right. He chose instead to be sentenced by the trial judge without a jury recommendation.

In preparing for the sentencing hearing, counsel spoke with respondent about his background. He also spoke on the telephone with respondent's wife and mother. . . . He did not otherwise seek out character witnesses for respondent. Nor did he request a psychiatric examination, since his conversations with his client gave no indication that respondent had psychological problems.

Counsel decided not to present and hence not to look further for evidence concerning respondent's character and emotional state. That decision reflected trial counsel's sense of hopelessness about overcoming the evidentiary effect of respondent's confessions to the gruesome crimes. . . .

Counsel also excluded from the sentencing hearing other evidence he thought was potentially damaging. . . .

The trial judge found several aggravating circumstances with respect to each of the three murders. He found that all three murders were especially heinous, atrocious, and cruel, all involving repeated stabbings. All three murders were committed in the course of at least one other dangerous and violent felony, and since all involved robbery, the murders were for pecuniary gain. . . .

[T]he trial judge found numerous aggravating circumstances and no (or a single comparatively insignificant) mitigating circumstance. With respect to each of the three convictions for capital murder, the trial judge concluded: "A careful consideration of all matters presented to the court impels the conclusion that there are insufficient mitigating circumstances . . . to outweigh the aggravating circumstances." He therefore sentenced respondent to death on each of the three counts of murder and to prison terms for the other crimes. The Florida Supreme Court upheld the convictions and sentences on direct appeal. . . .

Respondent subsequently sought collateral relief in state court on numerous grounds, among them that counsel had rendered ineffective assistance at the sentencing proceeding. . . .

Applying the standard for ineffectiveness claims articulated by the Florida Supreme Court in Knight v. State (1981), the trial court concluded that respondent had not shown that counsel's assistance reflected any substantial and serious deficiency measurably below that of competent counsel that was likely to have affected the outcome of the sentencing proceeding. . . .

The Florida Supreme Court affirmed the denial of relief. For essentially the reasons given by the trial court, the State Supreme Court concluded that respondent had failed to make out a prima facie case of either "substantial deficiency or possible prejudice" and, indeed, had "failed to such a degree that we believe, to the point of a moral certainty, that he is entitled to no relief. . . ." Id., at 287. . . .

In assessing attorney performance, all the Federal Courts of Appeals and all but a few state courts have now adopted the "reasonably effective assistance" standard in one formulation or another. . . . Yet this Court has not had occasion squarely to decide whether that is the proper standard. . . .

For these reasons, we granted certiorari to consider the standards by which to judge a contention that the Constitution requires that a criminal judgment be overturned because of the actual ineffective assistance of counsel. (1983). . . .

That a person who happens to be a lawyer is present at trial alongside the accused . . . is not enough to satisfy the constitutional command. The Sixth Amendment recognizes the right to the assistance of counsel because it envisions counsel's playing a role that is critical to the ability of the adversarial system to produce just results. An accused is entitled to be assisted by an attorney, whether retained or appointed, who plays the role necessary to ensure that the trial is fair.

For that reason, the Court has recognized that "the right to counsel is the right to the effective assistance of counsel." . . .

The Court has not elaborated on the meaning of the constitutional requirement of effective assistance in the latter class of cases—that is, those presenting claims of "actual ineffectiveness." In giving meaning to the requirement, however, we must take its purpose—to ensure a fair trial—as the guide. The benchmark for judging any claim of ineffectiveness must be whether counsel's conduct so undermined the proper functioning of the adversarial process that the trial cannot be relied on as having produced a just result.

The same principle applies to a capital sentencing proceeding such as that provided by Florida law . . .

A convicted defendant's claim that counsel's assistance was so defective as to require reversal of a conviction or death sentence has two components. First, the defendant must show that counsel's performance was deficient. This requires showing that counsel made errors so serious that counsel was not functioning as the "counsel" guaranteed the defendant by the Sixth Amendment. Second, the defendant must show that the deficient performance prejudiced the defense. This requires showing that counsel's errors were so serious as to deprive the defendant of a fair trial, a trial whose result is reliable. Unless a defendant makes both showings, it cannot be said that the conviction or death sentence resulted from a breakdown in the adversary process that renders the result unreliable. . . .

In any case presenting an ineffectiveness claim, the performance inquiry must be whether counsel's assistance was reasonable considering all the circumstances. . . . No particular set of detailed rules for counsel's conduct can satisfactorily take account of the variety of circumstances faced by defense counsel or the range of legitimate decisions regarding how best to represent a criminal defendant. . . .

An error by counsel, even if professionally unreasonable, does not warrant setting aside the judgment of a criminal proceeding if the error had no effect on the judgment. . . .

The defendant must show that there is a reasonable probability that, but for counsel's unprofessional errors, the result of the proceeding would have been different. A reasonable probability is a probability sufficient to undermine confidence in the outcome. . . .

When a defendant challenges a death sentence such as the one at issue in this case, the question is whether there is a reasonable probability that, absent the errors, the sentencer—including an appellate court, to the extent it independently reweighs the evidence—would have concluded that the balance of aggravating and mitigating circumstances did not warrant death.

In making this determination, a court hearing an ineffectiveness claim must consider the totality of the evidence before the judge or jury. Some of the factual findings will have been unaffected by the errors, and factual findings that were affected will have been affected in different ways. Some errors will have had a pervasive effect on the inferences to be drawn from the evidence, altering the entire evidentiary picture, and some will have had an isolated, trivial effect. Moreover, a verdict or conclusion only weakly supported by the record is more likely to have been affected by errors than one with overwhelming record support. Taking the unaffected findings as a given, and taking due account of the effect of the errors on the remaining findings, a court making the prejudice inquiry must ask if the defendant has met the burden of showing that the decision reached would reasonably likely have been different absent the errors. . . .

Application of the governing principles is not difficult in this case. The facts as described above make clear that the conduct of respondent's counsel at and before respondent's sentencing proceeding cannot be found unreasonable. . . .

Failure to make the required showing of either deficient performance or sufficient prejudice defeats the ineffectiveness claim. Here there is a double failure. More generally, respondent has made no showing that the justice of his sentence was rendered unreliable by a breakdown in the adversary process caused by deficiencies in counsel's assistance. Respondent's sentencing proceeding was not fundamentally unfair. We conclude, therefore, that the District Court properly declined to issue a writ of habeas corpus. The judgment of the Court of Appeals is accordingly

Reversed.

Source: United States Reports. Vol. 466, 668–92. Washington, D.C.: Government Printing Office, 1984.

DOCUMENT 62: *Doggett v. United States* (1992)

Marc Doggett, indicted for drug trafficking in February 1980, was finally tried in September 1988. He was convicted and appealed his case claiming he was denied a speedy trial. The delay of his trial was caused by his travels and the government's losing track of his location. Unaware that he had been indicted, he returned to the United States and lived in Virginia for six and one-half years before his arrest.

Even though he did not suffer the usual consequences of long delay before trial, such as imprisonment and the uncertainty of pending trial, and he did not argue during his case that the delay prevented him from having an effective defense, the Court ruled that the delay was a violation of his right to a speedy trial. The court reasoned that a delay of this type caused by the errors of the government can be presumed to have made a proper defense more difficult. Justice Thomas wrote a dissent, with which two justices concurred, that Doggett suffered no harm from the delay and therefore no violation of the Sixth Amendment had occurred.

* * *

Doggett v. United States, 505 U.S. 647

Justice Souter delivered the opinion of the Court.

In this case, we consider whether the delay of 8 ½ years between petitioner's indictment and arrest violated his Sixth Amendment right to a speedy trial. We hold that it did.

On February 22, 1980, petitioner Marc Doggett was indicted for conspiring with several others to import and distribute cocaine. . . . On March 18, 1980, two police officers set out . . . to arrest Doggett at his parents' house in Raleigh, North Carolina, only to find that he was not there. His mother told the officers that he had left for Colombia four days earlier. . . .

Doggett remained lost to the American criminal justice system until September, 1988, when the Marshal's Service ran a simple credit check on several thousand people subject to outstanding arrest warrants and, within minutes, found out where Doggett lived and worked. On September 5, 1988, nearly 6 years after his return to the United States and 8 ½ years after his indictment, Doggett was arrested.

He naturally moved to dismiss the indictment, arguing that the Government's failure to prosecute him earlier violated his Sixth Amendment right to a speedy trial. The Federal Magistrate hearing his motion applied the criteria for assessing speedy trial claims set out in Barker v. Wingo: "[l]ength of delay, the reason for the delay, the defendant's assertion of his right, and prejudice to the defendant." The Magistrate found that the delay between Doggett's indictment and arrest was long enough to be "presumptively prejudicial," Magistrate's Report, that the delay "clearly [was] attributable to the negligence of the government," and that Doggett could not be faulted for any delay in asserting his right to a speedy trial, there being no evidence that he had known of the charges against him until his arrest. The Magistrate also found, however, that Doggett had made no affirmative showing that the delay had impaired his ability to mount a successful defense or had otherwise prejudiced him. In his recommendation to the District Court, the Magistrate contended that this failure to demonstrate particular prejudice sufficed to defeat Doggett's speedy trial claim.

The Sixth Amendment guarantees that, "[i]n all criminal prosecutions, the accused shall enjoy the right to a speedy . . . trial. . . ." On its face, the Speedy Trial Clause is written with such breadth that, taken literally, it would forbid the government to delay the trial of an "accused" for any reason at all. Our cases, however, have qualified the literal sweep of the provision by specifically recognizing the relevance of four separate inequities: whether delay before trial was uncommonly long, whether the government or the criminal defendant is more to blame for that delay, whether, in due course, the defendant asserted his right to a speedy trial, and whether he suffered prejudice as the delay's result. . . .

[T]he Government claims Doggett has failed to make any affirmative showing that the delay weakened his ability to raise specific defenses, elicit specific testimony, or produce specific items of evidence. Though Doggett did indeed come up short in this respect, the Government's argument takes it only so far: consideration of prejudice is not limited to the specifically demonstrable, and, as it concedes . . . affirmative proof of particularized prejudice is not essential to every speedy trial claim. . . . Thus, we generally have to recognize that excessive delay presumptively compromises the reliability of a trial in ways that neither party can prove or, for that matter, identify. . . .

The lag between Doggett's indictment and arrest was 8 ½ years, and he would have faced trial 6 years earlier than he did but for the Government's inexcusable oversights. The portion of the delay attributable to the Government's negligence far exceeds the threshold needed to state a speedy trial claim; indeed, we have called shorter delays "extraordinary." When the Government's negligence thus causes delay six times as long as that generally sufficient to trigger judicial review and when the presumption of prejudice, albeit unspecified, is neither extenuated, as by the defendant's acquiescence nor persuasively rebutted, the defendant is entitled to relief.

We reverse the judgment of the Court of Appeals and remand the case for proceedings consistent with this opinion.

So ordered.

Thomas, J., dissenting.

Justice Thomas, with whom The Chief Justice and Justice Scalia join, dissenting.

Just as "bad facts make bad law," so too odd facts make odd law. Doggett's 8 ½ year odyssey from youthful drug dealing in the tobacco country of North Carolina, through stints in a Panamanian jail and in Colombia, to life as a computer operations manager, homeowner, and registered voter in suburban Virginia, is extraordinary. But even more extraordinary is the Court's conclusion that the Government denied Doggett his Sixth Amendment right to a speedy trial despite the fact that he has suffered none of the harms that the right was designed to prevent. I respectfully dissent.

We have long identified the "major evils" against which the Speedy

Trial Clause is directed as "undue and oppressive incarceration" and the "anxiety and concern accompanying public accusation." The Court does not, and cannot, seriously dispute that those two concerns lie at the heart of the Clause, and that neither concern is implicated here. . . . Indeed, as this case comes to us, we must assume that he was blissfully unaware of his indictment all the while, and thus was not subject to the anxiety or humiliation that typically accompany a known criminal charge.

Thus, this unusual case presents the question whether, independent of these core concerns, the Speedy Trial Clause protects an accused from two additional harms: (1) prejudice to his ability to defend himself caused by the passage of time; and (2) disruption of his life years after the alleged commission of his crime. The Court today proclaims that the first of these additional harms is indeed an independent concern of the Clause, and on that basis compels reversal of Doggett's conviction and outright dismissal of the indictment against him. As to the second of these harms, the Court remains mum—despite the fact that we requested supplemental briefing on this very point.

I disagree with the Court's analysis. In my view, the Sixth Amendment's speedy trial guarantee does not provide independent protection against either prejudice to an accused's defense or the disruption of his life. . . .

Source: United States Reports. Vol. 505, 647–71. Washington, D.C.: Government Printing Office, 1996.

DOCUMENT 63: *Lewis v. United States* (1996)

Ray Lewis was a U.S. Postal Service employee. Supervisors observed him opening mail and stealing its contents. He was charged with two counts of obstructing the mail, which is punishable by a sentence of up to six months. He requested jury trial but was denied one because the penalty was a sentence of less than six months. Lewis's lawyers appealed his conviction claiming that his total sentence of twelve months made him entitled to a jury trial.

The Court reasoned that the legislative intent was to categorize obstructing the mail as a petty crime by assigning a maximum six-month sentence. Although Lewis received a sentence totaling twelve months, the crime committed is still considered petty and therefore no jury trial is required by the Sixth Amendment.

* * *

Lewis v. United States, 518 U.S. 322

Justice O'Connor delivered the opinion of the Court.

This case presents the question whether a defendant who is prosecuted in a single proceeding for multiple petty offenses has a constitutional right to a jury trial where the aggregate prison term authorized for the offenses exceeds six months. . . .

Here, the maximum authorized penalty for obstruction of mail is six months' imprisonment—a penalty that presumptively places the offense in the "petty" category. We face the question whether petitioner is nevertheless entitled to a jury trial, because he was tried in a single proceeding for two counts of the petty offense so that the potential aggregated penalty is 12 months' imprisonment.

Petitioner argues that, where a defendant is charged with multiple petty offenses in a single prosecution, the Sixth Amendment requires that the aggregate potential penalty be the basis for determining whether a jury trial is required. . . . The Court must look to the aggregate potential prison term to determine the existence of the jury trial right, petitioner contends, not to the "petty" character of the offenses charged.

We disagree. The Sixth Amendment reserves the jury trial right to defendants accused of serious crimes. As set forth above, we determine whether an offense is serious by looking to the judgment of the legislature, primarily as expressed in the maximum authorized term of imprisonment. Here, by setting the maximum authorized prison term at six months, the legislature categorized the offense of obstructing the mail as petty. The fact that the petitioner was charged with two counts of a petty offense does not revise the legislative judgment as to the gravity of that particular offense, nor does it transform the petty offense into a serious one, to which the jury trial right would apply. . . .

Certainly the aggregate potential penalty faced by petitioner is of serious importance to him. But to determine whether an offense is serious for Sixth Amendment purposes, we look to the legislature's judgment, as evidenced by the maximum penalty authorized. . . .

The Constitution's guarantee of the right to a jury trial extends only to serious offenses, and petitioner was not charged with a serious offense. . . .

The judgment of the Court of Appeals for the Second Circuit is affirmed.

It is so ordered.

Source: United States Reports. Vol. 518, 322–43. Washington, D.C.: Government Printing Office, 1999.

DOCUMENT 64: *Dickerson v. United States* (2000)

Miranda v. Arizona (see Document 46), which required police warnings about self-incriminating statements and the entitlement to a lawyer during questioning, was an extremely controversial decision that changed police practice throughout the nation. Many objected to it, including William Rehnquist, then a lawyer. By 2000, Rehnquist had become chief justice of the Supreme Court. Many wondered if he would overrule *Miranda* when given the opportunity. The case *Dickerson v. United States* provided that opportunity.

In an attempt to undo the *Miranda* decision, Congress passed a law, 18 U.S.C. § 3501, that made the voluntary nature of an accused's statement the only rule determining its admissibility. If the statement was made voluntarily, it could be used whether or not the Miranda warnings were given. Dickerson was indicted for bank robbery and related federal crimes. He moved to suppress a statement he made because he had not received his Miranda warnings at the time he made the statement. The District Court agreed, but the government appealed, and the appellate court held that §3501 permitted the use of his voluntary statement. It held that *Miranda* was not a constitutional holding and that Congress could have the final say on the admissibility question.

Chief Justice Rehnquist wrote the opinion of the court. He forcefully reiterated support for the *Miranda* decision, declaring that the *Miranda* ruling was a constitutional decision that could not be changed by legislation. He further stated that the Court was unwilling to overrule *Miranda*. The phrase "stare decisis" is used in the decision; it means "to stand by that which is decided." Rehnquist and six other members of the Court concurred in strongly reaffirming the *Miranda* decision.

* * *

Dickerson v. United States, No. 99-5525

Chief Justice Rehnquist delivered the opinion of the Court.

In Miranda *v.* Arizona, we held that certain warnings must be given before a suspect's statement made during custodial interrogation could be admitted in evidence. In the wake of that decision, Congress enacted 18 U.S.C. §3501, which in essence laid down a rule that the admissibility of such statements should turn only on whether or not they were voluntarily made. We hold that *Miranda*, being a constitutional decision of this Court, may not be in effect overruled by an Act of Congress, and we decline to overrule *Miranda* ourselves. We therefore hold that *Miranda* and its progeny in this Court govern the admissibility of statements made during custodial interrogation in both state and federal courts. . . .

Given §3501's express designation of voluntariness as the touchstone of admissibility, its omission of any warning requirement . . . we agree with the Court of Appeals that Congress intended by its enactment to overrule *Miranda*. Because of the obvious conflict between our decision in *Miranda* and §3501, we must address whether Congress has constitutional authority to thus supersede *Miranda*. If Congress has such authority, §3501's totality-of-the-circumstances approach must prevail over *Miranda*'s requirement of warnings; if not, that section must yield to *Miranda*'s more specific requirements. . . .

Congress may not legislatively supersede our decisions interpreting and applying the Constitution. . . . This case therefore turns on whether the *Miranda* Court announced a constitutional rule or merely exercised its supervisory authority to regulate evidence in the absence of congressional direction. . . .

[F]irst and foremost of the factors on the other side—that *Miranda* is a constitutional decision—is that both *Miranda* and two of its companion cases applied the rule to proceedings in state courts—to wit, Arizona, California, and New York. . . . Since that time, we have consistently applied *Miranda*'s rule to prosecutions arising in state courts. . . . It is beyond dispute that we do not hold a supervisory power over the courts of the several States. . . . With respect to proceedings in state courts, our "authority is limited to enforcing the commands of the United States Constitution." Mu'Min *v.* Virginia, (1991).

The *Miranda* opinion itself begins by stating that the Court granted certiorari "to explore some facets of the problems . . . of applying the privilege against self-incrimination to in-custody interrogation, *and to give concrete constitutional guidelines for law enforcement agencies and courts to follow.*" . . . (emphasis added). In fact, the majority opinion is replete with statements indicating that the majority thought it was announcing a constitutional rule. Indeed, the Court's ultimate conclusion was that the unwarned confessions obtained in the four cases before the Court in *Miranda* "were obtained from the defendant under circumstances that did not meet constitutional standards for protection of the privilege."

§3501 reinstates the totality test as sufficient. Section 3501 therefore cannot be sustained if *Miranda* is to remain the law.

Whether or not we would agree with *Miranda*'s reasoning and its resulting rule, were we addressing the issue in the first instance, the principles of *stare decisis* weigh heavily against overruling it now. . . .

We do not think there is . . . justification for overruling *Miranda*. *Miranda* has become embedded in routine police practice to the point where the warnings have become part of our national culture. . . . While we have overruled our precedents when subsequent cases have undermined their doctrinal underpinnings, . . . we do not believe that this has happened to the *Miranda* decision. . . .

The disadvantage of the *Miranda* rule is that statements which may be by no means involuntary, made by a defendant who is aware of his "rights," may nonetheless be excluded and a guilty defendant go free as a result. But experience suggests that the totality-of-the-circumstances test which §3501 seeks to revive is more difficult than *Miranda* for law enforcement officers to conform to, and for courts to apply in a consistent manner. . . . The requirement that Miranda warnings be given does not, of course, dispense with the voluntariness inquiry. But as we said in Berkemer *v.* McCarty, "[c]ases in which a defendant can make a colorable argument that a self-incriminating statement was 'compelled' despite the fact that the law enforcement authorities adhered to the dictates of *Miranda* are rare."

In sum, we conclude that *Miranda* announced a constitutional rule that Congress may not supersede legislatively. Following the rule of *stare decisis*, we decline to overrule *Miranda* ourselves. The judgment of the Court of Appeals is therefore Reversed.

Source: Charles Thomas Dickerson, Petitioner, v. United States, Supreme Court of the United States Ship Opinion. Washington, D.C.: Government Printing Office, 2000.

Bibliography

Allen, Ronald J., Richard B. Kuhns, and William J. Stuntz. *Constitutional Criminal Procedure*. Boston: Little, Brown and Co., 1995.

Bartholomew, Paul C., and Joseph F. Menez. *Summaries of Leading Cases on the Constitution*. Totowa, N.J.: Littlefield, Adams and Co., 1981.

Beaney, William M. *Right to Counsel in American Courts*. Ann Arbor, Mich.: University of Michigan Press, 1955.

Beth, Loren P. *The Development of the American Constitution, 1877–1917*. New York: Harper and Row, 1971.

Bodenhamer, David J. *Fair Trial: Rights of the Accused in American History*. New York: Oxford University Press, 1992.

Cortner, Richard C. *The Supreme Court and the Second Bill of Rights: The Fourteenth Amendment and the Nationalization of Civil Liberties*. Madison, Wisc.: University of Wisconsin Press, 1981.

Cushman, Robert F., and Susan P. Koniak. *Leading Constitutional Decisions*. Englewood Cliffs, N.J.: Prentice Hall, 1992.

Epstein, Lee. *Constitutional Law for a Changing America: Rights, Liberties, and Justice*. Washington, D.C.: CQ Press, 1992.

Freedman, Warren. *The Constitutional Right to a Speedy and Fair Criminal Trial*. New York: Quorum Books, 1989.

Galloway, John, ed. *Criminal Justice & the Burger Court*. New York: Facts on File, 1978.

Gora, Joel M. *Due Process of Law*. Skokie, Ill.: National Textbook Co. and American Civil Liberties Union, 1979.

Hickoik, Eugene W., ed. *The Bill of Rights: Original Meaning and Current Understanding*. Charlottesville, Va.: University Press of Virginia, 1991.

Hyman, Harold, and William C. Wiecek. *Equal Justice Under Law: Constitutional Development, 1835–1875*. New York: Harper and Row, 1982.

Lockhart, William, Yale Kamisar, Jesse H. Choper, and Steven H. Shiffrin. *The American Constitution: Cases—Comments—Questions*. St. Paul, Minn.: West Publishing Co., 1991.

Maddex, James L. *Constitutional Law: Cases and Comments*. St. Paul, Minn.: West Publishing Co., 1974.

Morgan, Edmund S. *Inventing the People: The Rise of Popular Sovereignty in England and America*. New York: Norton, 1988.

Murphy, Paul L. *Constitution in Crisis Times*. New York: Harper and Row, 1972.

National Commission on Law Observance and Enforcement. *Lawlessness in Law Enforcement*. Washington, D.C.: Government Printing Office, 1931.

Padover, Saul K., ed. *Sources of Democracy: Voices of Freedom, Hope and Justice*. New York: McGraw Hill Book Co., 1973.

Peck, Robert S. *The Bill of Rights & the Politics of Interpretation*. St. Paul, Minn.: West Publishing Co., 1992.

Pollack, Harriet, and B. Smith Alexander. *Civil Liberties and Civil Rights in the United States*. St. Paul, Minn.: West Publishing Co., 1978.

Rutland, Robert Allen. *The Birth of the Bill of Rights, 1776–1791*. Boston: Northeastern University Press, 1991.

Schlechter, Stephen L., and Richard B. Bernstein, eds. *Contexts of the Bill of Rights*. Albany, N.Y.: New York State Commission on the Bicentennial of the United States Constitution, 1990.

Schwartz, Bernard. *The Great Rights of Mankind: A History of the American Bill of Rights*. Madison, Wisc.: Madison House, 1992.

Schwartz, Bernard. *A History of the Supreme Court*. New York: Oxford University Press, 1993.

Schwartz, Bernard, ed. *The Bill of Rights: A Documentary History*. New York: Chelsea House, 1971.

Sigler, Jay A. *Double Jeopardy: The Development of a Legal and Social Policy*. Ithaca, N.Y.: Cornell University Press, 1969.

Walker, Samuel. *Popular Justice: A History of American Criminal Justice*. New York: Oxford University Press, 1980.

Warren, Earl. "The Law and the Future." *Fortune*, November 1955, 106–7, 224–30.

Warren, Earl. *The Memoirs of Earl Warren*. Garden City, N.Y.: Doubleday, 1977.

Wiecek, William M. *Liberty under Law: The Supreme Court in American Life*. Baltimore, Md.: Johns Hopkins University Press, 1988.

Woll, Peter. *Constitutional Law: Cases and Comments*. Englewood Cliffs, N.J.: Prentice-Hall, 1981.

Index